FLYNN OF THE INLAND

AUSTRALIAN CLASSICS

FLYNN OF THE INLAND

Ion L. Idriess

ANGUS
& ROBERTSON

A division of HarperCollins *Publishers*

AN ANGUS & ROBERTSON BOOK

First published in Australia by Angus & Robertson Publishers in 1932
Australian Classics edition 1983
Reprinted in 1987
This edition published by Collins/Angus & Robertson
Publishers Australia in 1990

Collins/Angus & Robertson Publishers Australia
A division of HarperCollins Publishers (Australia) Pty Limited
Unit 4, Eden Park, 31 Waterloo Road, North Ryde
NSW 2113, Australia

William Collins Publishers Ltd
31 View Road, Glenfield, Auckland 10, New Zealand

Angus & Robertson (UK)
16 Golden Square, London W1R 4BN, United Kingdom

National Library of Australia
Cataloguing-in-publication data.

Idriess, Ion L. (Ion Llewellyn), 1890-1979.
    Flynn of the inland.

    First published: Sydney: Angus & Robertson, 1932
    ISBN O 2O7 14703 5

    1. Flynn, John, 1880-1951.
    2. Royal Flying Doctor Service of Australia.
    3. Aeronautics in medicine— Australia – Biography.
    I. Title. (Series: Australian classics (Angus & Robertson)).

362.1'092'4

Printed in Singapore

 7 6 5 4 3
95 94 93 92 91 90

FOREWORDS

THE names of John Flynn and those faithful workers associated with him in the work of the Australian Inland Mission will be ever remembered with sincere gratitude by the "outback" settlers and workers of Australia who have received and been helped by the kindly ministrations of this wonderful organization.

Only those who have experienced the dangers, discomforts, and difficulties associated with the outback country, especially in the earlier days, can realize what it means to have available at various centres the medical aid and nursing facilities provided by the A.I.M. During most of the many years I spent in the isolated portions of our great country, no such help could be obtained: it was a case of look after yourself as best you could. Visits from such a good Samaritan as John Flynn would have been more than welcomed. I never cease to admire the spirit and courage displayed by the pioneers of the great outback, especially the women folk, who ventured out to be with, and tend for, their men.

The marvellous strides made in the organization of this great Christian Mission are amazing and the efforts of its noble band of workers have placed the back country on a very much safer basis than ever before. The Flying Doctor Service has been the means of saving many lives.

Knowing the conditions existing in the interior as I do, and the need for means of communication in times of urgency, I commend to the sympathetic consideration of all true Australians the claims of the Australian Inland Mission for their loyal support and encouragement.

SIDNEY KIDMAN.

Adelaide,
S.A.

John Flynn has never thought himself great, and not even the great story so admirably told in this book will make him think so. He will remain the simple genial dreamer who will not let you go till he tells his latest dream, and whose dreams have a way of coming down from the clouds to materialize on earth. The unfading boyishness of hope and its vigorous irrationality are nowhere better illustrated than in the founder of the A.I.M. It is not what he does, fine as that is, it is what he makes *you* do. You listen to him thinking what an unpractical visionary he is, and before you know where you are you are helping him to do it.

And John Flynn's dream-land is the great sun-baked plains of Australia where the lonely pioneer and the still lonelier prospector and, noblest of all, the women who add the angel-touch to life, are doing outpost duty for civilization. The stormy seas and ice-bound coast of Labrador have their Wilfrid Grenfell. This book will reveal to Australia that her sunbeaten land has its John Flynn and his devoted band of workers, the Nursing Sisters and the Flying Doctors, who soften the tragedies of life to the men and women in the far outback: and it will also reveal that the human material to which he and they are ministering in soul and body deserve well of Australia. Unconventional and sometimes outwardly rough, but with a brave spirit, a generous heart, and a loyal friendship, they exemplify the words of one of our own poets:

> Two things stand like stone:
> Kindness in another's trouble,
> Courage in your own.

RONALD G. MACINTYRE.

Parramatta,
N.S.W.

AUTHOR'S NOTE

I HAVE written *Flynn of the Inland* in order that the people of Australia may learn something of the work which has been and is being done for isolated and suffering humanity by the Australian Inland Mission, its Padres and Doctors, its Sisters and voluntary workers—and by one Padre in particular.

This book is not a history; but it *is* a true story. The omission of the names of many good friends will, I hope, not be misunderstood. If it had been a history of the A.I.M., they would certainly have received the recognition to which their services entitle them.

A wanderer myself for many years in the Inland, I have seen the work of the A.I.M. there. This book is my humble tribute of admiration for John Flynn and his fellow workers. If any work bears the hallmark of the Master who inspired it, theirs does.

My thanks are due to the officers of the A.I.M. for allowing me access to official records, and the *Inlander*; and to the Patrol Padres and Nurses for help and inspiration in my work.

It would be ungrateful not to mention specially Miss Baird, the Secretary of the A.I.M., whose patience I fear I have more than once tried, but whose smiling face and unfailing courtesy gave no sign of the fact.

ION L. IDRIESS.

CONTENTS

CHAPTER I

THE CAMEL-MAN

THE Camel-man rode alone—or so it seemed! His back suggestively humped to the monotonous sway of the camel he gazed with eyes dream laden as the long miles crawled by. Following him, with ancient head held high, plodded another camel, attached by a line from its nose-peg to the leader's tail. It was loaded with water canteens, packbags, quart-pot, and swag. Its eyes too were dreamy, its step as unhurried as time.

Bright sunlight, clear air, fleecy white clouds drifting in a sky of blue: it was grand out here. Everything looked big, felt big; all except the Camel-man who had a big job—gigantic! Towards the ever-receding horizon, far away across a gibber plain bearded with tufts of spinifex, he gazed unflinchingly. That desert grass was bright green, for a passing shower had fallen only a month ago. The harsh-looking spiky tufts, snatching life from harsh surroundings, were long despised by men. Only now were they discovering that stock would thrive even on it. Here and there grew camel-bush near stunted mulga whose dwarf shapes seemed dancing in the hazy plain. In contrast to those hardy little trees a clump of lovely desert oak stood erect and graceful. Dimly to the right appeared low sand-ridges more suggestive of Sinai than Australia. Not even the hum of insect, or call of bird, broke the silence of that brooding solitude. Water, the life-giver, was far beyond the horizon.

Day after day the Camel-man rode. He had a thousand miles to go, but Central Australia shrugs at distances. Hours melted into days, days into weeks, and weeks into months. As he rode he dreamed, and the music he barely heard was the soft drumming of the camels' feet, the swish of water in the canteens, the squeak of cordage as the packs swayed right, left, right, left, throughout morning and afternoon.

One afternoon two white cockatoos flew low overhead to speed on into the evening. Man and camels watched their telltale flight, thankful that water must be close by. As afternoon merged into evening plain and trees and gibber stones softened in golden colours; these faded into lonely blue twilight; stars shone out, and the night had come. With soft footfalls they came to the water-hole, a muddy pool in an old river-bed that had been a flowing glory in the days when the world was young.

Two grey ghosts hopped from the pool to sit back on their tails and earnestly watch the camels loom up. The 'roos' ears were pricked and twitching, the big "old man" scratched his chest as he stared. Two emus stepped away from the muddy waters' edge with slow and stately tread, the old man bird clucking hoarsely, his solemn head upon its long neck a strange miniature of the camels that lurched down and forward, backward and down, down and forward, to finally settle with a rumbling of satisfied grunts.

The Camel-man stepped to solid earth and stretched his long limbs. He was a hefty lump of a young fellow though sparely built; a quietly determined chap already showing signs of the crow's-feet that were to wrinkle his face like the desert sands. A wry smile made wistfully pleasing a thoughtful face: his blue eyes were those of the born dreamer: his long brown hair was almost unkempt. But who cared out here in the "arid lands"?

From the water-bag he enjoyed a longed-for drink, then carried his two quart-pots to the water-hole, and bending peered searchingly across its shallow brown reflection. Fat black water-beetles were skimming upon it; tadpoles squirmed up and looked at him. He knelt down and sniffed the water.

Only a strong animal smell. Quite relieved he skimmed the surface with practised hand and filled his pots. You see, one darker night he had camped similarly, very thirsty. Next morning when the sun rose he smelt the dead man in the water-hole.

He unloaded his camels, watered them and turned them out to feed. One leisurely attempted to kick him as it lurched across to a tuft of camel-bush. He was always kind to his camels and they reciprocated by trying to kick or bite him. He boiled the quart-pot unhurriedly, for the job was a luxury: the little fire crackled cheerily to the craft of his lean brown fingers. He knew how to pick his twigs, did the Camel-man, and he knew just how to set on the quart-pot.

By the dancing fire he mixed his dough in a small dish, sifting in with his fingers the pinch of soda and tartar, pouring in the cloudy water (in small quantities), stirring and mixing it with his fingers to a firm toughness, giving it a light punch and a roll with his clenched fist before breaking it off in lumps and flattening each into a cake between his squeezing palms. The quart-pot had boiled so he made his tea, then raked out the coals and flopped the Johnnies on. While one side was cooking he sipped the tea with a sundowner's enjoyment.

He made a frugal meal—he had to—but was well content. Johnny-cakes with corned beef washed down by tea without milk, after twelve hours on a camel, is "luxury enough". He ate in peace and enjoyed it. Man is ever a discontented animal however: he wished he had a dip of treacle to sweeten the last Johnny.

With no washing up to do he rebuilt the fire and spread his blanket, craftily choosing a soft patch of red sand, one where no spiky spinifex could add point to his rest. But before he spread the blanket he dug out a hole under the middle, in which he could fit his hip. Then he sat down with something resembling his camel's grunt, ran his fingers through his hair, cocked his ear towards where the animals were feeding, took off his boots, and lovingly filled his pipe. It was an "old warrior" but the camels did not mind, and anyway he had to put up with many a whiff of them. He lit that pipe as if he owned the world, though he used a firestick to save a match—not because he was mean but because every match meant "carriage" out in the Centre. When a match has travelled three thousand miles it becomes valuable. Lonely women out there have cried when their last match was done—and the Camel-man had given away many matches.

With a sigh of content he stretched himself out, pillowed an arm around his neck and puffed up at the sky, smiling at the ambitious little puffs that tried to make a cloud. The stars twinkled back. They were far away but the longer he gazed the more intimately did each one twinkle. He wondered if, when the day came when "Time should be no more", would he ever wander among those worlds. Gradually a friendliness settled around him; a living friendliness it seemed; the silence whispered as if the heart of the earth was alive: one can *feel* silence out there. The little fire twinkled: the soft padding of reassured feet, and tails thumped as the 'roos assembled again at the water-hole: the annoyed grunt of a camel coughed from the darkness as he bit his itchy hide. Slowly the Camel-man's pipe burned out: lingeringly he puffed the last tasty whiff: sighing, he clung to the empty warrior. Tobacco means "carriage" out there in the Centre. He allowed himself one smoke at dawn and one smoke at eventide. From far away, with a note of unutterable longing, floated the howl of a wild dog.

"As a voice crying in the wilderness," said the Camel-man aloud, "as three thousand Australians cry in isolation out here in the Great Heart. As twenty thousand cry in the Inland!"

As he spoke his vision broadened from the Centre to the great North and far Nor'-west. Swift as the dawn spreads over those lands he visioned two-thirds of a continent, two million square miles with its frightening distances, its isolation, its people battling for a living against primitive conditions while the modern world presses a button and—'tis done!

It would not have mattered so much perhaps had it not been for the tragedy which those "press button" methods could prevent. For the Inland is a happy land; its sunlight is filled with song and the hearts of its men with cheery hope. The Camel-man wanted it all so. He saw the tragedy because it was his job to see it. His job was to help others; and in the helping he saw these things.

That vast land with its good country and poor, its areas often far larger than a European state, each with peculiar local problems of its own awaiting solutions that may release untold pastoral, mineral, and even agricultural riches: that land where a handful of scattered people battle for their homes, sometimes their lives, isolated in ones and twos, tens and twenties, hundreds of miles from medical, material, and spiritual aid. A handful of Australians making safe the "Never Never" for our grandchildren. We will want it then —badly.

One of the tragedies of the life is that many of the men of the Centre never marry. They dare not ask a white woman to share the loneliness—especially in these days when city life holds so much.

"And yet the cities want beef," growled the Camel-man. "They want wool to keep their factories going, timber and minerals for their houses and steel works and manufactories. They need the things of the Inland to build cities with, and the Inland needs the cities' help."

He was thinking of that blue-eyed youngster suddenly taken ill, with the nearest doctor two hundred miles away! Of the fearful drive through day and night; the change of horses at the station, then day and night again; the overturning of the buggy down that black ravine; the cry of the mother as she groped for the child. When the horses dropped the parents walked. It was terrible crossing the "Twenty

Mile" patch of rock and sand with the smell of dead animals down in the water-hole. At sunrise they saw the glint of roofs away down there in the tiny outback hamlet. Only one more hour to go—but the child was dying in the mother's arms.

The Camel-man moved restively: "It was not fair," he said aloud, "the child should have lived!" He sighed, settling back on his blanket. It could be such a happy land but . . . He was thinking of mothers, and fathers, with aching hearts sending their children a thousand miles away to school. After years of childish voices, empty rooms! Then those others who must grow into men and women, educated neither in spirit nor brain. There are very few schools where the Camel-man rides. His thoughts drifted to that lonely boundary-rider's hut he had passed two hundred miles farther east, where the little wife was standing staring towards the setting sun, waiting day by day, nay hour by hour, for her man whom she may not see for another month. There are many such huts out there in the sunset. Cannot we break that loneliness?

"Whatever man dares to do that he can," thought the Camel-man, "if he thinks long enough, wills sincerely, and works hard enough." These people deserve the help that only the cities can give; they are chancing their lives even in the cutting of tracks for our sons to follow at their leisure. Parts of these lands are capable of supporting far greater numbers of people. With population, isolation would disappear, roads be built, markets established, life made safe. In the interest of the Commonwealth these things should be.

If the wife gets sick! If . . . That "If" of the Inland spoilt the security, the strength and happiness of Inland life. No man in all Australia knew more of that "If" than the Camel-man. It was his job to blot it out: it was his life's work. Dearly he loved the happiness of the Inland, the brightness, the hope, the feeling of "life" in everything, from the insects' song and mountain range and sunlit plain to the laughter and the dry humour of its people. All would be like that "if—"

He brooded on the distances necessary to bring medical help when in pain or to travel stock to market—that twenty days' rough travel necessary to transport a sick person from Alice Springs to Oodnadatta railhead, for instance. Even then a hospital was six hundred miles farther south. The lonely tracks of the Kimberleys with two doctors in an area of 137,294 square miles! One tiny school at each of the three little ports, none inland. The Northern Territory with one doctor and one school in an area of 523,600 square miles! No wonder the sick ones seldom arrived. Distances—distances —distances.

How could those distances be eliminated; quick communication, quick travel be introduced?

He sighed. A man out here in the Centre, travelling with camels, planning to modernize three parts of a continent in a day! No wonder the very sands mocked him. As his fine face clouded over he saw again the lonely graves of a continent: rain-flattened mounds under coolabah, gidgee, and gum; wind-scoured mounds under desert oak; graves by creeks that seldom held water; grass-covered resting-places of the plains, and graves by the billabongs, resting-places of children and mothers and breadwinners who had fallen by the wayside. So many lives could have been saved, could now be saved if organized help, quick in action, were stationed within a radius even of three hundred miles.

How could it be done?

Scattered over two million square miles he visioned the tiny hamlets, the stations, the mining-fields, the little camps where the camel-teams bring food only once in six months, perhaps once in twelve; the camps where even a mailman is unknown, where another white face might not be seen in twelve months and more. He knew people who had never seen the sea, nor a town. He knew children reaching manhood to whom the outside world was but a name. He pondered on those lonely mothers bringing God's greatest gift into the world far from another woman's help and said aloud "Give every woman and child a fair chance."

And a voice said: "Cry not! the world is given you. Be up and doing lest you cry for the moon that it be put into your hand."

The Camel-man sighed. How *could* he solve a problem if he had not the brains? His mind cleared as he gazed around and listened. How utterly silent everything was! What a sweetly elusive tang of desert grasses was in the air! Pity the camels smelt so.

Lazily he arose, kicked the fire into flame, then strode out into the darkness. He had his ears and nose to guide him. Sprawling big heaps were the camels squatting among the shadows, strong jaws working as they chewed the cud. No fear of them making a noise to guide him, they'd lie as quiet as mice and let him walk right past. Well, the brutes seemed to have settled down for the night. He turned to his blanket, smiled lazily, and hitching his waggon to a star turned in till the coming of the dawn.

Sunrise in the Centre comes like the breath of God, pure and rich in life and hope, with a rosy glow that beautifies the sandhills before they turn hard and stern under the glare of day. Sleepily the Camel-man smiled and turned over, covering his head with the blanket. Chattering little wretches, waking a man so early. But the chatterers would not be denied so he threw off the blanket and yawned.

He was an object of interest to a swarm of finches, prettily coloured little mischief-makers, filled with noisy importance. They simply covered the scanty bushes around the waterhole: they swarmed over his pack-saddle twittering uncomplimentary remarks. The Camel-man sat up and glared, then laughed and whistled, and the chirruping rose to the skies. Others regarded him—two 'roos sitting back on their tails and two emus standing on long sturdy legs. Other things

of the Wild had seen him also but had scuttled to safety
before he woke. He knew, because they had left their tracks
in the mud of the water-hole. With the bushman's curiosity
he examined each one of those "visiting-cards".

He boiled his quart-pot, ate a careless breakfast, carefully
filled his pipe, watered his camels, loaded the protesting
animals, mounted, and rode into another day.

CHAPTER II

RIDERS OF THE PLAINS

ONE afternoon he saw wheel-tracks in the sand. His camels followed them and at sunset lurched up to the home of the Five Sisters. The old grey stone homestead looked beautiful with its veranda screened by creepers climbing up over the roof. A roomy stable was visible at the back, and a strongly built stockyard farther back still. Under the sunset the salt-bush plain in front appeared tipped with silver; the old white gums down at the creek were noisy with parrots coming from their evening drink. Hills that were only mounds rose up behind the homestead; a few cattle and some horses were grazing there looking nearly as big as the few shrubby trees.

Dogs ran out barking, a rooster crowed lustily, and as the camels lurched up a girl came on to the veranda, called over her shoulder, "It's the Padre", then ran out to quieten the dogs. A bare-armed bush lass with the imp of mischief shining from her delighted face. Strong-limbed, grey-eyed, with rich brown hair, she looked health itself as she laughed an eager welcome.

"You look in good form, Rene," smiled the Camel-man.

"So do you, Padre. You're the nicest looking man I've seen since you were here last. There have only been two others."

Another girl came running out followed by the mother. Bush life had dealt kindly with her.

"Jess and Bess and Tess are out on the run," laughed one of the girls, "rounding up cleanskins with Dad. What a yarn we'll have tonight!"

"Where did you get the new hat, Padre?" broke in the others. "You look scrumptious."

"Is it true Rolling Downs has a baby?"

"Did you bring on any mail?"

"What are they doing in Oodnadatta? What——?"

Those girls slung off the camel-packs as easily as a man could and the camels did not mind. Mother tried to corner him but the girls could talk and work too. All wanted news of distant Oodnadatta, the metropolis for an enormous district, upon which all things hinged.

"Here they come!" said Rene as the camels walked leisurely off down to the creek.

They came! with a rush of hooves and scampering of dogs and a wild yell of "up and over!" charging down on the Padre.

"Couldn't see your camels for the house," they laughed, "until we put the mob in the yard. Dad's coming. How are you, Padre? How's Oodnadatta? How's——?"

That evening he sat in the big roomy kitchen and smoked with the father, who was content to listen. The mother did little better. It was a happy home, the home of a pioneer made comfortable. The father had practically forgotten his only disappointment: just occasionally with wonderment he realized that his "boys" were girls. They did all the mustering about the place, all the branding, all the horse-breaking, in fact they "ran" the station. The father was only the manager. "I might be a blooming jackeroo at times," he complained.

But the dreamer realized that distance had caused these girls to miss a great chance in life. Rene could draw from her violin strings the soul of the bush—its longing, its loneliness, its joyousness, and its glory. She could play the song of a bird to its mate and make the strings cry to the lonely flight of waterfowl vanishing overhead at night. Bess could put the bush on canvas—its desolation in drought, its beauty after rains, the flowers of the desert fringe, and the fading sun in horizons far away. The other three sisters were born sculptors. They might have made world names If——

Laughingly next morning they took him down to see the latest "creations" in the studio they had dug out of the steep bank of the creek. Here on the shelves were the horses of the run, the cows and calves and bull of the milkyard, the homestead dogs, modelled in clay, perfect in outline and colour.

"I see you've Roger and Baldy immortalized now," smiled the Camel-man, "and there's the old black rooster and the cattle-pup I left last time. They're splendid. I could pick the originals in the paddock."

"Could you pick this?" and Tess laughingly drew aside from a shelf.

"Well I'm blessed," drawled the Camel-man. "Do I really look like that?"

"You said they are perfection," was the mischievous reply.

He was admiring the lifelike models of his camels and himself. There was even the scar of his riding beast where it had been bitten long ago. All these sisters had the makings of world artists. He wondered would they have been happier If——

They loved their models. They had complete mastery over the originals too, could ride any horse on the run, break in any "outlaw" and enjoy the taming; could ride from dawn till dark on a muster for a month on end and find only joy in it. They had galloped before the thunder of a cattle stampede in the dead of night, had swum flooded rivers while clinging to their horses' tails.

They were dare-devils right enough. He had seen them in the stockyard among frightened, plunging beasts and it fairly made his hair stand on end. He had sat on the rails with his heart in his mouth lest he should see those girls trampled to pancakes. They had laughed up at him and invited him to come down inside. Smilingly he declined.

The Camel-man enjoyed his stay at this station. There was always "something doing".

"I must push on tomorrow," he said when they urged him to stay another day and yet another.

When he did push on he rode in strange company, for three of the girls rode with him—on steers! Camels and steers hate each other, but the girls had sworn to visit an adjoining station on steers—and they did!

He waved them farewell and branched off into the open spaces, the days growing lonelier as he drew out towards Lake Eyre. One afternoon he halted his camels, glancing down at tracks plain on the sand, a horse's tracks, a shod horse: it had come from the east. His eyes followed those imprints vanishing into the west. Fresh tracks they were, firmly set; both beast and rider were well, neither leg-weary nor suffering from thirst. They knew too where they were going, by the tale of the tracks. Who might he be, that lone rider from the uninhabited lands going out towards Nowhere-in-particular? What was his business? By his own lonely fire that night he thought of the lone rider, for tracks in the sand speak a volume in the bush.

When the Camel-man neared Lake Eyre he rode up to a hut of saplings hidden among sandhills, the hut of a pioneer "just starting". How the early explorers would have turned in their graves if told that a human was actually battling for a living in "that land of desolation". The pioneer was a tough cattleman, a brown-faced chap with hard grey eyes. He stared at the visitor and came incredulously forward as the camels lurched down.

"You're a long way off the beaten track aren't you?" he asked as they shook hands.

"Well, no. Why?"

"There is no business in these parts. What firm are you travelling for?"

"I am not a commercial traveller," smiled the Camel-man.

"What are you then?"

"A parson on the wallaby."

"Good heavens!"

"Why?"

"Well—well, as a matter of fact a commercial would be mad to come out here, but a parson——"

"There is method in our madness," smiled the Camel-man.

"What is it?"

"Just to give you a hand in any way we can. Just to be a wandering link between you and civilization as it were— might come in handy sometime."

The cattleman passed a wondering hand over a wrinkled brow. "The church has never come out this way before," he said slowly. "Never bothered about us, and why should you bother now? Why, if you combed the country for two hundred miles around you would not muster a congregation."

"We do not expect them to come," replied the Camel-man. "There is the distance and they have their work to do. Our work is to go to them. Here I am."

"Come inside and have some tea," said the man. "It's rough but I see you won't mind. The dog is my only company. You've struck me nearly dumb with surprise, but you can talk to me all night and I'll listen."

The Camel-man left behind there a friend when he rode on. It was a strong handshake, just a smiling "So-long!" as he rode away, but he had left in the home of the pioneer the strength of a connexion with the outside world. It would be days now before he saw another human: he was riding north just inside from the fringe of that great salt lake. As he rode he fell to dreaming again. Distances! how could they be eliminated? He pondered on that thread of two thousand miles that stretches from Adelaide to Darwin carrying overseas news from north to south. At every hundred miles or so there is a little telegraph-station, in charge of an operator. From hundreds of miles inland, from east to west, sick people travel to these little stations as a last hope. The operator anxiously "tick tacks" a doctor in Adelaide, describing the patient's symptoms, then does his best to follow the advice over the wire!

There are some great campfire stories of cures effected that way. But of course where an operation or special medicine is necessary—! It takes months for medicine to arrive.

"Poor old Jim!" the Camel-man sighed. Though that thread of wire could not cure, it sometimes brought a last repose to those lucky enough to reach it. He was thinking of his friend the station manager and the men who carried him by day and night. But Jim was too far gone, so the officials in Adelaide brought his wife to the wires. Thus they spent their last forlorn hour together.

The Camel-man looked out across the plain with stern wonderment in his eyes. "These are modern days," he said, "and yet one telegraph-wire and mailmen driving camel-teams represent the communication for all this vast Centre!"

When he came to the fringe of the arid lands mountain-peaks loomed up. All misty in the evening they were throwing purple cloaks out across the plain. Next morning he rode through a gorge of primitive beauty, its towering walls so close that by midday he could imagine himself within a walled road. Here a shaft of sunlight shone down on a pool mirroring in eerie beauty the crags above.

He photographed the pool. Among other things he was an expert photographer; had taught himself; mastering the art, as he did most things he attempted. He had hundreds of unique photos, for long ago photography seemed to weave itself into the dream. He had, too, developed into a fine descriptive writer. That, also, he felt would help. He had a volume full of interesting things concerning a little-known country. Fine stuff! His dream was now part of him, *was* him. Now, to him, it was more a reality waiting fulfilment than a dream.

The Camel-man rode on for several days, satisfying himself of good water-holes, of pasturage that showed promise of permanence "farther in". He must know of these things, of lands where settlers might make their homes in time to come. Time! As he again entered the saltbush country he dreamed rather bitterly. A man had so much to do and so little time to do it in.

CHAPTER III

MAPS IN THE SAND

JOHN FLYNN, Australian born, was a dreamer of dreams. One dream has awakened joy in the heart of a continent.

It was a giant project, Flynn's dream. Nothing less than to establish help, communication, and transport throughout two-thirds of a continent, two million square miles peopled by an isolated few having no political voice. An Empire would hardly have tackled such a job. His dream hinged on the cradle. First ensure that every Inland woman could have her baby and her own life with it. Then educate those children, annihilate loneliness, and bring a feeling of security to the fathers, and see that all had that spiritual companionship which smooths the path of life.

As he dreamed so he built on national lines, visioning the completion of the great north-to-south railway, ports at Darwin and other fine harbours along two thousand miles of the coast, pastoral and mining activity in the empty lands, security and a nation-wide prosperity for Australia.

But he was merely a Camel-man with an empty pocket, this empire dreamer, riding alone in the brooding Centralian silence. How could *he* evoke the sympathy and active interest of the population hugging the rich coast-lands, without which his dream would remain only a dream?

They said he was "mad!" The very sands mocked his dreams with mirages of beauty that faded in the glare of day. The very drumming of the camels' feet crunched "Mad!" "Mad!" Mad!" "Mad!" day after day, now grown into year after year. That drumming was growing in his mind—Let them mock! But the nights did not mock—these Inland nights shedding a heavenly peace. All things seemed possible in these soothing silences—silences alive with whispered encouragement.

That day turned out brilliantly; a cloudless sky glinted on the gibber stones among tufted spinifex and saltbush, splendid feed for stock: a line of distant gums grew up sharp and clear upon some nameless creek: a desert hawk circled high up in the blue. No track other than the wild marked the brown and gold stretching all round. Little finches chirruped from a desert shrub, while a dingo, in leering hunger, followed up his tracks.

Presently a slight, glary haze spread across the horizon, but the Camel-man dreamed to the steady drumming of tireless feet, the swish, swish, swish of the water canteens and the whispering cordage, singing the hours away. On such a day as this the "unknown" had perished at Horseshoe Bend, with only half a mile more to crawl. The thirst madness dimmed his bloodshot eyes and he raved round and round in a circle—within sight of the hotel roof.

The Camel-man thought of the navvy's wife. She had never seen a church or a town. The husband was the roughest of the rough, but he asked the wandering parson to christen the children, terrified youngsters who had never seen a parson. What half-realized longing was it that had whispered in that untutored woman's heart and brought tears to her eyes as she clung to the children in the quiet of the hut? He had left her with the peace born of sympathy and understanding.

Hers must have been the same longing that the hawk-eyed bushman felt when he pleaded with young Rolland to visit a still farther district in extreme isolation.

"I am only one man," replied Rolland; "time, circumstances, and distance make it impossible!"

"Oh, well," sighed the bushman, "I suppose my soul ain't worth much to God."

The Camel-man smiled.

"He knows every grain of seed upon the earth," he whispered, "every bird. He knows of man out here in want of medical, spiritual, and practical help. But how to give it to him?"

For years thus he had dreamed, and the drumming of the camels and the distance and the sunlight all merged in the haze of his longings. Today there was a mirage in the sky. He hardly noticed it, they are so common in the Centre. The mirage showed a string of camels and their turbaned Afghan drivers taking supplies to some far distant station. That camel-team would be at least a hundred miles away. A mirage is a quaint freak of Nature, more elusive even than the artesian water which one day the dreamer dreamed would water this land. It vanished as he watched, like the fading of an eastern scene. "And the mirage shall become a pool, the desert rejoice." He hardly noticed a shimmering blur that masked the beginning of a range of sandstone hills. In the flickering haze the first hill took in the dreamer's eyes the form of a pyramid, sharp cut like the great pyramid of Egypt! Perhaps that pyramid, too, had been a dream before it was built! Then as the camels drummed to the swish of the water canteens, pain, and a sudden loneliness filled his heart.

But presently he smiled, for he felt that somebody walked down there beside him, a tall, brown man with bare feet, whom he could see with his heart alone. And the man walked on to the drumming upon the sand and he looked straight ahead, and when he spoke it was from the heart.

The Camel-man smiled and asked: "How shall I do it?"

And the voice replied:

"Send ye to your brethren!"

Then the Camel-man did a wasteful thing. He lifted his eyes to the sky, pulled out his pipe, filled it brimming full, and lit it with a match.

After this patrol was over he would send to his brethren!

This would be the last of his lone-man patrols! He would do something to start the dream. "The brethren" must do the rest: he knew not what the "rest" was: he only felt that if he started something the rest would build in.

Of nights now he was absorbed, drawing maps in the sand. They lacked foundation, like his castles in the air, but still were something concrete where before he had only built in his mind. Now he built in the sand. Australia was there: cheerily the fire showed its outline. He partitioned that map into states, the states into "thickly inhabited", "sparsely in habited", and "uninhabited" areas. Then he drew existing lines of communication, railway lines, telegraph lines, roads, stock routes, mailmen's tracks. The lines were very easy to put in when he got out towards the centre, the north, the nor'-west, and west.

This map showed him vividly what he already knew, how the population clings to a strip round half our coastline. How our communications, the railways and roads, and telegraph, follow the population. It showed him vividly the huge areas in the interior with a man scattered here and there along the spider-web of a track here and there.

One map led to another. He drew maps of the present holding areas of the country, of the people, cattle, sheep, horses, farming, mineral. Then maps of the carrying capacity of the country. Even he was staggered at the number of people Australia could support. The people weren't here yet, but they would come. The land would be ready—granted communication.

He drew, too, maps of artesian water possibilities and many other things. He became so interested, taught himself so much, that at times the sun rose before he had gone to bed. Perhaps no man knew more of the Inland. He filled those maps with facts, possibilities, and future developments. And yet he taught himself how much he had still to learn about the Inland.

But the map of his heart, the one built up in concrete

form last of all, had tiny circles over it in those places marked "sparsely occupied". The centre of each circle represented a hospital. The circle itself represented a radius of three hundred miles; the hospital at a pinch might serve all that country. Each circle touched another, and those circles covered all Inland Australia, except No-man's Land, Arnhem Land, and a portion of the wild "nor'-west corner". In these big areas no white man lived. The western coast of Cape York Peninsula, too, was unmapped.

Now, as he rode on day after day, he was happier. Though he built his maps on the sand, the day was coming when he would build on a continent. And he would know just where and how and what to build—when the brethren stood behind him!

CHAPTER IV

THE GIBBER PLAINS

JOHN FLYNN had dreamed for twelve years before he did things. As a minister of the Smith-of-Dunesk Mission in South Australia, he had toiled through the Inland, learning, growing certain that that country could support millions if its local problems were tackled sincerely. He believed that medical aid for the toilers, spiritual and material help was his job. Flynn is a lovable humorist, which is why perhaps the tragedy in the Big Places hurt him so. But often very humane things are born of tragedy—like the Smith-of-Dunesk Mission. A Scottish lad perished out in the Centre and the mother overseas left her mite to found a Mission to help other mothers' sons. That objective has been realized a hundredfold, thanks largely to the far-seeing work of Rev. F. W. Rolland.

Flynn's dream was to banish isolation. How, he did not know; people believed it impossible until Australia should attain a population as large as Canada. Message communication, even, could not be assured, let alone doctors, ministers, and transport. Flynn, when in civilization, has stressed the need at every opportunity, listening with a smiling seriousness to the objections raised, then carried on with his work and dreams. But he always left thoughts in the minds of the objectors.

He applied to his brethren down south. They grew into a band of enthusiasts, anxious to help, but—they had no money! A drop of water may swell into a river, one shot may start a battle. Flynn fired the first shot, a shot that was to heal many a wound. His sister wrote a letter to the *Messenger*, proposing "a quarter of a mile of threepenny-bits" to finance an inquiry into the spiritual needs of the Northern Territory.

Thereafter the little band saw that no week passed without at least one newly arranged "letter" accompanied by a subscription-list. Gradually, hundreds of readers became interested, letters and contributions began to come in. By 1911, £200 was raised, and John Flynn trod on air. He was detailed to travel through northern Australia and report on the possibility of practically benefiting the country in spiritual, medical, material, and national needs.

The man was quite sure his dream was realized; it was a dream no longer to him. How often sometimes in exasperation his friends have exclaimed, "Oh, man, man, come to earth! You are ten, twenty, fifty years before the times!"

As usual, he promptly started off. This time he arrived in Sydney and interviewed Rev. John Ferguson, Chairman of the Australian Board of Home Missions, who immediately decided that the project should be put before the General Assembly of Australia. Within three hours a meeting was held, Flynn's project was endorsed, and the scheme placed in the White Book of the G.A.A., and two hours later Flynn started on his twelve months' tactical trip across the continent.

He had awakened the sympathetic interest of a tiny few in Adelaide and Melbourne, and now won the official foundation—the mirage was becoming a fact.

Flynn acts when he sees his course clear: he goes straight ahead and nothing can turn him aside until that phase of the job is completed. Then he dreams again, sorts his dream into detail, and with a burst of energy carries on right through the next phase. A peculiarity of the man is that time in hours does not count. By the campfire or in city office he often works right through the night; works anywhere and at any old hour, quite losing himself in the job in hand, sometimes to the annoyance of his fellow-workers who toil more methodically.

As he works, so he travels. He has travelled innumerable miles of the Inland while others slept. Several times since motor-cars invaded the Inland he has come within an ace of breaking the necks of travelling sleepers. But he only smiled when they picked themselves up off the road: he was glad they were alive and pleased too that his own neck was intact.

So with concentrated energy he carried out this trip of trips, and twelve months later wrote from Darwin—wrote all day and hour after hour through the night preparing that momentous report, oblivious of the moths that burned their wings on the lamp-glass and littered his table with their bodies. He did not even hear the discordant squeak of a Chinese fiddle away down in Chinatown.

Flynn's report on the Northern Territory and Central Australia was presented in 1912 by the Home Missions Board to the General Assembly of the Presbyterian Church of Australia and created intense interest and sympathy. It was his dream put into concrete form before a body of trained business men. Flynn knew of difficulties, so many that he brushed them aside and carried on to do that "something". He has followed that course ever since.

But the members of the Assembly hastened more slowly; the foundations were planned by another, but they laid them, laid them so surely that in these few short years their bridges have girded Australia. Apart from the camel work of the patrol riders, there must have been tremendous spiritual power behind the movement.

The Assembly agreed with Flynn that the life of mother and baby was too precious a thing to throw away. They believed that the linking of inside Australia with communications and a line of hospitals was a national as well as a humane thing; they believed that the greater Outback would welcome Christianity when it came as Christ came, with healing for the body as well as for the soul. They also believed that it was a movement which would appeal to a continent and that we had the men and women of steadfast courage, endurance, selflessness, and love that would see it through. And they believed that the public would help by finding the money and some of the toilers as well. The difficulties in providing doctors were insuperable. But it was thought possible to establish Nursing Homes, each in charge of a fully-qualified nurse. So the Board voted to make a start. The work was to be quite non-sectarian: regardless of creed or none at all a sick man would be welcome to the best attention. To those who welcomed it, spiritual help would be ever ready, as well as material help, wherever possible. The work must have a national aspect, all was to be for Australia. In every way possible the movement was to help the nation and national life. It was a big project, embracing a continent; but then big things touch Australians.

The Board fired a canny shot in its first attack for the sinews of war. Headquarters issued an appeal for five thousand volunteers, each armed every year with £1, to form a Bush Brigade to get the Big Job moving. It moved.

Flynn was appointed Superintendent of Field Work. He left for Oodnadatta with a song in his heart.

From Adelaide he had ample time in which to plan as the little train crawled along on its six hundred and eighty-eight mile journey out towards the Centre. It was a fortnightly train, a three-days' trip. The train was crowded with returning frontiersmen who proceeded to make themselves comfortable —cattlemen, government officials, prospectors, settlers, well-sinkers, sheepmen, carriers, 'roo shooters, railway men, linesmen, shearers, station-hands, drovers, all the varied callings of the North. The dozen women travellers were the care of all hands aboard. A shy favourite was a young city bride happily curious as to the Inland, it was almost as a foreign country to her. Her future home was eleven hundred miles away, her nearest neighbour would be one hundred miles

distant. It had all been gravely explained to her by the sun-
tanned young cattleman with the understanding smile who
sat so protectingly by her side. The thoughtful expression
on the young husband's face was warmly echoed in Flynn's
heart. It was for such as these, for others coming, and for
those already "out there" that he would make the frontiers
safe.

Other faces were happy too, youngsters' faces returning
home after having seen the sea, and shops, and trams, and
people and "lots o' things". The mother's face told its own
story of a new lease of life, but Flynn saw the reason in the
eyes of the children, the telltale red rims now fast returning
to health from a doctor's care. It had been a fight to save the
freckled boy's sight, but he too would recover and return to
help Dad with the teams. Sandy-blight is a scourge in certain
parts of the interior, though cured easily enough if only the
right medicines are available.

To Terowie (139 miles) was a fast run on the broad gauge;
then came a change over to the 3ft. 6in. with Quorn (234
miles) reached at nightfall. With easy-going bustle the whole
crowd transferred to the Far-North express, which crawled on
through Hawker (275 miles), then Beltana (353 miles), and
puffed into Marree (441 miles) in leisurely time for breakfast.

Flynn had travelled the Centre through and across. All
hands knew him. He was "one of the crowd" with a thousand
questions to answer and ask covering men and women,
stations and mining-fields, across the entire continent. He
knew the man at the Ten Mile Tank on the South Australian
border, he knew the Afghan's dog at Angoranna, and the
boundary-rider west of Broken Hill. He had swopped yarns
with the cattlemen a thousand miles north at Pine Creek
and travelled with the mailman on the long southern tracks.
He had opened shell with the pearler at Broome and handled
the ribbons with the coach-driver two thousand miles back
on the Queensland side. He knew too as a continent what
many of his inquirers knew only in localities, the grazing,

pastoral, mining possibilities, and impossibilities of the whole Inland. He knew where fertile lands were, where real lesert and where desert in name only. And he knew that, inevitably, population was coming over all the land they were discussing, if not by our own race then by another.

On joining the "express" the passengers slung off hats and collars, produced books and cards and bottles and made themselves comfortable for the long trip up to Oodnadatta. Flynn then had a little leisure for his own thoughts as he gazed out over the country that inspired them. To the east stretched the abrupt line of the Flinders Range. Quite beautiful he knew that country to be. After long travel the ranges dimmed and a sea of plain crept towards the train. Speckled with gibber stones, saltbush and mulga, the plain looked dry and parched. When the rain came, it would look a wheatfield for hundreds of miles. Huge tracts of this land carried sheep, but the carrying capacity was limited. With communication and rapid transport would probably come artesian or irrigation water and the flowering of the land, large portions of it at least.

This railway was a magnificent enterprise; the attempt of a handful of people to build a line right across a continent for two thousand miles, and, at that, across the very heart classed "barren" for a decade.

Flynn knew that "barren" was a libel, but knew also that the Inland has tough problems, peculiarly its own. That railway when completed would help to solve some of them. From Darwin on the north the line ran south one hundred and fifty miles to Pine Creek, then followed a break of nine hundred miles right across the continent to Oodnadatta. To bridge that gap meant statesmanship and money backed by the determination of a people. The line must be finished—if we are to live as a nation.

Oodnadatta, six hundred and eighty-eight miles from Adelaide was the railhead, and this was the starting-point of Flynn's ambitions. He had to build his first Nursing Home

here. North, east, west, and a considerable distance south
stretched a country in which the British Isles, France,
Germany, Austria, Hungary, Luxemburg, Belgium, Holland,
Denmark, Norway, Sweden, Switzerland, Spain, Portugal,
Albania, Yugoslavia, Rumania, Bulgaria, Greece, and Italy
could be stowed with room to spare.

In that country lived fifty thousand Australians, and Flynn
meant to spider-web its vastness with Nursing Homes and
communications. What a problem faced the man and the few
behind him! Motor transport for the Centre was then thought
an impossibility, aeroplanes were hardly dreamed of as being
practical transport. When the train crawled into the little
railhead hamlet Flynn rolled his swag and stepped out
smiling. The future would take care of itself. This was his
country, these saltbush and spinifex plains, together with the
country of the mountains far away. Oodnadatta was the
farthest out place in the Inland where skilled medical help
was available. Sister Main had been installed in the little
Hostel just before Lady Dudley inspired the Bush Nursing
movement. Mr and Mrs Barr Smith were the good Samaritans
who had secretly assisted the Hostel. When the Presbyterian
Church stood officially behind Flynn, it took over from the
Smith-of-Dunesk movement, and Flynn stepped from the
train with his dream stretching continent wide before him.

A handful of little houses with white roofs. This, the
largest town for two hundred and fifty miles southward, five
hundred miles eastward, seven hundred and fifty miles west-
ward, one thousand miles northward. Back towards Adelaide,
twin rails merged into the horizon. A cloud of dust arose
from the trucking-yards, where a bellowing mob of unwilling
cattle, with horsemen galloping on the flanks, were yarded.
That mob had travelled a thousand miles from "the Queensland side" to provide rump steak for Adelaide. Life-giving
water from an artesian bore had made this hamlet of such
importance to travelling stock. Down by the old Neale River
clustered dark green trees around Hookey's Hole. The river

might be dry, but the pretty water-hole seldom was. In the haze out on the plain that surrounded Oodnadatta and spread beyond the horizon were big cattle herds, sheep too, though struggling under different living conditions to those obtaining in the heavier rainfall country of the coasts. Building up those herds were the present day pioneers. There was room for plenty more, and Flynn was convinced that the people of the cities would help, if they only knew how. It was a warm day; goats and donkeys sought the shade. The locked-up, deserted sheds, the rails, barrows, scoops, and idle tools at the railhead showed that the line had "ceased".

CHAPTER V

GRAINS OF SAND

FLYNN took off his coat and got right into the job of turning the little Hostel into a Nursing Home. He knew where the tool-shed was, and he started to build. He had willing help: people are not slow in helping those who are helping them.

One day he was sitting on the kitchen floor. So was Sister. So was an old kerosene stove, in pieces. Flynn was covered in soot from head to foot—so was Sister, to her sorrow. But Flynn exclaimed triumphantly as he clamped the battered thing together.

"There! It will go like a house afire now!"

"Like it went before?" questioned Sister meekly.

"Oh, no, it won't burn the place down now."

"I hope not," murmured Sister.

Out of a smudged eye Flynn gazed proudly at his handiwork, but sensing a lack of enthusiasm remarked, "You're a bit black, Sister."

"So are you."

"Oh," Flynn smiled, "a bit of soap and water will fix that—and the floor is nothing. But, why so troubled?"

"There's a family away out there," answered Sister, pointing towards the east, "camped at a water-hole. They worry me. A stockman in charge of an out-station with his wife and eight children. He's away weeks, sometimes months at a time, mustering. As the water gives out the family follow it. But the man has ridden in here—cancer on the face." She gazed appealingly at Flynn.

"What can I do for cancer?" she almost whispered.

Flynn's fine blue eyes clouded over.

"Won't he go south?" he asked gravely.

Sister shook her head.

"I tried to persuade him, but he just pointed east and said, 'My wife and children wait out there!' and rode off."

But the man rode in again—later. The agony had proved unbearable. Flynn was building a fowl-house. As he rammed down the mulga posts he dreamed: as he nailed the wire-netting he dreamed: and his dreams were of the saving of life. Sweat beaded his lean face as he punched the crowbar into the hard, baked earth. Digging these post-holes was laborious work, slow work. He was building a fowl-house and he had many hospitals to build—grudgingly he straightened his back, gazing out across the plain. Time and slowness! Time was flying, methods were slow while a continent awaited its hospitals! As the dream haze left his eyes he gazed steadily at a horseman coming—slowly. Loosely holding the reins, his shoulders drooping.

Flynn realized that for this man his hospital would come—too late!

With a cheery greeting Flynn walked to the horse, patting its muzzle while the man dismounted. He looked into Flynn's face.

"You are Flynn," he drawled as they shook hands, "the parson with the dream?"

"I'm he," smiled Flynn.

"I have had a dream, too," he looked into Flynn's eyes, "*my* dream will come true. I have a wife and children out there," and he stared hard.

"We will look after them," promised Flynn gravely.

Eventually Sister persuaded him to try the forlorn hope.

"Just try," she said. "The train leaves in a few days."

"I will give it a go," he agreed at last, and went south, leaving his heart behind him.

Later influenza came to Oodnadatta. While the township

was laid low a blackfellow came in with a message from the mother out at the water-hole. She asked for "medicine": all the children were ill.

A station-owner happened to be passing through; he had trained a motor-car up from Adelaide. A rescue party started out—it was only a thirty-mile trip. Eagerly Flynn watched the work of the car. It went merrily for fifteen miles, then it climbed sandhills, little ones 'tis true, but it climbed them, then jolted and bumped over miles of loose gibber stones. Finally it got to a water-hole at the foot of rocky hills. There was the shed of boughs and saplings, with a blackfellow boiling water at the fire. In two tents lay the children, all running high temperatures; the mother ill and worried. Sister got to work while the motor-man sent his car back for a relief party. Sister made her patients comfortable, sorted clothes, packed them, and made up a hamper. She spread her camp-stretcher under the sky, but did not use it: the night was bitterly cold and her patients were calling, calling.

At sunrise the motor-man harnessed up the old waggonette while Sister strapped the swags, dressed the children, and bundled the family aboard. It proved a creaky ambulance—its wheels patched with wire, its pole with greenhide. At the first steep creek the "old-timer" lumbered down the bank, bumped across the stones, and as the horses were straining up the opposite bank broke a back axle.

They comforted the sick people while waiting. When at last the car returned the worst cases were put aboard and it hurried off, leaving behind two pathetic little figures, one walking on each side of a half-caste with their hands clasped in his. The car returned at nightfall. The children had walked until they could walk no longer. They camped on a rise at the side of the track where the half-caste lit a little fire for each.

At the Hostel the Sister pulled them all through, though the mother nearly followed her baby when it was born.

Perhaps the father was waiting to greet it. But they did not tell her that—yet!

The dreamer sighed as he gazed north, and east, and west. The Nursing Home had saved this family, all but two, but how about those other families calling throughout five hundred miles of country to the east, over a thousand miles to the north, over a thousand miles to the west?

In the land of distances and lots-of-time, the dreamer again saddled up his camels, for he had to go on patrol. And to the drumming of the camels' feet and the swishing of the water canteens he rebelled against time and distance. "Faster transport!" he thought, while over and over again that steady drumming mocked him—"Slow but sure—slow but sure!"

"Ninety per cent slow!" thought he bitterly, "while Death flies on the wings of the Wind!" He held his breath and gazed up at the sky with a wild light in his eyes: "Aeroplanes! The wings of the Wind!"

His thoughts sped like lightning. "Why not! They were experimenting successfully with flying-machines in England, France, America, Germany. They were past the experimental stage surely. Flying doctors! Why not?"

For years he had dreamed it, now it struck him like a thunderbolt that this was the certain, the only solution. All his thoughts, time, and energy would be entirely wasted otherwise.

"The experience, the money to buy 'planes, the trained men to fly them?" But he brushed this thought aside. "It is the way," he whispered. "Hospitals stationed strategically over wide areas and Flying Doctors to connect with each. And it can only be started by 'doing something'."

Thereafter, day by day, as he crossed the plains, night after night, he pondered on those Wings of the Air, on a chain of hospitals connected by Wings of the Air. Vividly his maps explained that even if Australia were girdled with hospitals each would be hundreds of miles apart. What of

the sick, the urgent cases in between? A Flying Doctor with
Flying Ambulance to pick them up, a dream within a dream!
But how would the Flying Doctor know?

"Wireless!"

He looked to the skies and laughed. Dreams. Wireless out
here in Centralia! Why, wireless itself was still only a dream
of the Old World, being experimented upon by world-re-
nowned scientists backed by the wealth of nations!

Lonely were his camps—but he dreamed not alone!

He saw much of the Heart of Australia, a heart that a
man could patrol for a lifetime and not see it all. One day
he rode to a settler's home. Leaning over the gate was a
young fellow muscled like a draught-horse.

"Good day!" smiled Flynn. "I'm looking for a baby out
in these parts. He's never been baptized."

"Oh, that's me," admitted the Samson dubiously. "Does th'
brandin' hurt much?"

"Branding?" inquired Flynn.

"This baptizin'—brandin' a man with a name! Jerry Pent-
land out at th' Forty Mile has got th' marks on his arm yet.
Cripes! You oughter see them."

"Oh," smiled Flynn, "that is vaccination, not baptizing.
I'll have to call along and put Jerry through too."

From the plains he passed into the sand-ridges, those
parallel ridges like giant waves of a petrified sea stretching
beyond the horizon. Grim, waterless waves clothed with
desert gum and mulga, with creepers in vivid flower, the silent
valleys tufted with spinifex and sometimes with sweet grasses.
Thence he travelled on among solid hills into the mountains.
Queer mountains they were, the oldest in the world, standing gaunt against the sky, often in fantastic shapes like the
broken walls of age-old fortresses. Some mountains were timbered, and among the castellated shadows in the valleys wild
camels fed, wild horses, and even donkeys and kangaroos and
emu and queer "hoppy" things of the Centre As the miles

passed slowly by in their hundreds, he came on better grassed lands and even rivers, and then areas of beautiful timber. And nights came when instead of the desert silence he listened to the ceaseless squabbling of wild-fowl on the lagoons and breathed the fragrance of giant water-lilies that turned those lagoons into lakes of red and pink and blue.

Sometimes he would travel a fortnight without seeing a soul. He could have branched off at times and travelled for weeks without meeting man or woman. But he stuck to the "settled" routes. Even so, in places, he found the wild cry of the aboriginal company indeed.

Over those far-flung areas scattered white men were living, with a lonely mother here and there, blazing the pathways that our children might come and settle when our southern lands are over-filled. He passed through land that supplies us with much of our beef and sheep; he linked up with isolated mining-camps, with the sinkers of artesian wells, with teamsters and camel-trains loaded with wool shorn three months before! It would be late on the markets of the world. He came to a little bush home down in among the hills with gum-trees shading the back paddock and scarlet poinciana the veranda. He had lunch there. They were quiet folk the brown-bearded husband and the wife with brave, grey eyes. The children were somehow more quiet than shy, even though they only saw a visitor once in a year. Flynn rose with a tired sigh.

"Oh, well," he said, "I won't stay any longer. You have no need of me."

"Yes, we have," said the man quietly. And they took him down into the paddock where, under a pretty tree, was a wee mound with creepers already flowering upon it.

"There was no doctor," said the man. "We did not know what to do."

Flynn read the service.

Leaving the country of the saltbush he rode down a hill to a creek. The setting sun touched with beauty an old-fashioned house sheltered by a hill whose rocks poked up like a hand of cards. As the camel lurched down to rest, the man came out, a tall grey-beard, with a reminiscent smile, for he had met Flynn once, six years ago at Beltana, a thousand miles away.

"Well, Padre," and his brown eyes twinkled, "I haven't had a jamboree since! But where is the policeman?"

"Oh," laughed Flynn, "promoted: he is stationed in Adelaide, now."

"I'm glad to hear it, he could have got me into a heap of trouble if he had liked. And it would have served me right too. By the way, how is the dream?"

"Out of the chrysalis stage."

"It's true then that you've started a Nursing Home at Oodnadatta?"

"Yes."

The greybeard stared in mingled admiration and unbelief.

"It's hard to believe," he said earnestly. "We got the news by 'mulga wire' and I laughed—like I did years ago at Beltana—you remember?"

Flynn nodded and smiled.

"I am very sorry," the man said, "and though you cannot complete the dream I wish you all the luck in the world. But, come inside, the wife hasn't seen a stranger these two years past."

After the evening meal, it was a hot, airless night. No moon, but the stars shone diamond bright. On the veranda was a litter of bushman's tools watched over by Bluey, the cattle-dog. Beside the open door burned a lamp, with moths flying around it; in the doorway stood the dreamer, his sleeves rolled up, his face very earnest as he spoke. He might have been speaking to a congregation in a cathedral instead of an audience of three—father, mother, and grown-up son.

The son had never seen a minister, had never heard of things mentioned. After the service, he listened as Flynn spoke of the outside world, and his eyes grew vision bright. The mother said nothing: she listened and watched her son.

Flynn rode on through valley and gorge, where his camels' feet drummed not so rhythmically. The way was becoming rough and stony. Stunted scrub grew by the roadside until the country changed again. Precipitous mountains hemmed him in with rocks like grey houses clinging to their sides threatening to come rolling down. Fine trees grew up there, he could see their branches swaying in gusts of wind. Cockatoos made the valleys noisy and galahs swished by in screeching flocks of pink. Sweet grass overran valleys and hills, and on toothsome scrub the camels grew fat, though footsore on the granite rocks.

He camped at a mining-camp, a rough camp of sixty men, no women. They lived on a mountain side, in sheds of saplings. The smoke from their fires coiled lazily up amongst the bloodwoods; from down in the valley echoed the bark of a dog. The miners were mostly bearded, sun-tanned chaps; a self-reliant crowd, with an occasional noisy beggar among them. for yodelling rang out among the hills. Their stores arrived every six months, wet season permitting, creaking in over rough mountain tracks in high-wheeled waggons drawn by teams of patient little donkeys. Great pullers are the sturdy donkey teams. They have pioneered transport on many a lonely track, hauling through sand or over stone willingly and well. Their aggressive bray has awakened many a primitive gorge and startled the wits of myall natives.

Before a big bough shed were placed rows of boxes and kerosene cases as seats. Here the miners congregated around the Padre, an eager crowd, hungry for news of the great "Outside" and ravenous for the few books and magazines still in his saddle-bags. Then he rolled up his sleeves, gripped his favourite forceps, and the first victim opened his mouth. The audience watched feelingly, for the molar was rooted deep.

"You may swear if it helps!" he smiled grimly as the man held his head and spat and coughed.

When the bad teeth were all out, the Padre lanced a couple of boils, attended to a lad whose foot had been crushed by a fall of rock, then with the mate of a sick man walked up a winding gully to a bark hut hidden among trees. Someone was mumbling feverishly inside. With his hollow cheeks, staring eyes, and straggly brown beard, he looked rather awful. He smiled with grim interest as the Padre stooped in under the doorway.

"Old John Flynn," he said hoarsely, "the quinine-man! You saved my life once before. Who pays you to travel the country saving men's lives?"

"I have friends in the cities," smiled Flynn. "They are friends of all of you to as much as their purses can afford. And you know my great Friend."

"The Saver of Souls. It almost makes me believe in Him seeing that He has sent you to me twice."

That evening all hands congregated around the big shed. The church-bells were the camel-bells from the twilight in the foothills below. Silence spread over the mountain side, that silence when the earth seems hushed and listening. Gravely the Padre preached, bareheaded, with the light of the dreamer in his fine blue eyes. At a steady fire a little aside a miner boiled his quart-pot, quietly cooked his flap-jacks, and ate his meal while listening to every word.

Again the Padre rode away, among hills growing more grim and barren, until he approached yet another mining-camp. Here were the foothills, and beyond them, stretching away to the limitless horizon, the ridges of red sand. Again came the drumming of the camels' feet as they moved easy and contented.

Among knobby hills appeared the dumps and shafts with a rough camp here and there. From his perch high on the camel he could see as he approached the heads of a group of men. He wondered. They were hatless, solemn faced,

silently standing around a freshly filled grave. The two
shovel men stood uneasily staring at the mound, wishing
they had something further to do. At last one big rough chap
raised his threatening face and said:

"Well, boys, we can't say much, and we don't know what
to sing. But Jim here was a damn fine chap. We'll sing 'For
He's a Jolly Good Fellow'."

The speaker started the song and the solemn chorus
swelled until it rolled over the hills. The Camel-man understood. As his camels grunted down to rest he stepped off
and joined the circle and the song. When it was finished
he stepped to the centre and said quietly:

"Well, boys, I'm just in time. We'll finish the service
now."

He stayed a couple of days, for they made him very welcome. The morning he was saddling up he happened to
glance around at the little hills dotted with dumps like
ant-beds. Down a sandhill a miner was walking, the smoke
from his pipe curling blue in the clear morning air. As he
put his foot down a grain of sand gave way, others slid
with it, and the man slipped. He clutched at the sand, but
it moved with him. Down he went, clutching wildly, in a
chute of sand that emptied straight into an old shaft at the
foot of the hill. It was a shallow shaft and the man found
himself dumped into it unhurt. But as the trickle of sand
shivered down his neck he yelled and a dozen men snatched
shovels and came running to his cries and louder cries as the
sand flowed, then poured in, and buried him to his chest
He struggled like a trapped ant while his mates shovelled
and shovelled to turn the flow away; but the faster they
shovelled the faster more came down, until the plunging
victim was buried to his chin. Wild cries for help went
ringing across the hills. The whole camp came running:
they dug like mad men with the sun shining on their aching
backs. Two slow hours passed. They just held their own and
were tiring fast when the sand from above came with a shivery

rush, filling the shaft to a foot above the miner's head. With the strength of despair, some leaped down to hurl the sand from his mouth, damming the flow with their bodies while those above worked in gasping fury. They won the day: he was dragged out to lie white and trembling among his exhausted mates.

As the Camel-man returned to his saddling a fossicker strolled along.

"Why not take the buckboard, Padre? We've got one. The station is eighty miles in among the hills, and it's a rough track: horses will travel better. We'll look after your camels until you return."

Gladly the Padre assented and drove off, still thinking of that terrible struggle; of that grain of sand which had so nearly cost the life of a man. He thought of sand as he had known it for many years. He had eaten it in porridge and in jam, had eaten it raw despite his close-shut lips, had drunk it from his corked water-bag. He had dug it from the back door with a spade and dusted it from the church organ with a broom. He had seen it slithering across the road like little snakes, rolling up to the township like the smoke of a wild bushfire, blowing across the desert in a narrow blinding stream. He had seen it swirling across the plain in shrieking funnels two hundred feet high, had seen it blowing out like a pennon from the peak of a sandhill, and had seen in the morning a hill of sand where no sand had been before.

Sand grains! Oodnadatta had been his first grain of sand! The dreamer slackened the reins and the horses plodded on of their own free will. Oodnadatta! He would cover the continent with Oodnadatta hospitals built with money that must be made to flow like grains of sand! And the power to move the grains of sand? The hearts of men! Once touch the hearts of men and the money would flow.

He came to earth with a jerk as the buggy stopped dead against a rock. With smiling cheer he urged the horses round the obstacle. Plodding on, he looked longingly to the left, seeking a short cut.

A short cut! The elimination of distance!

He pulled himself together; he must cease dreaming for the time. Beside him ran the precipitous side of a dry creek; he had crossed it before and knew the creek ran for many miles barring his way. If he could cross it now he would save twenty miles. Suddenly he reined in the horses, gazing not at a miracle, but at grains of sand. A bend of the creek was completely bridged with sand! He saw it all—the bare patch away across on that little flat where had been the sandhill. A wind had come and blown it all into the creek. He drove the buggy across quite easily.

Grains of sand—the hearts of men! They would eliminate time and distance and bridge the continent. And his had been the foot that had started the first grain of sand that became Oodnadatta Hospital.

Dreaming fierce dreams he drove on. He must cease these long isolated patrols that ate up so much time: he would go back to the cities and fan the breeze that touches the hearts of men.

CHAPTER VI

THOUGHTS THAT WORK

FLYNN returned to Sydney eager to hurry his "grains of sand". He found with delight that the first grains were still slowly moving, yes, more people had become interested, more subscriptions were coming in; a scattered few in city and country were eager to help, while the Board had formed the nucleus of an organization which was already functioning steadily.

An accumulation of correspondence awaited Flynn. Eagerly he opened these letters, seeking in each a "grain of sand". Thoughtfully he replied to each, hoping to make five grains flow where one had flowed before. Then he sent out many more letters, always seeking "sand" but seldom asking outright. The object was placed before the recipient and if he was willing to help he did so.

Flynn planned and carried out his propaganda throughout the entire Commonwealth. He especially considered those men and women in particular walks of life, who, even though personally unknown to him, might be sympathetic to his ideal. He approached governments, officials, organizations, businesses, citizens—any person who might help in any way, if not now then later. Where he did not get immediate assistance he sowed the seeds of thought which, later, would fruit as tumbling grains of sand.

He worked, forgetting time, forgetting that he must eat, worked through the chill of an eerily quiet office often to the dawn. He slept when he felt like it; he ate when he must. With a deep satisfaction he pondered on seeds he had sown in those early years, which were returning a little harvest now. He had worked as a man seeing "through a glass darkly", feeling yet not knowing how numerous little actions of his, little well-thought-out conversations, would work into the fabric of his dream. On his infrequent visits south, in those early years, he had interested some kindly soul in a lonely family outback, had interested the public in lectures of his travels, and in conversation many others. At every opportunity he had told his dream to influential men, to scientific men, to government men, to men of the city and the bush. Some had smiled, others had treated him as a hopeless visionary. But he had spoken, patiently and with a smiling humour, cloaking his inner feelings on several bitter occasions.

But spoken words breed thoughts that fruit in action. And now that the Church was backing him, and he had the foundation for a working movement that should show practical results, many good folk were responding: some were sending "grains of sand" with which to build. He beamed over those painstaking photos and interesting descriptive articles. The press were sympathetically printing them now. What better agency than the press to put a dream before the people!

One drizzly morning he felt something scratching that was not the scratch of his pen. When sharp claws touched his leg he became aware of a kitten. He smiled down at the shivering little ball of wet fur gazing mutely up at him.

"Poor puss," he smiled. "Is it raining outside?" The kitten wrapped its tail around itself and shivered, too miserable to answer. Flynn glanced at the misty window, then at the clock. Three o'clock. Automatically he became aware that he had missed dinner.

"I'm hungry, puss. Could you do with a pie?" The outcast mewed miserably: it had never been asked if it was hungry before. Flynn stood up and stretched himself; then put the kitten in his overcoat pocket, turned out the light, and groped his way to the stairs.

"We'll have a pie down at the stall, puss. You can have the crusts and I'll have the inside. Yes, I'll have two pies unless the rain has driven old Joe away."

The rain hadn't. "Old Joe" was there under his flaring light, the coffee-pot steaming as he cheerily served those shadowy diners who eat in the night.

Flynn pushed in under the canvas roof that sheltered the cloaked forms from a drizzling rain.

"Peas, and sauce with mine," he smiled at Joe.

"An' a dash o' gravy," served Joe. "It warms a man's innards on nights like this."

"So it does," agreed Flynn, "and it smells O.K."

He had a pie and enjoyed it. He had another but hardly realized it, sauced as it was with his thoughts. "Now how about a lecturing tour, up through the largest towns of New South Wales, then on into Queensland and Western Australia? Could it be managed—an illustrated lecture in every large town in Australia? What a fine project to advertise the scheme, to bring the people of the Inland before the settled people, to make the 'grains of sand' flow." He ate the crusts, balanced the last pea on his fork, absent-mindedly paid the pieman, and walked off up the wet street. At his lodging door he searched for his key and found a reproachful mew.

"Poor old puss," apologized Flynn. "Why, I've gone and eaten your crusts and they represented the world to you."

He tiptoed down the hall, tripped over the mat, and sneaked into the kitchen, bravely aware that if the landlady was not in bed then she ought to be. Guiltily he crept to the cupboard and surveyed a large home-made meat-pie invitingly waiting beside a glass of milk. He winked at the kitten.

"It never rains but it pours," he whispered. "You started a lot of sand when you scratched my leg, puss!"

He left the kitten gorging and climbed up to his room, first thoughtfully leaving the kitchen door ajar so that the innocent might escape the wrath to come. Smilingly he pulled off his boots hardly noticing the awful row when he dropped them—he had decided on that lecturing tour!

From his very first dream right through the years Flynn fought a long fight, a dogged fight; but no one, in bush or city, ever saw him without a smile. There were times when he knew weariness of body and bitterness of heart. No one else knew.

Perhaps the wide spread of his thoughts saved much mental unhappiness: his mind was never idle a moment: even his dreams were really the necessary mental tracing of plans. Now, in his "spare time" he delved yet deeper into aviation and wireless. The only way, then, that he could delve was to watch overseas developments through the press and follow closely every development through British and American technical journal. Every scrap of information he could get, printed or personal, he sought with a searching thoroughness. Also he mentally marked out men and organizations in Australia whom he thought would be influential in our coming aviation and wireless world. In the furtherance of his flying-doctor dream he would approach these and surprise them with the thorough grip he had of aviation and the intricacies of wireless. Practical results would be some years in coming, of course, but then Flynn always looked "fifty years ahead". Meanwhile he sought to be prepared in any and every way that his mind suggested. Curiously enough, Fate in elusive roundabout ways had definitely commenced to work with him. The right word here and there had gained supporters whose work in turn spread and spread. Philanthropists were becoming interested though he did not know it; dreadful accidents were featured in the press and showed people vividly the menace of Inland isolation; while isolated acts of endurance shouted the silent heroism of it all. Such pen-pictures were only flashes on the sheet of public knowledge, but with gathering momentum they joined the cause for which Flynn was working.

In the midst of his fevered activities he forced time to let him bring out a magazine, the *Inlander*. A "quarterly" magazine, "a magazine with no magazine habits", "being a voice from the uttermost frontiers of settlement in Australia".

"Published by the Australian Inland Mission Board to Stimulate the Battle for a Brighter Bush. Edited by John Flynn the Inland Superintendent, whose home is 'The Wallaby' and whose postal address is Box 100CC G.P.O., Sydney."

Like other bush travellers the *Inlander* appears when best it can. It proved a bright magazine of unusual interest, illustrated by Flynn's photos, keyed up by his articles. Each number was only brought out after much travail of time, labour, and thought. Sometimes it appeared twice a year. But it soon attracted attention and collected numerous "grains of sand".

It was the tragedy of Hall's Creek which showed people of Western Australia, as perhaps nothing else could have done, the crying need for materialization of the very thing of which Flynn dreamed.

Young Darcy went amustering. It was a beautiful day in the heart of the Kimberleys. Darcy was an Australian frontiersman in the full strength of young manhood; he whistled carefree as, bridle on arm, he strode through the rich grass patch where his favourite horse fed. The horse was skittish and snorted, and Darcy laughed as he patted the trusting brown muzzle. He leapt on bareback and was away after the mob, his horse flying through the thick timber as only a trained stock-horse can. The mob wheeled for the camp to a snort of plunging heads and thunder of hooves as dry timber crackled under the tangled creepers. "Crash!" Darcy's horse thumped down and completely somersaulting threw the rider heavily. Weakly he raised an arm above the grass then lay quite still. Thus his mates found him. They raced to harness up the buggy.

The nearest man possessing some medical knowledge was at the telegraph station at Hall's Creek, three hundred miles away. That proved a dreadful drive. No road, merely a bush-track meandering over plain and along mountain valleys, crossing hundreds of gullies and unbridged creeks. When the pain became unbearable they would lift Darcy out on to the ground where he rolled in desperation while his mates silently watched. When his pale face set they lifted him again and drove on into the evening shadows.

Mr Tuckett was home when at last the buggy drove up. He examined Darcy gravely, recognizing with a sinking heart that here was a case far beyond his skill. The nearest doctor was two hundred miles away; impossible to get the patient there in time even if he could stand the added drive. But there was a wire at Hall's Creek connecting the tiny settlement with Perth. Tuckett injected morphine then called across the wire to Dr Holland. The line was "cleared" and they talked anxiously in slow dots and dashes. These men were 1100 miles apart as the crow flies, 1700 by man's quickest cut, 2283 by wire.

At last the doctor decided.

"Operate."

"What?"

"Yes."

"How can I?"

"You must!"

"I've no instruments."

"You have penknife and razor."

"I've no drugs."

"You have permanganate of potash."

"Oh, but can I do it?"

"You can try."

"Heaven! I might kill the man!"

"Well, if you don't hurry he will die first."

Simple preparations were made. Darcy clenched his teeth for there was no anaesthetic. His calm helped the amateur surgeon who worked steadily, making no slip, the only sound the "tick-tack tick-tack" of the telegraph instrument sending progress of the operation and receiving instructions from the doctor.

That operation proved succesful. But Darcy had only recently recovered from fever; his constitution had been further weakened by that dreadful drive. Complications set in. Two more operations under the same circumstances were necessary. It became evident that the man who had so gamely battled was going to die unless he received special medical attention. Dr Holland set out on his seventeen-hundred-mile trip in a race against time. Meanwhile a wonderful feat of endurance had been put up by Darcy's two brothers. When the accident occurred they were near Wyndham, two hundred and fifty miles to the north, in charge of a mob of cattle. They had been on watch all through the night but happening to visit the cattle port next day they got the news through the wires. It was dark before they could hand over their charges. Then they rode back into the darkness at that cautious, relentless pace of bush-bred horses. At Turkey Creek, one hundred and forty miles distant, they slept while fresh horses were hurriedly being run in, then rode on again. The last one hundred and ten miles were covered in fifteen hours.

The doctor left Perth by "express" steamer to Derby, thus cutting down time by half and saving three precious days. At Derby the tide was against them; the doctor waited hours, pacing the deck, staring across at the land. On landing, he was delighted at sight of a powerful car. They pushed her for a day and a half across country, racing when they dared. At Fitzroy Crossing the big panting auto was beaten, but a plucky little car waited there manned by Hall's Creek men.

That was a hell of a ride, across sandy creeks, down abrupt gullies, straight through bush, dodging stumps and fallen timber, creeping around the sides of spurs, racing across flats, tearing through the undergrowth on the maddest of short cuts, colliding with rocks, skidding off trees. Five times the engine broke down "completely"; but they jumped off and rushed into repairs, sooner or later getting her going again. Once the engine stopped for no apparent reason. The petrol was exhausted!

All hands gripped the car and heaving it over gently heard a little "swish-swash" in the bottom of the tank. Carefully they manipulated the car while one man applied a can to catch the precious drainings. When they righted her again the doctor pulled out his stethoscope and stripped off a rubber tube while the others removed the petrol pipe. Soon they had adjusted an ingenious contrivance to the carburettor and away they rattled to the next station.

Six days on the boat, a day and a half on the big car, five days on (and off) the little one and they chugged past Moolabulla station at sundown and on into the dark, only twenty miles from Hall's Creek. "Crash!" The car stopped dead with a tearing of wheels and grinding of broken gear. No one was hurt. They just gazed at one another, then walked back to the station homestead. Blackboys were hurried out and returned with the two first horses they could catch. It was doubtful if the animals had ever been in traces before but they were manhandled into a sulky and as the men jumped aboard plunged off into the dark.

When they drove up to the telegraph station Tuckett opened the door.

"How is the patient?" inquired the doctor.

"He died yesterday," answered Tuckett.

"Time wins!" said the doctor slowly.

CHAPTER VII

THE BOARD

FLYNN rapidly travelled the States, lecturing at church and hall, sowing the needs of the Inland far and wide. Many seeds fell on stony ground, but some took root and blossomed, and the Inland reaped the harvest—is still reaping.

The directors of this great scheme worked as a Board, with members in every State and an executive with headquarters in Sydney. Flynn, besides having a tremendous amount of organization to do, was in entire charge of Field operations. The men of the Board did their job in the city. They were church, professional, and business men. One is the head of a large pastoral concern, and his travels in the back country in connexion with his business had long ago familiarized him with the Inland problems. All were busy men with big jobs to attend to, and the time they gave to the rapidly developing activities of this new movement has had to be paid for in weariness and overstrain.

As the movement grew so State Councils were formed, one in each State, to direct its own organization and propaganda within the State—not for the State—but for all Australia. Each State Council, in addition to its own local activities, organized country and district centres, all of which were encouraged to send in suggestions for the broadening of the Australian movement. Each State Council was empowered to collect money and gifts of any kind, but all such were sent to the Board. The money was used by the Board for the betterment of the continent as a whole, concentrating its activities upon locality after locality of the farthest Inland, according to urgent and tactical needs and the money in hand.

They called the movement the Australian Inland Mission (the A.I.M.). The name was a little unfortunate, as it is hardly an inland mission in the generally accepted sense of the term: it also serves thousands of miles of coastline.

From the start of active operations, Flynn hammered at the Board for every move to be modern, right up to date, the latest in everything! He wanted modern cars instead of camels, little modern hospitals instead of small, old-time, rented buildings. He wanted, well—his dream.

And always the Board listened patiently; almost always it fully agreed it would be well for all concerned if all he wanted could be instantly materialized, but—Where was the money? So the Board built, slowly but surely, utilizing every shilling, and built exceedingly well.

When, however, they could first afford Flynn's craze for speed, they bought him a motor-car, an old Dodge, whose remarkable career is an epic in steel. After hundreds of thousands of miles over bad roads, dashed bad roads, and no roads at all, that old battler is still going strong. It should be honoured in the national museum, for no car has done more for Australia.

When they presented that old car to Flynn he shouted "Hoostha!" It was his farewell to camels. It was the first mechanical materialization of his taste for speed that was to make his dream a certainty. He got straight into that car. He pulled it to pieces right to the last nut; probed into its innermost secrets; laid bare its last speck of carbon. Then he worked at a car-repair shop until he learned mechanics and the handling of repair tools. He forgot all else in order to master this cog in his dream quickly and thoroughly. When satisfied that he could *build* a car if needs be, he set out on his first car patrol, chugging smilingly past the camel-team that was taking the mail to Alice Springs—only to learn that a car possesses a kick as well as a camel.

And what he learned of a car when crossing the roadless Interior wasn't learned all at once. He was bogged, burned, flooded, capsized—often. That car, overloaded worse than any camel, has creaked, groaned, and "raced" across Australia north and south, east and west. Its adventures in speeding up Flynn's dream would make interesting and humorous reading. Here it can only be given honourable mention. But it beat the camels out of sight. Its angry òld hum sang sheer delight to Flynn, material proof under his hand that quick transport could help banish distance and isolation. By its means he carried out many organized patrols where he had done one in loneliness before; and now he found a "mean-time" in which to scour the States on lecturing tours.

After each trip he found the ever-growing accumulations of city correspondence, necessitating a month's work until three in the morning to cope with it, a brake to his speed. It hurt him that valuable time was taken up by this routine work, necessary though it be. Staff work could accomplish it, but—— Where was the money? All cash was wanted for hospital work.

Flynn turned to his old foundation, the Church, where he had noticed many fine girls bubbling over with the desire to do things. On his long trips Inland he considered how he could advantageously utilize their superfluous energies. From these thoughts the Office Teams were evolved: a system which has spread and grown and produced remarkable results in willingness, efficiency, and warm-hearted help.

The O.T's were a success from the start. They were recruited from girls who could give an afternoon, an evening, each week, or more, from their daily work. These teams grew until, in Sydney, there was a team for each day. They attended to the clerical work, to organizing fêtes and functions, to propaganda work, to lecturing organization, to the "personal touch" work with lonely folk, to the sending of little gifts, letters of advice, of consolation, of comradeship; to the sending out of papers, magazines, and books. This last department soon grew so huge that a team had to be specially relegated to cope with it. It sends out every year literature in tons. Thus a heavy load was lifted from Flynn's shoulders: only correspondence needing his personal attention was reserved for him. He was free again to jump into the next step of the building up.

The members of these teams proved stickers. Many of the original members of the first teams are still working, still striving for "grains of sand" to further cement the bonds of goodwill which now join every Australian city with the farthest corners of the Inland.

Each State Council then adopted Office Teams. Over all was the Board; then the State Councils; under them the many O.T's; while in ever-growing numbers throughout the continent were the individual workers and sympathizers. To foster the spiritual part of the programme, travelling padres were appointed for the most isolated portions of the continent. These men had parishes far larger than Germany, Italy, and France combined. Their patrols were extended as time went on. The four main patrols covered Inland Australia in four huge territories: the Central Patrol, the Gulf, the Kimberleys, and Carnarvon.

The Central Patrol was originally based on Oodnadatta, running from south to north nine hundred miles, east and west two hundred.

The Gulf Patrol, as large as New South Wales, extended north and south nine hundred miles, and six hundred miles east and west. The Carnarvon Patrol was responsible north to Port Hedland four hundred odd miles, inland three hundred miles, south to Shark Bay eighty miles.

A wild patrol was the Kimberleys, embracing 137,294 miles, much of the country unknown. There were also smaller but huge patrols; in the Territory, for instance, and along the Transcontinental Railway.

These men travelled by camel, horse, donkey, and foot, according to the physical characteristics of the country, until

recent years when, where practical, they travel by car. They
necessarily had to be men of enduring physique, fearless,
and, above all, men of the world with a close insight into
human nature. This "human touch" in its Field workers has
gone a long way towards the rapid popularity of the A.I.M.

Flynn saw his second hospital looming up in the near
future. He was ambitious that it should be at Alice Springs,
the very centre of the Centre. A tiny township at the foot of
the Macdonnell Ranges, it was the hub of a large cattle
district. Sick people for hundreds of miles came to this town
preparatory to the three hundred and twenty mile drive down
to Oodnadatta railhead. A Nursing Home here would mean
the end of much suffering. So Flynn worked with a smile in
his heart, suddenly made anxious as war clouds spread over
the entire world. Working with the energy of despair lest
his dream be swept away, he realized as time passed, how
well the foundations were laid. For the dream survived; its
practical realization still worked for, though the entire people,
their energies and thoughts, were devoted to the struggle for
national existence. Flynn and the Board clung grimly to
what they had gained until the storm should pass. They suc-
ceeded, they actually built up a little, spurred by tales of
heroism other than the war, which spread a glow throughout
Australia. These unwitting helpers to a hard-struck cause
were the very beings for whom the A.I.M. were working
hardest—children.

It was a bright Saturday morning in the Pilliga Scrub
when a bush mother started to do the washing. She was
troubled, she had not felt well lately, and the husband was
away. Should anything happen to her, what would happen
to the children with help so far away? Anxiously she bent
over the tub, seeking in work to dispel these torturing
thoughts.

She straightened her aching back with alarm in her eyes
made pitiful by the childish voices playing out there under
the trees. An early morning breeze sighed among the timber

on the hillsides: a magpie carolled joyously: crickets were singing their hearts out. But the mother felt the loneliness. The children were playing without a thought in the world, secure in the knowledge that they could take all their little worries to Mum. She sighed as she bent laboriously over the washing. If Dad were only home, or nearer! It is the women who have to pay most in pain and heart-break for this pioneering.

She wrung out the clothes and carried them to the line. How unusually heavy the clothes felt! With a peg in her mouth she reached up to the line, then gasped at the stabbing pain, and collapsed with deathly face.

Young Billy, aged ten, came running across. Mother could speak only with her eyes. He knelt there and gazed, then tried to comfort her, forcing back his tears. Seriously he gazed at mother, his mind torn by conflicting emotions in this swift and terrifying tragedy. He hurried into the house and coming back tenderly placed a pillow under her head and a blanket under her body. He smoothed her hair aside and placed a wet cloth on her forehead. Then he put baby sister and little brother in a box with wooden wheels, provisioned it with two loaves of bread, some eggs, a billy of water, and a box of matches. He kissed mother once again, mumbled as he patted her hands, then hurried away lest she see his face.

He set out for Erdavale station, pulling the cart through the bush in the blaze of a midsummer day, cheerily comforting his dependent charges. They could not see his face, only when he stopped to have a little spell and give them a drink of water.

He reached help late in the moonlight.

With that strange coincidence that follows any particular type of tragedy, humour, daring, crime or almost anything, other deeds of childish heroism followed in quick sequence. And each vividly showed Australia the need of the A.I.M.

A blazing Westralian sun beat down on Billili station, some miles distant from Lennonville. Mrs Atkinson was working out in the yard, the children were playing in a group—all except Elsie who was helping mother. Presently she came running to the other children crying—

"Oh! Mum's lying asleep in the sun!"

Awe-stricken, they tiptoed across. Vincent felt his mother's pulse.

"Mother is dead!" he said quietly, and placed his old felt hat over the wan face.

Vincent's first idea was to follow the tracks of Dad, who was away prospecting. But he might never find him. He stood there gazing around, thinking. Would he run to uncle at the Five Mile? No, something might happen to the babies while he was away. He decided to take them all with him.

He fed the poultry, left them plenty of water, turned off the windmill, gave each child a piece of bread and butter and a drink of water and took a big drink himself to see him through. He then filled the water-bag, filled a bottle for the baby, put the baby into the go-cart, and, fearing lest it perish if left behind, took the puppy too.

The forlorn little procession started out for the Empress Mine, game little barefooted Australians, up against it at the start of life! Vincent was ten, Bobby eight, Isabel five, Arthur three, and Baby just seven months. Puppy was the first to knock up. His legs crumpled up under him and he lay there panting, red tongue hanging out as he gazed after them. He had to be carried. Then Arthur's feet blistered so badly that he had to be given a lift, the sand was awfully hot on bare feet. Vincent struggled on, the go-cart growing heavier as he pushed it through the sand. Baby presently felt the extreme heat, cried a little sometimes, and had to be given a sip of water every few hundred yards. The lad struggled on now in terrible anxiety lest the water should give out before they reached help. He dared not drink himself, he stared at the sand as he bent over the go-cart handle, his mouth so dry he could hardly breathe. Towards the last he had to carry young Arthur on his back and push the go-cart too. And Baby was crying more and more for water. He just managed the job.

These and similar cases helped Flynn with "grains of sand". The public began to visualize the position of the Inlanders under similar happenings—Inlanders who were hundreds of miles from help. So the dream just hung on, even though by a slender thread.

In 1915 funds had accumulated, not quite sufficient to start another hospital, but enough if granted help.—That came.

In far-away Port Hedland on the Western Australian coast the citizens called a meeting. They had a government doctor who in the course of his numerous duties inflicted their erring ones with fines. The citizens had long felt the need of a hospital as well as the doctor of whom they were secretly proud. They decided to try for a Nursing Home under this pioneer movement of the A.I.M. The State Government was immediately sympathetic and promised a subsidy; so did the Local Roads Board. The citizens passed around the hat with fruitful results. They wrote to Flynn. "Would he start a hospital?"

Would he! He grabbed the letter, forgot his hat, and hurried to the Board. He only wished for the chance to start a hundred hospitals.

Port Hedland lies one thousand and sixty-three miles by steamer north from Perth. It is the port of Pilbarra, where the gold comes from. Pearls are won from the ocean frontage, while inland is a vast district for cattle and sheep. The little town of pretty bungalows, housing two hundred and fifty people, is really on a low narrow island with the hills rising behind it. Tides there rise and fall twenty feet.

As the crow flies, the little pearling port of Roeburne lies some one hundred and thirty miles south; while the greatest pearling port in the world, Broome, lies three hun-

dred miles north. Along that way is the "Madman's Track":
its loneliness shouts aloud.

When the A.I.M. was born the terrible "Koombana
Blow" struck Port Hedland. That day the *Koombana* steamed
out of port and all that was again seen of her was a door,
a settee, a red cushion, and a teak panel. A lighter that had
started out to meet the *Bullara* went down with all hands;
and the *Crown of England* was wrecked on the ugly edge
of Depuch Island. During the blow the sea swept Port Hedland's esplanade and sprayed in over the verandas.

From the port a railway runs a hundred and ten miles
inland to Marble Bar gold- and tin-field. The country for a
considerable distance inland carries a hardy spinifex grass
on which sheep do fairly well. Areas such as the De Gray
River flats are exceptionally fertile. The hinterland at first
sight looks a rough land to the easterner; the men of the
nor'-west, however, know that with a large area around them,
and a large heart within, it is possible to do well on limited
capital. Thirty-seven stations, gradually abandoning cattle for
sheep, were scattered over the hinterland. In the wild places,
hardy groups of prospectors were seeking the yellow metal.
Some had wandered across from the Kimberleys and the
Territory, covering a thousand miles—sometimes through
previously unknown country. Some had fallen to the blacks,
others to thirst; but the wanderers still carried on, revelling
in the wild, free life and lured by the hope of gold. Men
like these laughed when first told that a hospital was coming
to the Kimberleys. But by the time they were told it had
come.

With a nurse installed at Port Hedland, the A.I.M. had
taken its first step in its merciful conquest of the wild nor'-
west.

As the war dragged on Flynn and the Board fought yet
more grimly, just managing to hang out. Flynn grew enthusiastically certain that his dream would materialize in its
entirety years before the planned time: the very holocaust in

Europe would help bring it about. Eagerly he watched the rapid discoveries in aviation and wireless, the perfection of motor transport and surgery. Once more out of great evil good would come. Closely he watched how the quickest brains of the world were competing to eliminate distance and time, making mechanics simple, cheap, and trustworthy. When the war was over, he would seize on these new discoveries and weld them into the materialization of his dream.

With a smile cloaking a heavy heart, he said *au revoir* to many of his city friends, to many lads of the Inland, to his own frontier padres and to nurses who, trained for the Inland, were now wanted at the war.

CHAPTER VIII

THE "BLACK CAMEL"

OODNADATTA lay bathed in sunlight that shimmered to the horizon. The railway line disappearing into the south quivered like moving steel ribbons. Sister came out to the veranda of the little Nursing Home seeking air not tainted with the dispensary. The men across at the hotel were watching the two billygoats of the village "settling it" in the main street: the clash of horns came from out of the little cloud of dust raised by the fight. Sister knew from the attitude of the loungers, the lazy pointing of pipes, that they were betting drinks on the result. What goats men were! But she watched the fight until an excited dog rushed in and chased the combatants away. She resented that dog's interference. Why shouldn't the goats fight, anyway? Down by the store a camel-train was just setting out loaded with the quarterly supplies of a station away out east. How calm and imperturbable the turbaned Afghans looked as they strode off beside their lurching beasts. Sister gazed to the far horizon where sky met plain and wondered what lay beyond. She wondered, too, if ever the railway line would creep farther north to Alice Springs. Would it ever reach Darwin, a thousand miles away? Sister decided she would be a long time dead by then, so looked to immediate affairs—across the yard to where a man was hammering, sweat trickling down his temple. He screwed up his eyes as she watched, wiped his forehead with the back of a hairy hand, swore at the flies, and gazed longingly at the pub. It was nice of him to build the washhouse, especially when he could have been over at the hotel drinking beer. Lots of people had built little things for her, been considerate of her comfort in many ways. It was nice to know her work was appreciated. That tall thin man who had planted the garden, working until well into starlight each evening, while all the time he was anxious to be away on the roads. And that big brown well-sinker with a hand like a ham, who had railed in the veranda and nearly swallowed a nail when she brought him morning tea. And quaint old "Dad" with the feathery white whiskers who had enlarged the kitchen and chopped off the puppy's tail. Then there was the bush lad who had built the bathroom. Sister smiled: he had forgotten to put in a window but remembered a lock for the door, and screwed two large bolts on the inside as well. The copper for the washhouse had come all the way from Adelaide: the men over at the hotel had passed around the hat. They would not be thanked. "Our own coppers are so often hot," they had said bashfully, "an' we know you want one!" Whatever they meant by that.

Yes, many things had been given, little thoughtful acts, helping so much to make life bearable.

Sister went indoors well content. It was cool inside and she did not have much to do: the patients were practically con-valescent, and she had finished cleaning the ward and dis-pensary and the rooms and had sorted out the washing for the coming week. She hoped a black gin would stroll along on washing-day. Only the dinner to get ready for the patients, then attend to the distribution of those books from the A.I.M., and she would be finished until after "eat-up" time.

But, in the afternoon she was kept busy. Two children came in with sore eyes from sandy-blight; a stockman had received a nasty kick from a horse, and an Afghan had to be treated for camel bite. Then three men came slouching along, with an uneasy glance backward, as they shouldered one another in through the gate. Sister diagnosed the symptoms and was out on the veranda before they decided to slink away.

"Come in," she called.

In shamefaced manner they crept up the path, Sister wondering how she was going to pull the teeth of that one with the thick bushy beard—she hoped the molar was not as firmly rooted.

"Toothache?" she smiled sweetly.

They nodded in surprised recognition of her discerning faculties. She waved them into the surgery with a wordless invitation towards the chair. No one was keen of first blood, but eventually the bearded one "chanced it", only to shy at the forceps. Sister manhandled his head under the crook of her arm and yanked the molar out. He grunted a bit. When the others took their turn he looked on gloatingly. They slouched away gladly apparently, gulping to hold their spit and language until they got clear of the garden path. Well satisfied with herself, Sister cleaned up the mess the men had been in too much of a hurry to notice, had a wash, fed the fowls, then prepared the patients' evening meal. She slept soundly, thankful for a quiet night.

Early next morning the 'phone tinkled: it was the railway doctor south travelling among the line-construction gangs. He rang from Williams Creek, a hundred and twenty-five miles down the line. "Child sick; serious. Can you come?" Sister thought in seconds. Her patients could nearly look after themselves: she would ask the townspeople to give a hand. "Coming," she answered.

She packed a basket and hurried across to the rails. A linesman waited there with the government motor-tricycle. Once aboard and the rails hummed under the wheels, the motor chug, chug, chugging sharp and clear. Sister watched the rails closing in to where away across the plain they joined in one, but though the tricycle travelled fast they never caught up to that join, it remaining always the same distance ahead; the rails ever spread out and hummed. She enjoyed

that ride though she had to sit tight and very still without a
back rest, or an umbrella as shelter from the sun. Only a few
stunted gidgee-trees now and again relieved the monotony
of the poorly grassed, sombre gibber plain. It was drought-
time. When the rains did come Sister knew that lonely
barrenness would be a smiling plain of grass and wild-flowers.

The tricycle hummed with a long rumble over twenty
bridges, the Algebuchina bridge of nineteen hundred feet
showing that man knew what to expect when rain did flood
those dry watercourses. Dead stock lay along several old
creek-beds where the beasts had ended an agonizing search
for water. Hard luck on the stockowner, looking forward to
trucking those cattle that very year! Occasional living rabbits
were seen, those hardy root-grubbers whose long curved teeth
enable them to seek deep in the earth for roots. Some rabbits
became confused at the hum of the rapidly approaching
tricycle and just "froze" right on the line, three goannas, too,
could not get out of the way fast enough: they became para-
lysed, and lay quite still with their heads on the line.

At Mt Dutton a railway gang was stationed: they had the
billy boiled with a brownie spread all ready beside the line.
The smiling cook strolled over from the camp wiping a sweaty
brow with a floury hand: he had a reputation for making
a brownie. Again the tricycle sped on in a swift fifty-mile
run, then Sister enjoyed a back-stretching rest and cup of
tea at Mrs Whitten's. On again into the afternoon and tea
with the gang at Anna Creek—a proud gang with a table-
cloth as white as snow and a china cup and saucer as extra
frills. Those boys knew how to entertain a lady. In the
evening, after a record trip of a hundred and twenty-five miles
in eight hours, on a tricycle with a woman aboard, "the angel
with the lamp" reached her patient.

Sister made the little patient comfortable, then feeling a
bit tired had just sat down to enjoy a well-earned meal when
a horseman came cantering into camp. A man was lying with

broken ribs and apparently internal injuries some fifty miles out. Was there a possibility of medical help?

Half an hour later, as Sister scrambled into a buggy, they let the horses' heads go and leapt aside as the animals plunged forward with the driver clinging to the reins, his foot ready to the brake, staring ahead into an inky night. The lamps only emphasized the darkness; they could hardly see the horses' heads let alone the road with its stones and ruts. Suddenly they lurched down into a dry creek, the brakes screaming, Sister hanging tight.

"It's pretty dark," drawled the driver.

"Yes."

"Th' horses are fresh."

"Yes, but we'd better not talk; you've enough to manage."

"Oh, it's not as bad as that: we're all right so long as a wheel doesn't fall off!"

Sister clung on through the miles until the horses steadied down into the sharp, swift trot of bush horses when driven in a careful hurry. They had branched off from the road into the merest track, and Sister wondered how the horses kept to it. They rattled down into a creek. "Snap! Clatter, clatter, clatter."

"Hold tight!" shouted the driver, as to a scream of brakes the horses gathered themselves up, "a pinbolt's broken loose from the swingle-bar!"

Then the horses bolted and Sister clung tight. Sparks flew from the brakes and hissed from the galloping hooves while the driver pulled on the reins, jamming his weight on the brake. Sister clung to her breath as well as to the seat, staring into blackness while the buggy swayed and lurched on the heels of the maddened horses. "Whoa! boys! Whoa!!" as the driver struggled to hold the mad things in check. Sister marvelled that his head clung to his hat. She gasped after they had raced past a black vacancy that was an old quarry bank. She awaited a crashing capsize with a flying trip through the dark and just couldn't believe it when the buggy rattled to rest among the gibber stones. The panting of the horses was echoed by the driver's deep breaths.

"Hold the ribbons a moment, Sister—Tight! Hang on while I jump down and catch their heads. They're over the traces and we'll have to mend the swingle-bar too."

Sister hung on while he quietened the panting animals and swiftly undid the traces, then she breathed easier—she had wondered what would have happened had they bolted with her clinging to the "ribbons". How extraordinarily quiet it was out here! A hushed silence in the darkness, with stars twinkling from other worlds. Sister had lived during those few moments, anyway. He repaired the swingle-bar with the bushman's companion (fencing wire), re-harnessed the brutes, and led them back until they struck the track again, then drove on.

"That livened things up a little," he remarked cheerfully.

"It did!" agreed Sister, "now I come to think of it."

He laughed.

"It would be all right in daylight," he explained, "but it's a bit nervy at night: there are a lot of deep gullies around here. The track winds in and out among them. Hullo! we've lost it again."

Thankfully Sister got out with a hurricane lamp and walked off into the night looking for the track. It was a bit eerie, peering back from the brink of those black gullies, stubbing her toes on gibber stones that rattled against their mates. The man's shouted directions seemed an alarmingly long way off before she found the faint wheel-tracks. She had crossed them and not noticed. She held the lantern high above her head until he loomed up.

Four times that night they lost the track.

"It's like life," said the driver. "We must go on although we get bushed now and again."

"But we'll get there," answered Sister cheerfully.

"Where?"

Sister hardly knew. She was thankful when a fiery sun

made beautiful that sombre land. A rider came out of the sun, his horse all burnished with gold.

"It's someone from the camp," stated the driver. "Either your patient is dead or they're bringing him along."

They were bringing him along in a dray. Five hours later the dray arrived, Sister took charge, bandaged the man, and transferred him to the buggy. Then started the slow drive back to the railway line.

Sister got her patient "home" and sighed with relief. It had only been a small trip compared to some of her trips. But for all that home was home. Besides, during these sudden calls outback she was always apprehensive lest some desperately ill patient be brought to the Home in her absence. One was arriving now, an old miner from the Arltunga goldfields; his buggy ride had meant a hurried three weeks of atrocious travel. He needed all nurse's skill. Anxiously she waited for the fortnightly train; it hurt her so to have a patient die on her hands. When the train came he was sufficiently recovered to travel with skilled attention. Sister had to take a chance. The townspeople volunteered to look after the hospital. She put the patient on the train and stayed with him during the five-hundred-mile trip to Port Augusta, the nearest "doctor's" hospital. She had over a week to wait for the return trip, then arrived back in time to greet a new patient. Her heart sank at sight of his yellow-white face. He had travelled over four hundred miles on a camel, three weeks of swaying torture in summer heat. There was no entraining this man, he would either walk away on his own legs, or——

Next day when Sister had a few moments to look over her Home treasures she nearly wept; the white hen was dead—the busy cackler that laid so regularly. With harried feelings Sister went to the meat safe. The ants were in it. Then just because all troubles happen at once the primus stove refused to light. Sister hardly knew which way to turn and had no time to waste lighting a fool of a primus. She called in a man who was walking past the window with hands in his pocket and a pipe smoking like a stove.

Of course he would light the primus! He smiled a man-sized smile and seized his matches. He would light the primus. He did! The explosion rocked the hospital.

With jumpy nerves Sister administered first aid, then hurried to prepare a bed for the new case. She opened the linen press and stared aghast as her hands touched sheets and pillow-slips as hard as cardboard. That fool of a black gin had starched them!

Busy days passed. The patient of the long camel ride held grimly between life and death. Sister sat up all through the night fighting for his life, dreading lest the "Black Camel" come. The hospital voiced the quietness of all hands, united to give the stranger a chance. In between, Sister attended to her duties, snatched an occasional sleep, and grew new skin on the face of the man who had lit the primus stove.

She feared lest an urgent call come from the "back of beyond", and wished she had a companion who could mind the hospital in case of eventualities. She wished above all that she could save this stranger's life.

But one dark night the "Black Camel" called and took him away. Sister was too weary to think. Mechanically she went about her added task, registration of death, fumigation, and etceteras. Then she looked up the burial service.

She read it in a sand-storm.

Back at the hospital, too tired to do anything but fall into a chair and close her eyes. There was a parcel awaiting her. A big parcel, done around with hessian carefully corded with knots that betrayed the cattleman's craft.

They opened it for Sister. She leaned forward in the chair and exclaimed in delight. It was a present of wild-dog skins, beauties; the ranges had been combed for those choice russet huskies. Just a token from the "Away Beyond": a remembrance from a cattleman whose life she had saved.

It was good to be able to save men's lives.

CHAPTER IX

FEVER

John Flynn was tired. He did not care. There was no one to see, no one to remark: "By Jove, did you notice how tired John Flynn looks? First time I've ever seen him without a smile. I wonder if all is going well with that A.I.M. business of his?"

Many a smile of Flynn's had brought its "grain of sand" —he must keep on smiling! The streets were chilly at three in the morning, footsteps echoed hollowly. He felt, too, his boots were overdue for repairs. He caught the glint of a policeman's cap: the steady eyes of the Law searched his face as he passed. He had recently returned from a hurried patrol of six thousand miles and was coping now with special correspondence. He called briskly at a newspaper office and smilingly bought a paper hot from the press. When in a city he always read the paper before calling it "a day". Quite often, through this habit, luck and forethought had enabled him to accomplish two days' work in one through information contained in tomorrow's paper before today was done.

Walking up Hunter Street he heard thunder dully rumbling along the street ahead. He sighed. As he approached the street rang out to the rhythmic tread of iron-shod hooves, the heavy rumble of shadowy guns as long lines of them swung by *en route* to some troopship waiting at the Quay. A kindly smile touched Flynn's face as he watched the great-coated figures ride by. He was proud of the boys. Australian blood was his and theirs. Keenly he peered, wondering what

lads were of the Inland and from what parts. He scanned
the clean-cut young fellows as the fours went marching by,
and his heart responded to the song of their rhythmic feet.
He searched the expression in the shadowed brown faces—if
it was only daylight he could "pick" any faces from the
Centre.

How he wished the war would end! Thankfully he remembered that the A.I.M. was pulling through. He watched until
the last Section swung past, then dreamed along and entered
his hotel.

He read yet again a letter from the Front, from a young
Australian Flying Officer Clifford Peel. It set out in approxi-
mate detail how Flynn's dream of flying doctors for Australia
could be realized, going into details, types of machines, costs
and reliability, petrol consumption, distances, bases, etc.

How eagerly Flynn had seized on that letter: craftily he
had had it published and discussed far and wide. It was not
from him, the dreamer, this letter: it represented a clear-cut
statement from an expert in aviation: it carried weight.

He mused, sitting on the bed holding the letter in his
hand. How everything was fitting in through the years! How
the seeds he had sown in the minds of men had germinated!
And now this letter through the press would soon sow more
seeds—"flying" seeds.

He took off his clothes and lay on the bed smoking, his
mind whirling with details, sorting them out and systemati-
cally dovetailing them into workable plans that would
materialize into that portion of his dream concerning the
Northern Territory.

That area of the Inland 523,600 square miles; as large
as France, Germany, Belgium, Holland, Switzerland, and
Italy combined. The population of the Territory was one
inhabitant to every one hundred and eighty square miles.
What a temptation, this practically uninhabited land to
over-populated powerful nations! How understandingly that
school child had answered its teacher: "There is a good deal

of nothing in the centre of Australia." There was much of "nothing" in the North too; but, also, several thousand whites and a great land waiting for our descendants.

There was only one railway line, from Darwin to the Katherine, a hundred and sixty miles as the crow flies. Then straight down through the continent came a gap of more than nine hundred miles to Oodnadatta. National safety and development both demand that the north-to-south line be finished. Peopling of the country would help bring that about. The A.I.M., by making the country medically secure, by bringing universally applicable means of communication, would help people the country.

The Territory might be one of the greatest cattle countries in the world. Sheep-farming and agriculture, too, were suitable over certain areas. Mineral wealth would be exploited when transport came. Australia's scanty population, lack of Inland communication, and great distance from markets, were the main causes of delay in the Territory's progress. In time it would support thousands of Australians.

Flynn planned to better conditions for the pioneers battling out there; and by doing that others would be encouraged to come too. After all, much of the beef those pioneers grew fed Australia, paid taxes, and helped to provide work for the south. Yet only one doctor was stationed in all that 523,600 square miles. He was at Darwin, the one real town.

Flynn's plans concentrated on Marranboy, a new tin-field two hundred and fifty miles from Darwin, fifty miles from the tiny Katherine railhead. Several years back a keen-eyed stockman, tracking cattle east of the Katherine River telegraph station, had specked some tin specimens. Richardson and Sharber in May 1913 prospected the payable lode which had led to the present rush. The field lay among the hills in the basin of a creek which flows into the Roper River—the beautiful Roper with its unique red water-lilies blazing upon leaves larger than soup plates. The price of tin being high pointed to a possible rush of population. Marranboy now represented the largest aggregation of men outside of Darwin; it was the strategical and most needed spot at which to start the next A.I.M. hospital. The Board had almost enough money in hand.

Before Flynn picked up the newspaper he had his plans sorted out to minutest detail. Given the slightest opportunity he was ready to start a hospital in that far-away spot. With a smile, as from work successfully accomplished, he opened the paper. Dawn had long since lit up the window-blinds.

Bright sunlight bathed all Northern Australia. Over the hills of Marranboy it kissed the leaves of the cypress pines and threw trellised patterns of filtered light upon the waters of the jungle creek. Forty miles away, toiling up a steep forest spur was a team of twenty-six donkeys, three abreast, straining at the traces as they hauled their load to the new tin-field. Stores arrive there every four months or so, dodging the wet season which makes the countless gullies impassable. The hills of Marranboy were dotted with shafts and windlasses; fresh red earth from growing dumps shone on the gully sides. Birds whistled cheerily among the trees; others cheekily fossicked round the paper-bark shacks. Scattered tents too shone white among the timber; natives talked gutturally round smouldering fires down by the water-hole. But the shafts appeared abandoned, no toilers at the windlass handles, no hauling of buckets to send the red earth tumbling down the dumps. No roar of stamper, no tapping of pick, no clanging hammer from a miner's forge. Apparently a mining-field abandoned in the first rush of its prosperity. Around the tents and huts too there was a stillness, a seeming absence of life and movement until a man emerged and staggered weakly to the creek, a bucket in his hands. His mate lay inside craving for water. Then here and there appeared a man walking quietly, talking quietly, going from camp to camp lending a helping hand.

Marranboy was stricken with fever. Malaria! From whence

it had come into that healthy climate, no one knew. But it had come, had registered already. As they toiled at a new hole the diggers knew that tomorrow others might be digging for them. A lanky miner chewing a gum-leaf strolled across to the diggers and surveyed the hole critically.

"Who are you planting today?" he drawled.

"Shorty."

"It's a bit too short!"

They ceased their labours, glad of an excuse—even a touch of fever tires a man quickly. They scanned the hole.

"It looks long enough," replied one. "We measured Shorty too."

"He won't fit in," drawled the tall man. "Sometimes they stretch."

"I thought they shrunk!"

"Depends. Most do. Others stretch. All grow fat."

A thin digger reached for his pipe.

"It'll be the first time I've ever been fat in my life," he remarked thoughtfully.

"An' th' last," sighed his mate.

They smoked silently. A bell-bird called in liquid notes from far up the gully.

"You'd better dig it a bit longer," drawled the tall miner as he dawdled away, "or Shorty'll stick."

Wearily the thin man lifted his pick and marked the end of the hole six inches longer.

"It'll be a hell of a long hole we'll have to make for Lofty," he sighed, "if he pegs out."

"Perhaps that's why he's so particular about Shorty," replied his mate. And they resumed their labours.

Inside a large paper-bark hut were two rude bunks, the men, lying there with a fortnight's growth of beard, appearing yet more unkempt in the shadowed light. One man was very far gone. From under the rough blanket his hand hung helplessly, the finger-bones visible under the tightly drawn skin. The hut was scrupulously clean and very quiet. A billy simmered on the ant-bed fireplace, a freshly-cooked damper showed in the camp-oven. Some miners' tools lay in the corner, two saddles and pack gear hung upon forked supports, several books and some six-months-old magazines rested on a bark shelf above a rough table. Two other men were whispering as they brushed the flies from the sick men, trying to keep them cool, trying to coax them to eat a little soup made from recently shot birds.

"How far is Oodnadatta?" whispered a man.

"About a thousand miles south."

"Isn't that where the A.I.M. hospital is? That church crowd that talks about putting hospitals in the farthest out?"

"Yes! It sounds like a mulga wire to me, but the Darwin people think there's something in it. We'd never get a hospital out here, though; the Territory is too big, too far away. The votes of us chaps don't count."

"From what I've heard, they don't go in for votes. Seems to be something different. I wonder would there be any hope of getting them interested?"

"I wonder!"

Silence in the hut.

"They say they've got a headquarters down in Sydney."

"It mightn't do any harm to drop a line."

Silence again. Presently a big fly buzzed in and a sick man moaned.

The two men were thinking perhaps they, too, would be gone long before letters could travel three thousand miles to some "queer" people down south. But what matter?

They wrote.

The miners passed around the hat—it brimmed over.

The government offered to erect a hospital. Would the A.I.M. find the nurses and maintain them?

Flynn smiled with joy in his heart.

CHAPTER X

THE CALL OF THE KIMBERLEYS

WITH delight Flynn farewelled the nurse and companion appointed to the new Marranboy Home. A crowd of chattering O.T's were farewelling too, but Flynn got in a word edgeways. The two girls set out on their three thousand mile journey enthusiastic over the great adventure. An abrupt transition lay before them. They would journey very near the primitive, would live right against the heart of things. They were going into the wilderness; would be cut off from civilization; find themselves in an untamed land among seventy rough men—some among them as wild as the hills, some who for years did not see a white woman.

But Flynn saw in the girls not only the messengers of healing and hope and warm womanly comradeship that they would bring to a stricken community, he saw them as a symbol to be followed by hospitals, communication, and flying doctors, that would help make habitable a vast territory for the Inlanders and for Australia. When he had smiled his last farewell he turned away with his mind immediately busy planning the next link.

His thoughts sped to the Kimberleys in the farthest north of Western Australia, another huge area with its own localized problems, its fine possibilities, its few people who would grow to many, once means of communication banished personal and business isolation from the south. He longed for the money to erect a hospital there right away.

"Grains of sand" were coming in surely and steadily,

helped considerably in the Marranboy venture by the miners and government. The Kimberleys now was the next link in the chain.

Long since he had thought it out on his space-registering maps, had drawn a line from south of Broome on the nor'-western coast and carried it straight over country into the Northern Territory. That corner block to the north of the line represented the Kimberleys—one of the least-known but one of the intensely interesting undeveloped areas of Australia.

There is East Kimberley and West Kimberley. The East embraces 78,414 square miles; the West 58,880: a total of 137,294 square miles, or half as much again as Victoria. The white population of the East was (there has been a considerable increase) 358, including 34 white women; and of the West (with Broome the pearling port) 1604, including 431 women. A well-grassed country, well watered, fairly well timbered, and mineralized.

A fascinating country, that wild nor'-west corner, its coast walled by bold cliffs that hold the rush of a phenomenal tide. It is a country of rugged ranges, many of weird grandeur and fascinating colouring. Where the ranges break are well-grassed plains interspersed with others that grow a rank grass which sways above the heads of horse and rider. Creeper-draped valleys with rock-walled gorges, here and there cut the land into a series of chasms: fine rivers tumble over rock-strewn beds: lagoons stretch inland, their miles of water-lilies a homing Bedlam for countless wildfowl. The plentiful timber everywhere (much of it valuable) is striking in its beauty and occasional quaintness.

In parts of the Kimberleys the river-flats and valleys are covered with extensive deposits of quartz gravel and drift, proved gold-bearing. These will be dredged when roads or aeroplanes are ready to transport the machinery. And the huge conglomerates of the Nullagine will be worked as are the famous Banket deposits of South Africa. Deep drill tests have proved the strong probability of areas being oil-bearing.

There are still areas of that wild country where white man has not yet ventured; where powerfully developed natives, eager fighters, roam in undisputed mastery. That is the land of the wild-cattle camps; the land of sure-footed horses able to race through timber and scrub and down breakneck hills in fearless chase after runaway beasts. It is the land of superb horsemen, tough prospectors, and some fine Australian women. It already sends away great numbers of cattle yearly: the time is fast coming when it will help feed the world. Its long, rough coastline sees few ships except the venturesome sails of pearling luggers. When we presently realize its immense value to Australia, ships from the Seven Seas will be loading in its harbours.

The Kimberleys' three ports are Broome, Derby a hundred miles farther north, and Wyndham three hundred miles farther north again. Broome is the world's greatest pearling port. Derby and Wyndham are the cattle ports. When shipping came to help the pioneers, Derby and Wyndham put up world records for the time shipment of sheep and cattle. Wyndham put aboard during one year 30,000 head; Derby 22,500. That from a country with less than two thousand white men in it! Australia will draw richly from the Kimberleys when she develops it earnestly and sympathetically. It has some fine harbours.

The pioneering already done in the Kimberleys has been only fragmentarily recorded. If that romance had concerned other countries, the world long since would have been flooded with its moving stories. Apart from the exploring ventures of Gregory and Forrest, and the scouting ventures of the Gordons, Buchanans, Duracks and others, is the stirring story of the four great treks. In separate parties, reminiscent of the great Boer treks in South Africa, these started out from Queensland with cattle, mobs of 2500, 1500, 2200, and 2000 head respectively. They covered two thousand five hundred miles in two years and eight months, battling into "No-man's" country, and got through with half their cattle to form the nucleus of the Kimberley herds. From the mental depression following fever and scurvy, two men committed suicide. Others were killed. In places they fought their way through country inhabited by the toughest blacks in Australia. They found and crossed rivers; fought flood and bog and fire and their own isolation; and penetrated a thousand miles of country upon which no white man had yet set foot! And they made no noise about it, leaving us to send to America for our pictures of pioneering! Silent, too, were the prospectors and those other pathfinders, the tale of whose deeds has been left to the campfire sagas.

This was the country now due to materialize in Flynn's dream. Not only medical help, but an accessible means of communication to every man and woman. Something by which swift help could come when needed; whether doctor, stores, business, transport, or relief from loneliness. Engraved in Flynn's heart is one bush mother he knew out there. He closed his eyes to picture her sitting at his dream wireless machine. How her face lit up as a voice spoke out of the distance!

If only his wireless dream could be realized! It would have vast economic importance upon the lives and finances not only of persons, but of the Commonwealth, making the Kimberleys safe for Australians and for Australia. Wireless would give the cattlemen, in addition to the news of the Continent and outer world, daily information of prices and movements of stock, of drought and grass. Thus in bad seasons they could save themselves and, incidentally, millions per year to the Commonwealth. Wireless communication for every home would bring security, hasten prosperity, help open up roads, and roads would mean motor transport. As it is the isolation of the Kimberleys is a national menace.

Flynn reached his hotel rather tired. "What a lot a man can think of in a little walk." This had been a great day, but he could not call it "a day" yet for he had not read the paper, and besides he had numerous details to think out. He was troubled, too, by news of his padres killed and wounded at the war—special men specially trained in the great Inland patrols. Nurses too: those young women he had been counting on, just when they grew highly skilled they were wanted at the theatres of war.

He lay back on the bed feeling a bit lonely. His mind was working fast but confusedly, his thoughts refusing to go into detail; they would not "stick" for more than a fleeting moment. They wandered to the northernmost Kimberleys, to the Bastion Range rising six hundred feet sheer behind the houses at Wyndham. Cattle were being loaded with great speed into a cattle boat. But Flynn swept inland over tree-lined billabongs and creeks and lagoons filled with barramundi, honking with pigmy geese, cackling with nesting wildfowl, and shadowed by whirring flocks of pigeons. Osprey cranes fished there; parrots and galahs and cockatoos with birds he did not know circled and alighted in clouds of colour. Momentarily his heart softened as he remembered four thousand finches taken from those honeyed lagoons in one shipment. He smiled again to the dance of long-legged native companions.

His mind travelled over grassy plains, wooded hills, and mountains rising like mediaeval castles, with frowning battlements, stretching far into the rock-girt haze. He saw some of the roughest country in Australia, some of the hardest, and some of the fairest. He saw the undisputed haunts of the wild man; saw him emerging from his fastnesses to spear the unprotected settlers' cattle feeding out on the plains. Then in a flash his mind showed him the white-roofed buildings of Moolabulla government cattle-station among its scattered trees: a great humane enterprise of the Western Australian government, not to raise cattle for profit, but for the blacks, to try and wean them of their spearing raids on settlers' herds. Word has been spread among the savage tribes to come in and eat their fill when they wish. Two hundred natives a day are fed without stint, sometimes five hundred turn up. One hundred miles north is the out-station Violet Valley, where many more hundreds of natives are fed—all from the great herds reared by the government. The Kimberley natives have no excuse for their many years of cattle spearing.

Pictures flashed through Flynn's mind like a racing cinematograph. He saw a neat bark homestead, a homestead he knew by a billabong gay with water-lilies. The homestead windows were flaps of heavy wood, loopholed and ready to be bolted on the instant; a heavy hardwood beam was set to fall and bar the door. A young wife had a revolver strapped to her waist as she worked, and as she worked she listened to the call of birds out on the lagoon or the merry chatter from trees near by. Among bush birds are those that give warning should anything unusual come sneaking along. Once, she came to the veranda and looked long and steadily towards the wild gorges leading into the mountains. Around the homestead all undergrowth had been cleared; in daylight at least anything that crawled would be visible. She was alone. Flynn knew her husband's work sometimes kept him away for weeks, especially if the "wet" should catch him unawares.

Flynn coupled her need with his sympathy. He saw her sitting by his Baby Transmitting set, smiling as a voice spoke through the ear-phones, laughing as she tapped out an answering message.

His mind flickered as he tried to detail a plan for making and spreading cheap wireless receiving and transmitting sets throughout the Kimberleys. A little unhappily he touched his brow. Wireless was in its infancy. A transmitting set was a huge apparatus necessitating skill to work it, costing big money. It was so hard to think out in detail how to make that dream machine, his Baby Set. And time sped so.

He wandered again and visioned the drovers with their mobs far and wide. One mob as it moved lowing down a

valley with grey-green hills on either side was spread out
for over a mile. There were only four men in charge, intelligent, far-seeing chaps. They would have to constantly
visualize a hundred miles ahead, planning and being prepared as they encountered drought and fertility, flooded
rivers and dry water-holes, bog and desert, and grassy plains;
wisely setting the pace of the mob according to the country,
the seasons and passing showers of rain that had or had
not fallen a month ahead. In places there would be blacks,
poison weed, bush-fires, famine and plenty, perhaps accident
and sickness. For long periods they would be lost to the outside world. Despite everything, they were pledged to bring
every hoof possible to market. Many months would pass
before that mob reached the trucking yards. A splendid type
of man the drovers, but what a slow method of transport!
Abraham travelled his flocks that way.

Again in imagination Flynn swept over the frontier places
where men settle by the billabongs and on the grass-swept
plains with their dreamy distances. He passed rivers where
crocodiles lie in wait for cattle, and tropic sunsets turn pink
and red the cliffs and tip the grass with gold. By a stout
post on a plain was a little heap of wood and a man was
bending over branding-irons beside a small fire. Close by
stamped an uneasy, lowing mob with horsemen keeping
them moving in a circle. A rider dashed in and lassoed a
cleanskin on the outskirts of the mob, whipped the greenhide
rope around the post and threw the beast to one frantic
bellow as it felt the hot iron. Quick workers are the boys
of the plains! Flynn spied distant homesteads, lonely mining-
camps, and a white mother here and there waiting for the
mail—the six-weekly mail! There were babies, too, soon to be
born. People wanted communication—communication.

Before he realized it, his mind had slipped again from
details as he saw a bewhiskered settler riding beside a station
manager. Across a grassy plain a line of Bauhinia trees stood
like sentries. The smoke from the men's pipes coiled lazily
past their friendly brown faces. They had chummed up,

although the station manager had only recently "taken over".
They were discussing a coming muster, an important event
out on the unfenced frontiers where the cattle herds sometimes become "boxed". Whoever musters, informs his neigh-
bours on all sides beforehand; each sends a representative,
and all work together. At the muster, they draft the cattle,
so separating any mixed beasts.

Of course, as in every walk of life, a man here and there
may do a little muster all on his own. Sometimes he gets
hopelessly confused with his brands, which explains why a
proud cow branded by station A will be leading about a fine
calf now branded by station Z. Mistakes will happen. Once
the calf is branded, all doubt of ownership is settled—legally
anyway.

After a thoughtful silence the settler observed:

"I'm glad this is going to be a friendly muster."

"Why?" asked the station manager. "Haven't the musters
always been friendly?"

"Oh, yes, but your predecessor used to get his brands mixed
—on my calves. You see, we never hit it too well. I used to
get on his nerves for some reason or other."

The new manager was genuinely angry, for he knew that
the station owners were averse to smart practices.

"I'll let the owners know about this immediately the mail
leaves," he said. "H—— won't gain by it."

"Oh, it's quite all right; let the matter drop," reassured the
settler, "I only wanted to know your policy. I've no time
myself for funny business with brands." He looked steadily
at the station manager, then added in a slow explanatory
smile: "Of course you understand I didn't lose in the end."

Flynn's thoughts flitted over that country as fast as wireless: a big lump of Australia about which few Australians
know anything. And yet it holds two world records: Broome
with the greatest pearling fleet in the world; Wyndham with
its record of cattle shipping.

How could he build hospitals, and give every home a transmitting set, in this land capable of supporting the big white population for which tracks are being blazed by the men battling out there now?

"Oh, call it a day," growled Flynn as he chased his thoughts away and reached for the paper. An early morning tram rattled down the street.

Perhaps even so Fate called it "a day" for the "Scrub Bull". The Kimberleys know him so well that they will not mind the "Last Post" being sounded by his old friend Fred C. Booty of Lambo station, Hall's Creek.

The "Scrub Bull" was crossing his last ridge.

Fifty years ago when Queensland was young and cattle was her chief industry, when Mt Cornish was a mighty cattle run and fences were almost unknown, "Scrub Bull" was a smart youngster on Thylungra cattle station in Queensland. Nearly thirty years ago, he had worked as head-stockman on Ord River in nor'-western Australia, mustering cattle, and branding calves at the rate of one a minute. Something about the man reminded one of Falstaff—an unconscious swagger that suggested ancestry from some old soldier of fortune.

Now after twenty-five years on other stations in the Kimberleys, he had returned in the sunset of his life to Ord River to die and be buried in the station cemetery alongside the man who had been speared to death at his side.

I can see "The Bull" galloping up to the station on a foaming Macarthur brumby with the news that the blacks had speared Tudor Shadforth as he and Shadforth rode together down the Osmand River; telling how, with the spear in his heart Shadforth had ridden his scared and bounding horse for seventy yards, and then in a fallen heap gone out, muttering only "Oh, Christ!"

One likes to think of "The Bull", with whiskers bristling,

revolver levelled, unconsciously controlling his excited brumby, standing guard while the black boy of his dead mate carried him out of the gully to a safer place.

After twenty-five years, the two splendid horsemen are to lie side by side where, maybe, they can talk of the animal they both loved.

CHAPTER XI

THE WILD NOR'-WEST

A BELL-BIRD called in the ranges: his clear, sweet notes were answered from far out towards the Black Elvira. Down below, as if planted amongst the hills, shone a clump of white-roofed houses—the court-house, post office, hotel-store, store, police station, Miners' Institute, and an odd cottage. The sharper gleam of white down by the creek was the prospectors' tents, a band of hardy roamers who had just come in from Dead Finish Creek with news of good gold being got in Grant's Gully. Running west from the tiny hamlet, until it was swallowed by the hills, one glimpsed a dusty road that led to Fitzroy Crossing, a smaller hamlet a hundred and fifty miles towards the coast. East of Hall's Creek only rough tracks led out to lonely stations or mining-camps. Up among the grassy ridges horse-bells tinkled; the clang of a bush-smith's hammer echoed from the township. A fluttering, like wee white handkerchiefs, showed where a woman was hanging out washing.

Among the ranges big felsite dykes showed up, landmarks that told of queer upheavals when the earth was young. Perhaps the earth is still young "under below". When the Gordon Downs station people were putting down Euortoo bore a strange fish with no eyes, but having well-developed eye-sockets, came up from the bowels of the earth. That is a well authenticated fish story. Euortoo bore was the first put down in the East Kimberleys.

Such is Hall's Creek, the Inland outpost in the Kimberleys over three hundred miles from the nor'-westralian cattle port of Derby.

The day was one of those Kimberley winter days when it felt good to be alive: brilliant sunshine, the air from the hills like champagne. In the township a cloud of dust almost hid a mob of bellowing cattle. The cracking of whips rang sharply above the cheerful shouts of men as the mob moved off, followed by calls of goodwill from the tiny outpost. A new stock route had been discovered across the wilderness of hill and mountain towards the south, and this mob was going to "try it out".

The hamlet quietened down again with the going of the cattle. Men grouped about the store as they discussed the possibilities of the mob getting through. Droving of cattle through new country is a serious undertaking, no matter how spiced the adventure.

Time passed and Hall's Creek jubilated, for the mail had just got through after an extra solid wet season—the first mail in five months. Teams were away back along the road, coming with flour and sugar. The supply famine was over.

One day a rider appeared along the track, swaying upon a weary horse. As the policeman hurried down to meet him the rider's bowed head swayed over the horse's neck; he clung desperately to the saddle, had clung so for days now—he did not know how long.

They lifted him off. His face was thin and drawn; his eyes were screwed up and he shivered violently. Fever? Yes, badly. He was one of the drovers and had to turn back. He had left the mob going along all right; they were in wild country now. The flats were waving with tall grass through which no horned beast had ever pushed before. They had met no "poison" country yet, but a few of the beasts had knocked up and had to be abandoned when travelling up a great valley paved with stones like a cobbled street. Nature had played a queer rough prank there. Up to the day he left them the drovers had not seen a solitary nigger; but the previous afternoon the boss had pointed out the wild men's smoke signals coiling up from the peaks ahead. The mob would get through all right, but the going was tough. He was sorry they had made him leave the mob, but a sick man was a handicap.

Hall's Creek was busy, energetically so; a race-meeting was being organized. Though men on the committee might live a hundred miles apart, they organized just the same. Although the object of these meetings was the raising of money for some deserving cause, the essence of each was the happiness of human comradeship, the pleasure felt at the smiles on the faces of women when they met other women for the first gossip in twelve months.

The meeting was held and lasted two heavenly days: the heart to heart talks lasted longer. There were six races and ten babies. The people gathered from a radius of over a hundred miles and numbered, including jockeys and babies in arms, just sixty-five white people. And in those two days they raised £512 for patriotic funds. That district occupied by a little over a hundred whites raised £5000 for patriotic funds when we needed it. A wonderful record, especially considering that Australia hardly knows she has a Kimberleys, either an East or a West.

To return to that mob of cattle. They never got through! The remains of the drovers were found with the spear-riddled carcasses of their horses beside them. The ambush had been a complete surprise.

How John Flynn would have been delighted had he heard of another meeting being organized far away up there in the Kimberleys, all because they, too, had heard a whisper of the ideals of the A.I.M. If the little they had heard were true, this movement meant the longed-for chance to get medical help into the country. With the promptness characteristic of the Kimberley Inlanders when they see a chance for progress, these folk decided to "try the scheme out".

F. W. Tuckett, the man who had operated on young

Darcy, took a prominent part in the meeting at which £100 to carry on with was immediately subscribed, and a race-meeting was voted in the near future as a means of raising funds. The old Miners' Institute was declared fit and available to be utilized as hospital until funds were sufficient to build one. The people wished to raise the money themselves if possible, but in the meantime decided to ask the Government to lend a hand. Soon all plans were completed and it only remained to be seen what the A.I.M. would do about it. Would they really send nurses—trained nurses?

They wrote John Flynn (Sydney, N.S.W.) stating their case and asking particulars of action if any. That letter happened to be posted on the same date that one for Flynn was leaving London, twelve-thousand miles away. The mail from London arrived just a month before the Kimberley letter. Flynn read that letter with smiling face. This meant a permanent foothold in the Kimberleys. To think that thoughts could do things like this!

The A.I.M. had money on hand, just enough "grains of sand" to mix with the Hall's Creek quota. He hurried the matter to the Board; the Board moved quickly but deliberately, making firm the foundation for the new venture. For Flynn, however, the hospital was already built; he immediately passed on. Soon afterwards two men with the unmistakable stamp of the far-out bushman walked into his office. One was Mr Haly, of Moolabulla station. Haly had been holidaying in Brisbane when his Hall's Creek friends wired him to go personally to Sydney and get particulars from a Mr John Flynn, A.I.M.

Shortly afterwards the Western Australian government offered £125 per annum towards the new Home. A little later two plucky girls set out on their long trip to the frontier outpost. They went by train to Perth, then nine days by coastal steamer, then a four-hundred-mile ride into the rugged but grand heart of the true nor'-west.

"I am going," said one, "because I think Australia is such

a grand country and I am proud to have a hand in developing it."

Another link had been forged in Flynn's chain. In the quietness of his room he felt that each one of those links was forged round his heart.

Port Hedland was dozing. Sister May came to the door of the trim little Nursing Home and gazed out to sea. Calm as a blue lagoon, no stranger would dream that a "Cock-eye Bob" could whip that water into fury, and perhaps drown a pearling fleet, within minutes.

"It's a beautiful day," thought Sister, "feels good to be alive."

Sister felt particularly happy for the letter she had in her hand contained a £50 cheque "For the Sisters' Xmas". So wrote the De Gray station people from back there over the hills inland. It was grandly encouraging—this and other proofs that the bushmen appreciated so the work of the Nursing Home. A riot from the fowlyard urged Sister to hurry through the little hospital. If that dog is chasing those laying hens again——

But Fido wasn't. Sundry small boys, bare-legged and freckled, were chasing the squawking fowls over the sand while Sister Grace directed operations.

"Warm work," thought Sister May as she walked across to give a hand.

Sister Grace sat with a fire blackened bucket before her in which was hot fat. A triumphant boy came running up holding an outraged rooster by the legs. Sister Grace seized it and ducked its neck in the fat. Stupefied silence from the rooster. It emerged with open beak and staggered expression; its feathers glued to its neck as it walked weakly away.

"Them ticks are gettin' a hot time!" gasped Ginger admiringly as he rushed with a hen victim.

"Keep erway from th' bucket, Ginger," yelled Skinny from

across the yard. "If they takes you for a rooster you'll set it afire!"

"You come here and I'll dip *your* head," threatened the redhead. With flushed face he stood by while the hen was dipped. It emerged bleary-eyed, open-beaked, emitting a feeble cluck as it staggered after the rooster.

"Gee!" declared Ginger, "youse Sisters are nuts on ticks! If Dad only knoo that hot fat stuff he could ha' sat down in a bucket. You orter seen th' ticks on him when he come in from th' scrub."

Sisters were relieved when Nipper raced up and butted in with the story of a bigger tick. Soon a knot of youngsters were heatedly arguing, regardless of their stranglehold on sundry fowls' necks. Sisters settled the argument before the barnyard was seriously incapacitated and the ducking went on apace.

Later the Sisters gazed professionally from the veranda. A man was walking up the sandy track from the town. He hesitated at the gate, then threw out his chest and marched on. "Good day," he remarked to the sisters with a flourish of his hat.

"Good morning."

"Sorry to trouble you, Sister, but could you pull a bloom—a tooth?"

"Certainly," said Sister, "if you are sure it is the tooth troubling you."

"Sure as me conscience!" he replied earnestly.

"Then come in."

He followed the Sisters gamely enough but shied at the surgery.

"Come right in!" encouraged Sister.

He did so and stumbled over a chair as he glanced nervously round and coughed. An odour of recent beer blended harmoniously with the smell of chemicals.

"Sit down," ordered Sister. He did so, somewhat unsteadily. His eyes rolled as Sister opened the tray of shiny forceps, and he glanced furtively towards the door; but Sister Grace stood there, eyeing him.

"Open," ordered Sister.

"Seems to me, Sister, it's not achin' nearly so much as it was," he observed earnestly, "now I come to think of——"

"Open!" ordered Sister.

Meekly he obeyed, getting a grip on the back of the chair. Sister squinted professionally at the tooth, sniffed and reached for the forceps.

"Struth, ain't you goin' to give me painkiller?" he protested wildly.

Sister got a half-Nelson around his neck and jerked his head back remarking, "You've had too much 'painkiller' as it is. I'm not wasting our good anaesthetic on you!"

She got to work, and the tooth came out to a stretching groan that ended in a howl.

"Spit in this!" ordered Sister Grace.

"Struth!!!" spat the victim.

He crept shamefacedly away. The Sisters watched from the veranda. Away down the track he was surrounded by a mob of small boys. The hunch left his shoulders, he spat for their benefit, he opened his mouth and "showed them". They escorted him to the pub.

"Anyway we saved that cocaine," said Sister May.

"He will get as full as a tick,'" laughed Sister Grace with a glance at the dispirited hens in the fowlyard.

A quavering yell brought the Sisters into the ward with its eight spotless white beds. The Koepanger was at it again. He had been dropped ashore from a pearling lugger. No one understood his language: it was hard to fathom his wants. They had brought him a hard-boiled egg one day when what he wanted was a knife to cut his toenails.

He was sitting up smiling now, bright brown eyes triumphantly shining from his creamy brown face. Sister felt the bed—wet! Proudly he showed her how he had done it— by balancing the water-bottle on his head. Patiently the

Sisters tried to understand what he wanted now. Vehemently he tried to explain. At last Sister Grace held up a glass of water, energetically he nodded. Sister held the glass to his lips but he snatched it and poured it over his head in smiling delight.

"We can't have any more of this," said Sister. "We'll have to tie him down and bathe him in a civilized way otherwise we'll need a drying line for him alone."

The Koepanger had been a problem: All his life at sea, he had been used to diving into it whenever feeling the hot touch of fever. His convalescing had been the worst. One day he had crawled across the floor and caught the cat. He had bitten its tail trying to make them understand he wanted a mouth organ. Thank heaven he was getting better now.

The Sisters stripped the bed, nearly having a fight with the laughing Koepanger when they rolled him back into the dry sheets. When Sister Grace was hanging out the wet sheets she glanced down the track towards the township.

"Sister," she called out, "come and see what the last 'willy-willy' has blown along."

Sister May did come and surveyed a figure rolling up the track, three seas over. His hat clung tipsily to the back of his head as he steered a wavering course, determined to get there somehow. He did, negotiated the gate, cautiously essayed the path, and triumphantly braced himself up before Sister.

"Goo'-day!" he smiled with a dab at his hat.

"Good morning," replied Sister. "This is not the hotel."

Intense surprise lightened his face.

" 'Course not!" He pointed. "Pubsh down there!"

"Well what is it you want? You are not sick, not yet, anyway."

"I wantsh toosh out."

"What for?"

He screwed up a bewildered eye, scratched his head, dropped his hat and picked it up and fell on it.

"Go away and have a sleep," advised Sister.

"But my toosh," he wailed.

"Come back later."

"But ain't you goin' to pull it?"

"Certainly not in your condition."

"But you pulled Joe's," he wailed.

"He wasn't as bad as you," replied Sister.

"Oh, washn't he!" He stepped forward confidentially. "My toosh so bad a team er horshes couldn't pull it."

"You go away and have a sleep," ordered Sister sternly.

"Oh, Sishter," he implored, "you ain't goin' to turn a man down?" In pitiful plight he held his hand to his jaw. "If you only felt thish agony!"

"Nonsense!" replied Sister. "You're imagining it." She turned resolutely away.

"Oh, Sishter!" he implored, "you ain't goin' to turn a pore bloke down? Ush coves shinks you Sishters wunnderful!!!"

Sister hesitated, she regarded the tempter with a cold eye.

"I'll just look at it," she capitulated. "Open your mouth."

He shut his eyes and opened his mouth to the skies.

"Just look in this!" nodded Sister to Sister.

Sister Grace peeped. Slowly the victim's eyes opened; his mouth shut and he looked foolish.

"You haven't a tooth in your head," said Sister sternly. "Go away."

Solemnly the Sisters marched into the hospital.

CHAPTER XII

THE DEAD HAND

Beltana Nursing Home was opened in 1919. Beltana is a little might-have-been town three hundred and fifty six miles north of Adelaide. The quaint township of little houses of wood, iron, and stone is bounded on the south by the beautiful old gums lining Wariotta Creek and on the west by Puttapa Ridge with tent-shaped hills in the distance. Away to the east rise the peaks of Flinders Range clad in their mantle of mysterious blue.

Round and north of Beltana are the "arid lands", huge belts of saltbush and gibber plains, of sandhills and spinifex. And yet that "arid" description is partly deceptive. Sheep and cattle stations are scattered north, south, east, and west throughout that country. Even parts of the desolate regions round Lake Eyre are inhabited. An empty patch lies directly north of the Lake, another begins a hundred miles west of Oodnadatta.

The saltbush is the marvel. It is splendid fodder and thrives on six inches of rain per year, holds its own on three, and persists on nothing for twelve months, to immediately spring into vigorous life when rain comes. Those so-called arid lands will become fertile when the water supply has been solved. At present it is the land of large holdings.

The man who has partly solved the problem, who has gone out and battled from "scratch" and fought to be beaten and rise again and yet again is Sir Sidney Kidman, the "Cattle King" of the world. He plays chess with Fate. Flocks and herds, his brains, and the bushmanship of his men are his pieces against droughts and flood, heat and cold and distances, while the Northern Territory, South Australia, Queensland, N.S.W., and even Victoria, marked out in station boundaries, represent the playing board. He watches the seasons a season ahead, moving his vast herds across the continent from station to station, "following the grass", checkmating dry times here, there, a thousand miles away; shifting his herds to grassy lands, always ahead of old man Drought. Other men have won success by following his example on a much smaller scale. Probably Australia will eventually solve the water problem for the arid lands and then the small man's turn will come.

It was with an added delight that Flynn saw the Beltana Home opened. To him it was the hand of Fate that opened that hospital, a hand stretching down through the years, silent and invisible but stronger far than links of steel, the spiritual hand of a woman dead nearly sixty years ago.

Beltana was not, strictly speaking, in the country of the A.I.M. It lay just outside their southern boundary, in the Smith-of-Dunesk district. The residents had subscribed liberally towards a hospital, then approached their committee, but the job was too great so the problem had been laid before the A.I.M. The Board had been delighted at the opportunity of thus helping "an hundredfold" the deed of the dead woman of Dunesk.

The story of that woman's legacy takes the polish off the accepted notion that a Scotsman "smells money". The legacy that started the Smith-of-Dunesk Mission lay forgotten among the papers of Scotsmen for over forty years.

It was the Rev. F. W. Main of South Australia who one day examining an ancient Blue Book raised his eyebrows and paused in doubt. It was true though, for when his two years' investigation was completed it was proved that Mrs Smith of Dunesk had bequeathed to the Free Church of Scotland certain sections of land, the income from which was to be devoted to humanitarian work in the colony of South Australia. After all these years accumulated rents and interest had provided additional capital of over £2000.

The Beltana Home was named "The Mitchell Home", after the old giant who had carried the church on his back right into the hearts of the Beltana people and far beyond. Perhaps it was fitting that at the opening of the Home the crowd, gathered from a radius of three hundred miles, were driven indoors by a dust storm that came rolling down upon them in sullen red clouds. The storm passed but the hospital stood, augury of that brighter future when men will combine for good in the land.

Flynn greeted with a sad but deep thankfulness the end of the war. Looking back over the years he marvelled that the Board not only had held on but had gained. The A.I.M. now was almost "solid"; its ideals were creeping into the hearts of the people. Now that the guns were silent and the people's ears receptive to other sounds, the voice of the A.I.M. might be heard crying in the wilderness. A cry did not suit Flynn: he wanted to make it roar. So did the Board. But their methods were entirely different. The methods of this furiously-travelling dreamer were at times a little exasperating to the Board. Often no one knew where he was. He just disappeared to turn up months later, perhaps in the heart of Australia, perhaps in the farthest north, maybe the farthest west. He would reappear next in Sydney, Adelaide, Perth, no one knew where, to perhaps vanish straightway again in the silence of the Centre.

When he did reappear in the Sydney office he carried that winning smile of his, that softly spoken word and a head full of data and the strangest plans that, yet, had to be sorted and worked out to the minutest detail. The Board gave up all attempts at scolding. What was the use? When Flynn, all in his own good time, was ready with his very latest plan, they listened quietly, looking into the speaker's eyes across the long table, as earnestly and with ever ready smile he gave them his own idea of details that represented conditions of life present and future, possibilities present and future, and certainties present and future of a hundred thousand square miles of country away out "Inland". Then he would show how the scattered few out there could best be helped, how communication and lots of etceteras could be established for the eventual good of all Australia.

The Board would listen patiently, then ask questions, and be answered with unfailing courtesy. But the Board used often to sigh, sometimes in lively exasperation, when the dreamer vanished again leaving them with a gigantic undertaking to sort out and build upon in sure and methodical business-like ways.

After Beltana was established the movement had progressed to such an extent that a permanent secretary was appointed for Flynn. The Office Teams were re-organized and others appointed. In numerous country centres committees and Voluntary Teams were organized to spread the ideal far and wide. "Districts" of the Inland were mapped out, different committees and workers being responsible for different districts; sending people reading matter; attending to postal business and shopping; corresponding with them in letters of advice, sympathy and understanding; giving all the help they could—written and other.

Private individuals, too, took up the cause and corresponded with the lonely wives of far-out settlers, even educating their children. Australia does not know the stories of these people who, for years, devoted nearly all their spare time to educating by correspondence children who probably would never see a school. Quite a number of private individuals undertook the work. Each would "adopt" some family, perhaps two thousand miles away, and be responsible for the education of children whom they would never see. They have had their reward in letters of thanks written from the overflowing hearts of grateful mothers.

Flynn's maps became a feature of Inland publicity. That

the maps would be true in minutest detail, he made a friend of Norman Orr, a master draughtsman. It was characteristic of Flynn that he studied the draughtsman's craft until he too was a draughtsman. And a tribute to Flynn's personality is the fact that when Orr retired from business he worked doubly hard for the A.I.M.—is still working.

Again Flynn disappeared from Sydney. Eventually he was located in Adelaide, "lost" in the intricacies of wireless telegraphy. He was now an expert, but desired the help of successful experimenters; so he approached them in that quiet way of his, helped by his ever ready smile. He wanted something badly. A Baby Wireless Transmitting Set, so inexpensive, light, and simple that every bush mother could handle it.

What a madman's dream!

But the wireless men could not resist him or the dream, though they doubted its realization. It might come fifty years hence. But he was terribly keen on what they were terribly keen on—this wireless craze. Why, he could talk it—understand it—nearly as well as themselves! They took this new enthusiast to their hearts: each had a little something to teach him. Then seriously they set to work, each in his own way, in his own time, in his own "workshop", to try and help the dream; to fashion some gadget or other that the dreamer could weave into his dream. Men who have since made great names in the Wireless World are among those who worked throughout the quiet hours of the night trying to "make the Inland speak".

Flynn worked with a concentrated intensity through experiment after experiment: nothing could turn him aside. As always through life, when once he started practical work on a thing he saw it right through, allowing no distraction, no business, no anything, to interfere.

Not only did he toil with a file rasping a bit of steel, he enlisted the sympathy of the Postmaster-General's Department and a great wireless corporation, E. T. Fisk, Barker and Kauper, D. Wyles, the staff of the A.W.A., and those crafty amateurs, the ants of the wireless world, who make such big noises with a bit of wire and a bottle of juice.

As Flynn toiled with heart and soul and mind, so others toiled on his long patrols. A camel-man stared across a desert silence in the stillness of the night. The only sound was the merciless drumming of the driven camel's feet. The rider was riding far and fast, driven by a sick child's wail, "Daddy! Daddy!" Savagely he urged the camel, he who had never been cruel before, and the brute reared its head on high and roared and gurgled upon the sands.

"Travel! Shah! Travel!" urged the man in a dry harsh voice, and he thrashed the beast, struck again as it savaged back with its wrinkled neck. As its eyes blazed in fury to bite he struck again, sick at heart that he must thrash a tired beast that was a friend.

He was the padre of the Central Patrol, riding now to save the life of a child. He had ridden up to the homestead by the coolabah creek, riding proud Shah, savage beast but friend of many thousand miles, Ameer and Kabool lurching along behind under their packbags and water canteens, Doctor leisurely padding in the rear under his two big cases.

With slathering grunts of thankfulness the long-necked beasts had folded their great legs under them and lurched down to rest. Even camel legs grow weary after twelve hundred miles.

But the woman ran out from the homestead crying "Quinine!" and her eyes told the need.

"Plenty," answered the padre and hurried to the cases on Doctor.

It was the youngest boy—malaria—a week of it and not a grain of quinine in the house. He bent over the child and forced the quinine between the tight-shut lips and washed it down with lemon-juice, for lemon makes the quinine act quicker. He gave the child repeated doses, strong doses. Quinine is a miracle worker against malaria. It pulled the child round, but with the first cry that followed the searching of the dull childish eyes, the weak thrust of the thin hand, the padre recognized a serious complication.

"Daddy! I want Daddy!"

The child was inconsolable, refused all endearment, all promises; refused everything; just turned his face to the wall. It was simply a phase of weak humanity, a longing of the heart to which nothing else mattered.

The padre looked at the woman. She pointed out, her eyes asking what her lips trembled to say.

"He is out there somewhere," she whispered, "a hundred and twenty miles away—across the Forty Mile desert, repairing an old well."

"I'll travel as fast as I can," he promised. "Shah is a good camel: rest assured he is very fast."

Shah had roared and shook his head and refused to budge without his mates. He had done his stage and every camel knows when he has done a stage. He had come close to running "macnoon" when the man thrashed him to his feet. And now the padre stared across that desert stretch hoping to see figures looming in giant shape towards him. Vain hope, that a father would come when he did not know his son was calling. As he strained to the utter silence a voice wailed "Daddy! Daddy!"

"Go! Shah! go!" he answered, and Shah roared his slavering protests over the voiceless sands.

He did not know where the well-sinker was, but he was hurrying for the police. The police of the great Inland! What tales of our farthermost frontiers those splendid men could tell! Recorded on musty files and locked in the hearts of men, their deeds would stir a continent if only given voice.

A week before the padre had met a Police Patrol returning successfully to Alice Springs after a chase of nearly two thousand miles. The constable had mentioned he would be camping on a certain day a week hence at the artesian well east of "the desert"—providing nothing unexpected turned up. Tomorrow would be the day. The police would find the well-sinker no matter where he be.

"Travel! Shah! Travel!" urged the rider low and urgently and the sands squelched from the beast's forced feet.

He was still crossing the desert at dawn, a wonderful dawn that brightened into a pink glow until the leaves of the bushes shimmered like lace. In the east needles of liquid gold quivered up into a cold, steel-blue sky: the needles spread in a fan that touched the sands with gold: a molten disc swimming in a golden glow shot up and it was day.

The padre crossed over into the desert fringe and saltbush appeared and camel-bush and herbage: desert oaks stood upon a plain with hills in the distance: the heat poured relentlessly. Two emus strode with stately tread from the bushes as the rider hurried by.

They came to the remains of an abandoned stockyard. Shah made for it. The rider tugged at the nose-peg, but the camel trod doggedly to the gate and lurched down. It was midday and this was the time to feed. But there was a stronger hunger with the beast; it wanted to get away back to its mates and feel their companionship and join in their guggling talk. So Shah "stayed put", he refused to budge no matter how the man struck. With a sound like a sob the padre pulled out a dog-chain. He thrashed the camel and it swayed its neck to the blows, snarling, roaring from open mouth with bared yellow fangs. It lumbered up, eyes gleaming hate, lurched on a few yards, then swung round and ran straight into a needle-bush tree, the rider bending low, arms thrust forward, to ward off the branches armed with needle-sharp thorns. Then the camel suddenly flopped down —a horrid sensation from that great height—and roared like a mad beast. Up swung the chain to cut down in blow after blow that ceased only when the camel rose. It tried to bolt but the pull on the nose-peg through that sensitive nose held it roaring back to flop down again. In maddened lunges it rose to the chain and backed again and again against a tree, seeking to smash the man. Twelve times that raving beast flopped down, until beaten at last it trod doggedly forward, groaning its rage, biding its time.

The man wiped his bloodstained face, his eyes nearly as mad as the camel's, the knotted chain round his wrist quivering from his trembling arm. An hour later they came to a winding creek: tall red gums shadowed water-pools where birds chattered among the reeds. Crossing the creek the camel, without the slightest warning, lurched down instantly and attempted to roll upon the man. But he slid off sideways and seizing the nose-rope held the big ugly head under water until the savage eyes glared up in silent appeal.

At sunset he saw the poppet-head by the trees around the well, horses were drinking at the troughs, two black troopers stared towards him. As the camel lurched down the policeman stepped forward. The padre told his tale.

"The man is timbering an old well fifteen miles farther east," said the policeman. "I'll write a note and send it by the lightest trooper on the fastest horse:"

CHAPTER XIII

THE PATROL RIDER

WITH an easy heart the patrol padre saddled his camels and rode out towards the horizon. His job was to be here, there, and everywhere in the Centre: he had recently left Oodnadatta on a two thousand five hundred mile journey. His district embraced an area almost twice the size of Victoria. He was going now as far north as Tennant's Creek, a telegraph station up in the Territory: he might cover the mileage in six months. He loved his job. That job was to meet every man and woman, strengthen the ties of friendship and sympathy on the patrol of last year, to help all in need in any way he could. And to help his country should opportunity occur.

For the furtherance of the work of the A.I.M. he must report on the country traversed, its physical nature and its present and future possibilities, on land suitable for closer settlement, the people now in occupation, their needs; and particularly on the most suitable and necessary localities for Nursing Homes. He must register lonely womenfolk so that their city sisters could write and help them. He must remember the scattered children so that those same sisters could send them toys and books and educate them. A big work had this rider who followed in the Camel-man's footsteps. Here and there in the unmapped places, among the wild blacks, he must carry his life in his hands. Rather fine men has Australia bred in her sons of the A.I.M. patrols.

Cheerily he spoke to Shah for he had saved the life of a child. Shah, back once again with his mates, moved con-

tentedly in long, lurching strides. A good-looking camel, and
he knew it; dark brown with black points and curly hair
and a head that in repose looked wise as the Sphinx.

What desert man in long vanished ages, thought out the
simple nose-line and peg? This Australian's nose-line was a
piece of light rope doubled so that one end passed over
each side of the camel's neck. Each end was tied to an
end of a short wooden peg which passed through a man-
made incision in the nostrils. The right-hand side of the line
was fastened to the smaller end of the peg, the other end
was shaped like a large flat button. This prevented the peg
being pulled through when the rider tugged the line. A
camel's nose is sensitive to the slightest pressure, so the line
levering on the note-peg drives him whichever way the man
wills.

The rider as a rule did not bother about the line; he carried
a light stick and tapped the beast's neck according to the
direction in which he wanted him to turn. But when the
camel "plays up", should the rider sharply tug and break the
line or pull the peg out—then the camel is master.

Ameer's nose-line was tied to the rear of Shah so he lurched
along behind, great head on high, his big fierce eyes with a
calculating glint in them. Ameer, who could snap a nose-line
with the ease of a child breaking cotton, would wait until the
Master was crossing some critical stage in the track. Kabool,
steadily munching his chops, followed Ameer. Kabool could
kick with lightning swiftness in any direction, whether standing or kneeling. A man loading him needed to be an acrobat.
He moved with the air of the most long suffering creature
in the world: when he looked to be suffering most was when
he could kick the farthest. Doctor, the surly pack-brute
farther back, was the biter. When he reared his savage head
and snarled the others snarled back while edging away, for
even a camel's hide will tear under such terrible fangs.

But now the string moved on contentedly, and the whispering of their feet and the swish, swish, swish of the water

canteens was music to the rider's ears. He smiled as Shah's long neck shot out and the leathery mouth fastened on a limb of a thorny shrub running the branch down to its extremity, stripping every leaf as it calmly strode past. The longer the thorns the better these beasts liked them.

The patrol padre straightened his back and with shaded hand stared north, over plain country thick with spinifex and mulga towards low hills that were appearing north and east. Around him, too, was camel-bush and a dwarf species of Mitchell grass relished by stock. He was out past the exact "Centre" now, travelling a wandering route north of Alice Springs until he would pull in towards the Overland again.

At sundown of a lovely evening his camels lurched down before a little bark hut over which a flowering creeper grew. Lazy blue smoke coiled up from the chimney, an important chimney, squat-looking, built of red clay and grey granite stones. A dry gully ran past the hut: in its steep brown bank right under the twisty roots of a gnarled red gum was a black tunnel mouth. Gold might lie deep in there—and it might not.

A quaint old figure heartily welcomed him, an old prospector whose face would have been a cherry red had it not been tanned by many suns. He was a short rotund old man, his patriarchal beard touching the belt buckle which held up clean dungaree pants. A galah was perched upon his shoulder, a cockatoo raised its yellow crest and waddled screeching out of the hut door, while a cat with tail mast high stretched mewing at the old chap's feet. A dog with intelligent ears and lordly air walked across to inspect the camels, and sniffed disdainfully. Fowls that were going to roost changed their minds and came clucking across instead.

The padre spent a pleasant night with this congenial old hermit whose pets listened to the evening's theological discussion with varied expressions of disinterest. It was not the first time they had been talked to. When at last the padre was allowed to climb to bunk the galah was asleep, the cockatoo was asleep, the cat was asleep, the dog was asleep, and the padre nearly so.

Next day he followed faint tracks that wound in and out amongst the mulga to vanish at times. Those tracks had been made a fortnight before by a rider from an out-station passing by the old hermit's house. The hermit had told his visitor of a woman "out there", with eight youngsters. At sunset the padre camped by a rock-walled creek where plain ended and hills began. The setting sun clothed the plain with a soft pink cloak; the queerly twisted limbs of the trees on the hillsides took on fantastic shapes in the gathering twilight.

As he unpacked the camels and hobbled them Kabool chanced a lightning kick—and missed. Shah grunted scornfully and made straight for a sweet-flowering acacia-tree. He raised his great neck and seized a branch as Doctor ranged alongside and seized another. The beasts surrounded that green-leafed tree and fairly pulled it to pieces, noisily breaking the branches and stripping them of every leaf and flower.

Next evening the padre rode up to a homestead whose untrimmed timbers appeared rough as the land. Smoke coiled from a mud-and-stone chimney, under the bark veranda hung a row of pack and riding saddles with a long-lashed stockwhip and lariat of plaited greenhide. Branding-irons hung from a nail, and a giant pair of bullock horns was nailed over the door. Inside, over the open fireplace of the big kitchen hung slices of beef, slowly smoking. But for all its rough exterior it was a happy home—would have been happier still but for that dread fear of illness or accident.

The father was away, camped out on the run, but the mother greeted the visitor with gladness in her eyes. The eight children stared with the quietness of young humans who see a stranger perhaps twice a year.

After the evening meal the mother said, "Tell them something!"

He looked at eight pairs of eyes staring at his. They understood the wild things of the bush, the sun and moon and stars and the winds, and the rains and the laughing happiness of perfect health but of other things—nothing. They had not had even one school lesson in their lives. He watched their faces as he felt his way. He told them of the raising of Jairus's daughter—and the Roman soldier's child lived again in the breathless silence of the big dark kitchen. It was the first story the children had ever heard.

They wanted more; they asked with shy, eager eyes and funny little movements of the hands for they could not find the words they wanted. In this fruitful field he planted stories they would never forget, about a man born under an eastern star who went out as a great healer of men. He gave them short word-pictures of David and Goliath, Samuel, and the wise men of the east. Then he told them stories of modern life. And a new world and life had opened for these children of the sun. Their life could never be quite the same again.

He stayed a few days he could ill spare, he gave the children school lessons and wrote out the alphabet and lists of figures, and left several simple books with the mother that she might have a chance of carrying on the work. Later on, school-books would be mailed to her with the help of some kindly woman down south.

Some evenings later the padre camped with an artesian boring-party. They made him welcome and he yarned around the campfire long after the mopoke called. A young chap hinted at a theological question, the padre took it up—it was the opening he had been "fishing" for. When he rolled himself in his blankets he smiled up at the stars. He had preached a fine sermon over the solution of that problem. And they had listened to every word, appreciating the discussion, absorbing the teaching that under other circumstances they would have resented as "preaching".

East towards Queensland lay two hundred miles of country

unoccupied by white man, so he turned a shade north of
west and travelled in the direction of the Overland Telegraph Line. In two days' time he arrived at a little station
and was greeted right royally, white children running to
meet him, a crowd of curious natives, and a yelping rush of
dogs.

He was a wonderful man, for his camels carried a doll for
little Gertrude. The doll did not weigh much but it had
travelled seven hundred miles by train and four hundred by
camel. The Sister away back at Oodnadatta had sent it. On
Doctor, too, swaying in their little box, were two pussies, a
present from the police trooper at Alice Well. There were
other things carried by these Camels of Dreams. There was
the dog Streak who would sit up on her hind-legs and clasp
her paws with bowed head when asking for meat; there were
dress things for Mum and books for Dad.

The padre baptized the baby, married Billy and Mary the
half castes, gave the youngsters some school-lessons and the
father and mother news of Oodnadatta railhead, four weeks'
buggy ride away. All hands lined up to farewell him on his
ride to the next station. Here he learned of a man camped at
a well a hundred miles farther north. He reached that camp
and had a long quiet talk at the campfire. He set out again,
his only company the camels until he reached Stirling station. He was glad to hear a man's voice again—and that
man was the cook. The others were all away mustering, but
the cook was an old friend.

He wandered on through well grassed plains growing
occasional patches of mulga, then drew in east towards Wood-
ford Creek and followed it for forty miles, again through
richly grassed plains to near the base of Central Mt Stuart,
with the great untamed lands stretching far to the west. He
had glimpsed the mysterious peaks of ranges, purple and
pink and red under the rising sun, stretching far away into
that grim, intriguing country. Often he wondered just what

lay out there in "No-man's Land", as sometimes men called it.

Near Central Mt Stuart his camels browsed awhile along the rich banks of Hanson Creek. This big creek carries permanent water a few inches under the sand. He moved on and crossed Stirling Creek, then under good grass; crossed the Forster Ranges and rode down on to richly grassed plains timbered with gidgee and gum; and eventually headed towards the abrupt little hill frowning behind Barrow Creek telegraph station. In the early days the blacks mustered behind that hill before swooping down to kill the operators. The padre reached the station just in time for the excitement of the six-weekly mail.

CHAPTER XIV

LANDS OF THE SUN

THE padre left with the mailman travelling to Taylor's Crossing well where he was greeted with veiled enthusiasm by one of the telegraph line repairing gang; the man had a poisoned hand and the padre had a lance. From here he must recross that desert strip; so he spelled the camels on good feed, repairing the saddles, cooked a supply of food and got in two quiet campfire talks with the gang.

In the sunrise of a beautiful morning he rode away to farewells calling to return again. Forty miles of sand, stunted bush, and porcupine grass stretched away in flat monotony though possessing a harsh interest of its own. Heat rose from the sands until the camels' hides warmed so that the flies upon them dozed like things well doped. A day and a half brought him to Murray Downs Creek where he filled the water canteens, thankful that that desert was only a "baby". He carried on east, Mt Skinner standing up sharp and clear with a broad valley green with vegetation across its foot. Where Skinner Creek ran through the Murray Downs, fine sheets of water glinted in the sun and birds called cheerily. The padre was now zigzagging about the country trying to locate a nomad whom the police had smilingly told him had built a shack away "out east". He rode into poison-bush country. Uneasily he noticed those ominous shrubs among the healthier vegetation, but was dismayed to see that terror of poison weeds—the deadly indigofera. When he camped he tied the camels up and cut their feed lest he awake one morning and find them dead or mad. He searched for two days in the poison-bush country and on the third afternoon spied the shack down by a creek with water in it. Fading into the distance he heard a galloping horse.

It was a new hut, raw looking, its splintery slabs roughly seasoned, the bark sheets on the roof wired down under saplings. A primitive home, but many such have grown to great station homesteads. The owner had not even slammed the bark door nor snatched his rifle. Inside were some cattle-man's tools, a sapling bunk, some tinned provisions, and a billy on the fire. The lid lay off the camp oven which was brown inside with freshly burned flour. So he had snatched the damper! Yes, and a hunk of cooked beef from the tin plate on the rough bark table. Shreds of tobacco and knife cuts in the table showed where he had been filling his pouch when his dog gave warning of the camels.

The padre sighed, then set out on the fleeing tracks. He followed them several miles only to lose them on rough country. He did not trouble much. He tugged at Shah's nose-peg and turned east again, the sinking sun playing with the camel's shadows. He camped five miles from the shack.

Shortly after sunrise the padre walked a mile back along his tracks then hid in the bushes. An hour later he heard the hoofbeats of an approaching horse preceded by a prick-eared dog poking through the bushes, green suspicion in its eyes, its lips curled to a throaty growl. The man sat still even when the rider reined back in utter surprise.

"Good morning!" smiled the padre.

But the black-bearded rider stared with stupefaction in his eyes, his spurred heels outstretched. His broad-brimmed hat had a thong of greenhide twisted round the crown and his strong arms were burned nearly black from the sun.

"I've lost a camel," said the padre, "a big beast; curly brown; savage head. Have you seen him back along the tracks?"

"No."

The padre sighed.

"I'm a poor hand at tracking," he lamented. "I'll be in a bit of a fix now. Apparently he has gone east from the camp, I thought he must have doubled back. By the way, I met Jimmy Macdonald at the telegraph line; he said you would tell me a short cut to Spencer Creek and from there across to the Frew. I'd like to have a look at that country; they say it's good cattle country. Have you ever been across?"

"Yes," replied the man with the "cattle" interest in his eyes.

"Good!" exclaimed the padre enthusiastically as he jumped up. "Come along to camp and I'll boil the billy; we can have a yarn over breakfast. I'm jolly glad to meet a man who knows the country; it's a wild place out here."

They stayed yarning until midday. Then he helped the padre pack up and rode with him showing him the way. At parting he earnestly invited him to "Call again, and camp until I come if I'm not there, I'll leave plenty of tucker in the shack."

They had started a friendship which has grown stronger with the passing years.

That man had always had the deepest distrust of parsons, the queerest imaginings of what a parson could be—understandably so in a man who had only seen a white woman about once in three years—never a parson. But he was a pioneer doing his bit, who might get married some day. That was where the A.I.M. would come in, the children would need them.

The conversation had been as bushman to bushman. On his returning patrol, the padre would call again with books and messages, and, in his assured welcome, interest the man in other things besides "cattle and country".

The patrol rider kept east and camped on Spencer Creek, by a quiet water-hole half a mile long, walled with tall gums, hedged with green rushes, gay with water flowers. He rode along with bright eyes, experiencing a quiet joy in the beauty around. And wondered. Rain had not fallen recently, and yet luxuriantly foliaged trees grew along the valley, riotous grasses spread over ferns and trailing creepers, galahs and cockatoos flew overhead, while flocks of parrots could be heard screeching half a mile away, and a kingfisher, a living bit of rainbow, flew from its tunnel in the bank. Away to his right rose an abrupt range of hills. Where they overlooked the valley the white trunks of lime-trees stood out against the darker background, and higher up splashes of scarlet and yellow showed where flowering creepers draped the rocky ledges. He loved this beauty, but he knew the Centre. He would like to see this country in the grip of drought. Would its beauty wither then as did so much of the beauty of the country farther south?

The padre struck a rough pad seldom used; grass covered it in numerous places. It led his way, towards a range that divides the Murray Downs country from the Frew, and he let Shah follow it. The camels laboriously climbed the rough path that grew rougher, grunting protests in gurgling anger at the roughness to their feet. When a camel's feet grow tender his temper grows worse.

They entered a gloomy gorge whose black walls looked like velvet draped with green. Boulders like tumbled houses lined the way, and among these the camels twisted and turned with a roar from Ameer as his nose-peg tugged when Shah slid down a washaway. Lace-like vegetation hung from clefts in the walls and high up an eagle had built its eyrie of big sticks, piled like a woodheap upon a jutting ledge of rock. The savage bird looked down on the camels toiling below.

"I'm glad there are no Pathans up there," smiled the padre to Shah. "What a place for an ambush!"

But Doctor bit Kabool, Kabool bit Ameer, Ameer bit Shah, and Shah lurched forward and roared. Angrily the man twisted around and roared back at his innocent-eyed beasts. Doctor gurgled at him.

Rising through several gorges the sore-footed beasts felt

their way over the Dividing Range and then tiptoed on the long climb into the Frew country. The Frew River rises on a rocky hill where water trickles to join other trickles that grow into a stream which flows singing into a valley. That first night over the range the padre camped in a gorge by a rock-girt water-hole, long and deep, reflecting shadowed trees from the cliff above.

This was the first water-hole of the Frew. The campfire crackled merrily and threw dancing flames across the pool. Little fish swam up and cruised in the reflection, a frog with big eyes flopped right up to the fire. The padre boiled his quart-pot and ate his Johnny-cakes in a chilly silence, made weird by the croak of a mopoke. As the camper listened for the answer, there came a gurgling grunt from Kabool nursing his sore feet in the shadows.

As the padre travelled down the valley of the Frew, making for Frew Head station, the stream grew into a rocky river and the valley broadened out, showing ranges spreading in many directions with peaks like spiked helmets. All was so beautiful that again he surmised how this country would stand drought: he must not send in a misleading report. Over many miles he registered the grasses in growing surprise: the far-famed Mitchell grass, blue grass, silver grass, mulga grass, barley grass, herbage, and that "harpoon" grass with its stalks pointing down like a poised harpoon. Such evidence was against recurrent drought. Suddenly he listened to the ring of a tomahawk coming from somewhere over in that range. "Natives! cutting out a 'sugar-bag'. Were they myall or tame?" He came on quinine bush, halted the obliging Shah, pulled some of the leaves and bark, and thoughtfully chewed them. "Yes, bitter as gall." He rode on again well pleased. A man must travel with his eyes open in new country. Who knows but in a fever case this bush might make a substitute for quinine! Life hangs on a thread of bark, sometimes, in the Inland.

The leafy foliage of these trees was welcome to the eyes

after the mulga and spinifex of the gibber plains. Here were
bean and corkwood, ironbark, beefwood and lancewood, and
trees he did not recognize. He was pleased to see a stretch
of the old familiar saltbush, and, yes, bluebush too: fine
drought resisters.

The Frew Head station people insisted that the padre "spell
a day or two". Thankfully he accepted.

The river had widened out down by the station: a particularly fine long sheet of water a native pointed out as
"Tootoowa". He fished there one glorious evening and the
fish were ravenous. The river of course would eventually peter
out into water-holes and vanish in the plains country.
Refreshed in mind and body, as his camels were in feet, the
padre saddled up and made off down the Frew towards a
"lake" some twenty-five miles away.

"Two of the boys are building a yard down there," the
manager had explained. "One has got an 'old man' toothache.
The station smithy broke the tooth and the chap is growing
cranky with pain."

As the valley opened out the ranges spread from the river
only to close in again in the distance. The level country was
delightful under a mat of grasses, and the climate was
delightful; the padre smoked the pipe of peace. But Shah
grunted his disdain—the desert and the camel-bush for him
every time!

He arrived at sunset at the little lake, Arralooloola the
aborigines called it. A beautiful two-mile sheet of pale blue
water turning to rose under the setting sun. Along its banks
big gum-trees threw weird shadows. Emus and 'roos watched
the solemn camels tread past; flocks of wild duck sped down
to water with a hissing splash; wood duck, like soldiers in
line, perched solemnly on tree branches, while other trees
blossomed white and pink under cockatoo and galah. The
sun set to a cool breath from the water and a noisy farewelling
from the birds. As in long solemn strides they travelled along
the bank the grotesque shadows of Shah, Kabool, Ameer, and

Doctor faded from the water; on the opposite bank a fire leapt up and sent a pink ribbon flickering upon the lake.

The padre wound round the shores towards the fire. At the grassy rustle of his camels' footsteps the men stared up as if at ghosts.

"Good evening!" smiled the padre.

The man with the swelled face just stared, but he of the frying-pan ejaculated:

"Stone th' crows!"

"You don't mind me camping in company?" laughed the padre.

" 'Course not," they declared and dropped the frying-pan and the face and stepped over to help him unpack.

"Where on earth did you spring from?" asked he of the frying-pan.

"Oodnadatta originally."

"What?"

"Oodnadatta!"

"Hell! Where the crows fly backward."

"Not exactly," answered the padre politely. "Bedourie, I believe you mean—I have not been to the other place."

"There's plenty of time. What's that about 'when we all go where we all must go'? But what on earth are you?"

"A parson."

"Cripes!"

"Now we're introduced," laughed the padre, "I'll pull that tooth, then sit by your fire and show you how to eat fried duck."

"Get to it!" laughed the one with the pan as he grabbed it. "If you really can pull molars, Jim here'll reckon you're an angel—from Oodnadatta or otherwhere. He hasn't slept a wink these last three nights."

CHAPTER XV

THE WAY OF A DOG WITH A MAN

THE traveller enjoyed that meal. Juicy duck goes well after a long ride, especially when eaten at night by a moonlit lake mysterious with croakings, honkings, and whistlings. These two new friends were hungry too—for news of the outside world. The man with the tooth out fell asleep over his meal, but his mate held the visitor talking until nearly dawn.

A few hours later despite all urging he saddled up again. Time was precious, distances were great, humans few and far between.

"There's a prospector somewhere away out in the Elkedra country," they told him at parting. "He's in the rough country, heaven knows where exactly, but he's got packhorses and had twelve months' supply of tucker, so probably he's still somewhere about. He's got a black dog too, and they just about love one another. But you'd never find him, the country is as rough as the hobs of——"

"Oodnadatta!" finished the padre.

"Well, thereabouts!" they laughed.

"It is my job to find men," smiled the padre, "even if they be in—Oodnadatta, which is a rather decent little place really."

They laughed him farewell and he set off towards the Elkedra, where sharply outlined hills loomed up. Happily he rode: he had made yet two more friends for the A.I.M. His joy now was to find a seeker of gold.

The padre crossed the Divide and wandered for a week, solid going up along fertile valleys between rocky ranges, crossing from valley to valley, winding in and out among the hills, seeking a seeker after gold. Scanning the ground for tracks of horse or man or dog, seeking traces that might betray the work of a white man's axe, seeking cold ashes that might have been a campfire. Closely he scanned any creek, because the water would come down cloudy if a man were washing dirt up-stream. He skirted every water-hole seeking the tiny pile of gravel that would show where a man had washed a dish, he searched the big water-holes on the Elkedra even, looking for a camp. Horses must come to water. A man who travelled by horse must camp near it—particularly a gold-seeker. He would seek mostly in the gullies for alluvial and he must wash his dirt.

It was good country here, well grassed, flowering-trees and birds in plenty. Euro and wallaby hopped among the hills; kangaroo, emu, and pademelon browsed among the foothills. It appeared a happy land.

Often the seeker listened for the blow of a pick, the ring of a dolly-pot, the cracking of stone. He heard plenty of sounds from the feathered world. Often he listened to the far-away call of the bell-bird echoing in a lingering tinkle from hidden gullies—so suggestive of a distant horse-bell. But he saw no sign of white man, at night caught no gleam of campfire among the hills. A precious week passed and he drew farther into the wildest country in the ranges, searching from dawn till dark with all the bushcraft he knew.

A day came which the padre knew spelt the last of the search. Unwillingly he camped, boiled his quart-pot and thoughtfully ate a late meal, listening and watching, hoping, even at this last moment, for a whistle, an echo, a campfire gleam that might put him on the track of the prospector. Only a sighing came from the timber up on the rugged hills, a soft whispering from the light breeze wafting down the valleys. Down where the lone camper listened was a stillness broken by a swish and vanishing whistle as wildfowl sped overhead. Then came a savage sound, sudden and menacing, the song of wild men triumphant at some primitive deed. He jumped at the sound and stood still. Natives! A mile away perhaps, out there towards that ironbark gorge! Had they seen his tracks? Were they a war party or wandering hunters? He doused the fire while listening.

In rising and falling cadences came that savage song. There was something of the earth "earthy" in that throaty chant, a feeling in it carrying the growl of the primitive beast that reacted on the listener's spine. Then came the rhythmic thump of feet to the "Whouff! Whouff! Whouff!" of their stamping grunts with the sharp clap of palms on thighs. There would be no sleep for the listener this night—especially towards the dawn!

He gasped and jumped when it touched his leg—like the creepy touch of a hand!

"Oh, doggy, doggy!" he exclaimed, "you scared me. Why didn't you bark, you old woolly-skin!"

The dog gazed up with a piteous pleading in its big brown eyes. As he knelt to pat it, it licked his hand, his face, it stared into his face, its eyes talking. It was a dog with a curly black coat and waddled a little—lived on the fat of the land; maybe dined when its master went hungry. It turned back into the darkness listening, but not to that distant song; then turned again to the man, its eyes imploring, its absurd tail wagging. It waddled out into the dark and whined, asking him to come. He smiled as he blazed up the fire, whistling low.

"The boss will see and hear," he reassured; "he'll be here in no time, doggie!"

But the dog whined, hurried back, took his trouser-leg and gazed up as it gently tugged. When he took a step forward it released its hold and joyously ambled back out past the firelight, gazing back, wagging its tail, urging him to come.

Unhesitatingly the padre followed; he had seen much of bush dogs. Something was seriously wrong. Had the prospector been speared? Had he fallen down a shaft?

"Don't go so fast, doggie," he called. "You're black as the ace of spades!" He followed it amongst the timber, stumbling across gullies and through long grass that swished above his knees. He wondered that such a fat dog could have worked its way through. It must have smelt his campfire in the first place, or more likely the camels. Fainter grew that chant away behind. Uneasily he hurried on, making haste with caution lest he break a leg. His camp was now entirely at the mercy of the blacks should they come. In that case they would raid it, spear his camels, and leave him stranded, perhaps worse.

But he followed the dog.

It vanished into a thick clump of shrubby trees. He could barely distinguish the white of the tent even under his outstretched hand. He crept inside.

"Hullo!" he said softly. "Are you there?" He lit a match in time to see the sick man's eyes, he lay on a rude sapling bunk, his face deathly in the matchlight. "Dying!" thought the padre as the match burned out. He struck another and saw a slush-lamp—melted fat in a jam-tin. He lit the flannel wick and the thing burned dully. The dog was standing on its hind-legs by the bunk, its head on the man's chest. His thin fingers had not the strength to stroke the curly head.

"Is it fever, old man? I have quinine."

"No," he whispered, "just—sickness. I'm—done."

"I know quite a lot about medicine," assured the padre. "Never give up! Tell me what is wrong."

The sick man searched the padre's eyes, then weakly whispered:

"You can see—I—am—done. Any moment——"

The padre knew the truth.

"Will you—do—something for me?"

"With all my heart, old man. What is it?"

"Look—after—Ronnie!"

The man's eyes were the last of him to die. When his fingers were dead upon the head of the dog he was still staring at his visitor. The padre bent over and gently closed the eyelids. The dog leapt up to his master's chest, whining frantically, shivering as with fever, licking the ashen face. Then it lifted its head and howled. Hurriedly the padre stumbled out into the darkness.

It was a lonely burial service, just the man and the dog, the trees and the birds and the sunlight. The prospector had dug his last shaft. When the padre slowly filled it in the dog crouched on the mound, and howled.

With a heavy heart he packed up and moved on again, and Doctor carried a woolly, black dog that had to be tied up in a bag. He struck nor'-west through the hills towards Taylor's Crossing well, and from there to Bean Tree Creek, another eighty miles, made lonelier still by the tracks of natives whom he knew were dangerous. The padre had met no white man since the burial. He was worried about Ronnie. The dog would not eat; at nights it just gazed at him.

Gladly he came to Bean Tree Camp. Here were some wolfram prospectors. They greeted him heartily and came forward to help unload the camels. He went to Doctor first, a foreboding at his heart as he lifted off the bag. Ronnie was dead.

The Hatch's Creek camp was a rough, good-hearted camp, echoing to the song of men who were busy and happy. They were energetically digging out the recently located wolfram. The field was new, junks of the dull black stone lay scattered over the tree-lined hills for the picking up and bagging. And the market price of the metal was "up". The old Afghan merchant prince who was fathering the field had just arrived with his great camel-train loaded with stores. His half-caste men were unloading the camels while the Afghan was surrounded by diggers. Newcomers were riding in from the Queensland side; rough bush anvils clanged to the hammer as "Jacky Howe"-clad men sharpened the steel. Now and again gelignite explosions rocked the immemorial hills.

The padre left Hatch's Creek, carrying with him the goodwill of all, besides a sum of money to help the A.I.M. and the promise of a substantial amount if the wolfram-field thrived. Before him now was the last stretch, a hundred and twenty miles of unknown country north nearly to Tennant's Creek. It proved a hard ride over stony country, sometimes through scrub, and glad were the camels when they saw the little telegraph station. The padre was going no further north on this patrol. From here he would turn back, seven hundred and fifty miles to Oodnadatta, choosing another route. Every patrol seemed very long, the way hard, the results meagre. Sometimes he felt discouraged. But by such work has the A.I.M. been built up.

CHAPTER XVI

THE DREAMER REAPS

THE dreamer rejoiced over 1919. The war over, the foundation of the A.I.M. assured, the opening of the Mitchell Home, finance, organization, Board and Field work, gaining slow but sure momentum. And on the financial horizon appeared rays that might spring into a sun to help gird all Australia—legacies.

The dreamer thought over this progress with a glad heart. As to legacies, if people would only think of the A.I.M. their thoughts would live long after them—in hospitals, in spiritual comforts, in the alleviation of pain and loneliness, and sometimes hopelessness, among those who will be living when we are dead.

This year, the Board decided to found a strong Building Fund, from which loans without interest could be made to Field Committees, but returnable in regular instalments. In this way the self-help which the Inlanders had increasingly displayed since 1912 would be fast developed: all moneys would be utilized to the greatest possible advantage; and givers would know that their money would be used over and over again as the years went by.

Another factor which would give momentum to the gathering tide of success, was the buildings themselves. Buildings "speak", and the hospitals away out there were eloquent advocates for the work of the A.I.M.

This year, too, marked the definite departure of a second nurse to assist every nurse in the Field. An additional nurse was needed, not only to care for the patients on those too frequent occasions when one nurse was called to distant cases, but for companionship. Ten women were now actively on the Field Staff with four more appointments to be made before the year was out.

The one big difficulty was to replace the padres who had been lost during the war. These men must have special qualifications. Apart from spiritual qualifications they must understand all animal transport and be able to travel and find their way and live, often entirely on their own resources, over thousands of miles of country, some of it, perhaps, the wildest in the world. Only bushmen born could hope to succeed under such conditions. And the A.I.M. padres had many other jobs to attend to as well.

Peculiarly gratifying to Flynn was a collection taken up throughout Scotland in the Sunday Schools of the United Free Church in ard of the A.I.M. It showed strikingly how his work was being recognized and approved in the Motherland. He wondered if the spirit of the Woman of Dunesk knew what her mite had set rolling.

With a smile on his fine face he thought of the work the Australian Sunday Schools had done. He loved children. The youngsters throughout the continent were constantly organizing little schemes of their own, planning them and carrying them out to the successful result of a stream of pennies flowing to the A.I.M.

And the *Inlander* was doing great work. Well illustrated and full of authentic information covering all parts of the Inland it was eagerly read whenever infrequent opportunity allowed of its production.

The press, too, both city and country, gave sympathetic space to the movement—had done so willingly since its beginning.

The voluntary Office Teams were growing in every city, the Country Centre teams were spreading, numerous private individuals were enlisting, work was spreading everywhere. The gift-book department had grown enormously. Books sent out were marked "Please pass on when read", and were being handed all round Australia. Flynn glanced again at a bushman's letter: "I've found the A.I.M. books in many a camp. There is more in the book-chain than merely novels to read. I've thought them like cobwebs floating in the air. Their starting-point is a kindly thought, but the most careless may look where that thought comes from. The thread leads back to the web; there is a real connexion, however frail."

Then the Nursing Homes, besides proving hospitals, had turned out to be centres of social service, the very presence of the Sisters proving a definite uplift on the spiritual side in those areas where men greatly predominated. The Homes, originally rented, were being rebuilt and modernized for the up-to-date treatment of sick and injured. With the coming of these Homes, too, a feeling of faith in the future was being generated among the people of the frontiers, of brotherhood between the city and the bush, of real goodwill between men and an appreciable impetus to belief in the "Unseen".

Flynn rejoiced as he counted the roll of the "Bush Brigade", those five thousand "Old Guards" who had started the campaign with twenty shillings a year each. Never did Army Commander gloat over his strength as Flynn gloated over that roll-book. That first five thousand were his "shock troops" with which he had set out to win a continent. Lingeringly he locked the well-worn volume safely away: it had fought the good fight—and won! He bought a new roll-book to hold reinforcements for his Bush Brigade was fast growing into the Bush Legion.

But to the dreamer in the quiet hours of his planning there came the conviction that the work had created something stronger far than the powerful organization itself, more enduring than the bricks and timber of his hospitals, more certain than the mechanism of his motor-car—the spirituality that was springing up wherever the A.I.M. set foot. The heart of man craves for more than material things, and the lonely Inlander, seeing men coming to help him materially, was realizing the power behind it all.

An event of personal importance to Flynn was the appointment of Thomas Ramage as a resident Secretary at Headquarters, thus relieving him entirely of important secretarial work. He was free to concentrate on his Field Work and organization of Home Bases in the different States.

There were enormous tasks before the movement; their strength for the job ahead was very limited; but as that strength increased so the work to be overtaken grew smaller and beautifully less.

Flynn dreamed with the certainty of the dreamer whose dreams are coming true. Whatever men dare they can do! He toiled to generate a National Will in the hearts of many individuals and his storm troops now were the Inland Legion. His wireless experiments were actually shaping into something that looked like a practical invention: that to Flynn meant a certainty. Of his flying-doctor scheme he felt assured. Aeroplanes could fly!—Well, get an aeroplane.

He put the scheme to the Board: "A flying doctor, called as occasion required by the wireless of the Inlanders, to serve a radius only limited by the flying capabilities of the 'plane. The 'plane to be fitted as a flying ambulance. The Baby Transmitting Sets used would need to have one powerful station which they could call when in need. At this station would be an aerodrome with a flying doctor in attendance."

That was to be the starting-point of the scheme. As it developed stations would be erected at main ports and railheads. He wanted flying doctors ever ready to answer the S O S until the complete Inland was linked up.

The Board listened as always. It was a grand scheme and gained their fullest sympathy: they would carry it out—if practicable. At present, the scheme, apparently, was years ahead. For instance:

"Where are these Baby Receiving and Transmitting Sets?"

"We are still experimenting. They will be invented in time."

"Where, then, is the money to buy and equip the necessary Mother Station?"

"It will come."

"Where is the money for an aeroplane?"

"It will come."

So Flynn left for parts unknown to scatter his faster dreams that they might hasten the hearts of men to provide the "grains of sand".

And grains came in—one grain from C. Alma Baker, multiplying in a separate fund year by year to initiate the wireless experiments six years later.

With his genius for interesting men who could help, Flynn counted Dr George Simpson as a pal. The doctor had grown up on a station familiar to cattlemen for its studstock. A city man now, he knew the needs of the Inland from experience. One of his brothers was an Ace in the A.F.C. The doctor started in right away to forge what links he could in the Chain of Dreams.

In 1920 Flynn saw the formation of the Queensland and Northern Territory Aerial Service Ltd (QANTAS). That he should see such an epoch-marking event in a few short years gave him great pleasure. He flew back to his dreams of the camel-days when the very sands, though mocking, seemed to whisper that these things would come. Whatever he had *felt* out there in the Centre *had* come true!

Very sincerely he wished the company success. Very soon people would learn it was safe to fly, and would realize that a flying ambulance was not a dream at all. It was only a matter of time now when the flying doctor *must* fly.

CHAPTER XVII

THOUGHTS THAT BUILD

In 1923 Flynn was happy because all was well with the Frontier Service. The Inlanders were doing great work organizing their districts, helping those who were helping them. Funds had come in from country and city, almost sufficient to start two more hospitals. Flynn radiated the good humour of the Board. The hospital sites, selected according to necessity and strategical position, were Birdsville and Alice Springs. Birdsville is Queensland's "farthest out" town, a thousand miles from Brisbane, down in the south-west corner within eight miles of the South Australian border. Its temperature, some years, is 40 degrees in winter and 114 in summer. It is the centre of a land of extremes: its average rainfall is six inches, but one year brought twenty-six. The people are very happy with six inches: then herbage grows magically. Some years, unfortunately, it forgets to rain at all. But the grass-seeds never die: they spring up immediately with the April or November showers. The town, consisting mainly of police station, hotel, store, and several dwellings, nestles among sandhills with big old gums lining the banks of the Diamantina close by. The people share their meat and milk—there is none for sale. When someone kills a beast all hands roll up for their cut. The A.I.M. proceeded to convert the old hotel into a Nursing Home. The country around for a radius of some hundreds of miles is sandy, with low hills here and there and dry creeks lined with trees: a "dry" country, but growing the drought-resisting saltbush together with good herbage that comes with the rains. People who have lived there a lifetime love that country as if imbued with the vitality that breathes in its soil. Cattle and sheep stations are widely scattered, all necessarily large holdings.

Birdsville is a strategic centre, big mobs of cattle pass it droving down the lonely Boulia-Bedourie-Marree track, six hundred miles, with neither telegraph nor telephone. At Marree in South Australia the cattle are trucked to Adelaide. Stores for the stations covering a huge area of country all came rolling in through Birdsville. Occasionally sick people came drooping along, too, if they thought there was a chance. Anything the policeman and the publican could do was theirs, but the nearest doctor was at Boulia, two hundred and fifty miles north.

Work at reconditioning the old pub went on apace. It was a comfortable enough stone building: there is a quarry near at hand from which the present hotel and police station are built. And a boat is there, too, tied to a handy tree, waiting for the Diamantina to come rolling down. When the Birds-ville folk decided to establish a permanent water-supply they built a large tank—then waited four years for the rain. An old-man drought came instead, even the town water-holes went dry. But the world carried on. Children were born at Birdsville. When the rain *did* come hissing down the children howled: it was a strange, wet phenomenon seen and felt for the first time. A few days later they were squatting for delighted hours watching the miracle plants springing up.

In the old days before federation, Birdsville was a customs town, but contraband troubles the border no more. Sand occasionally "raises Cain" when its swirling legions come howling down at man. Several stations have been blotted out by it; the sand gradually covering the very homesteads. Today two homesteads are watching the sand creeping to their wall-plates. Still, the country has its compensations;

pests that devastate more favoured rainfall districts are absent. And, in time, man will beat even the sand.

Two fully qualified Sisters were appointed to Birdsville. The Sisters set out on their long train and longer buggy ride of hundreds of miles. Very different country and a very different life to that they had known lay before them.

These girls of the A.I.M. were doing a great work; leaving their homes, their friends, and the comforts of civilization to go out, as a rule, into extreme isolation, quite shut off from the world. In some cases they would not receive mails oftener than once in three months. Sometimes they must suffer shortage of foodstuffs. They may know heart-ache and loneliness now and then, but they must never show it. On occasion they would have to travel day and night, by horse or vehicle, over the roughest of roads or none at all for a fortnight on end. And the heart-break would be all theirs if they found the man just dead as they arrived. In some districts there would be no other white woman than themselves. Naturally they had to be of enduring physique and cheery disposition; be ready to adapt themselves to environment, and to uplift that environment if possible. Two other qualifications are required of them: they must be Christians, and they must be thoroughly qualified for their job. The nurses come from various denominations.

The success of their work is proved by the growth of the A.I.M. and the esteem and affection they have won in the hearts of the people outback.

Flynn returned from a long motor organizing patrol to joyfully see the inception of the Birdsville Home. Then he got out his maps and studied what the few short years had built. Two Nursing Homes in the north of South Australia, another on the Westralian coast at Port Hedland, one right in the heart of the Kimberleys, one at Marranboy in the Northern Territory and, now, one in the south-western corner of Queensland. The links were stretching across the continent

—permanent links built by "grains of sand". Over hundreds of thousands of square miles those tiny hospitals had already cast a feeling of security. Not only material results in the healing of the sick and the succouring of the crippled had been accomplished, but Flynn's reports showed him a slight increase of population. Men are not afraid to take their families into a frontier district when medical help is within reach.

How surely the dream was building into fact! Now the Flying Doctor and the Wireless Transmitting Sets were wanted, then all Inland Australia could be made safe for the settler.

Flynn sighed. The Dream Set was still a dream: its invention was taxing some of the brightest wireless brains in Australia. This Baby Set seemed as elusive as the foot of the rainbow! Experiments so far had been a chain of failures. What these men were working to create was not a wireless set like that in every city home today—not a listening-in set —but one which would *send out* messages as well as receive. They wanted to build a tiny *transmitting* set, a baby transmitter capable of doing in a small way the work that the huge wireless transmitting stations do.

"If a man only *thinks* hard enough, *wills* hard enough, *works* hard enough, he will accomplish any dream!" murmured Flynn. He pulled himself together with almost a frown, resolutely squaring his shoulders. This was not the time for dreaming; he must concentrate on details for the next hospital. He put his finger right on the centre of the map.

"Alice Springs!" he said aloud and smiled. He loved the Centre. It has a fascination that creeps into the very blood of a man: it seems to be living: the farther you ride into its great silent heart the closer it enfolds you.

But—"Man proposes: God disposes." A sudden outbreak of malaria occurred at Victoria River Downs in the Northern Territory. Eleven per cent of the tiny population were sud-

denly carried off. A rider galloped to the Overland Telegraph
line at Daly Waters. News was wired to Darwin. Two relief
Sisters *en route* for Marranboy had just landed from the
monthly boat. One immediately took the tiny train to the
Katherine, then drove to Victoria River Downs—two hundred miles by rail and another two hundred by buggy. Thus
the A.I.M. took the field. The big station homestead on the
banks of the pretty Wickham was turned into a hospital and
the epidemic was fought as it had been fought at Marranboy
a hundred and eighty miles away, and with the same success.
No further deaths occurred at Victoria River Downs. In
course of time a Nursing Home was erected there.

Victoria River Downs station is the largest cattle station
in the world, thirteen thousand square miles carrying one
hundred and thirty thousand head of cattle. It is the "Bovril
station" four hundred miles inland from Darwin. Without a
doctor, and with no telephone to call one up. The Victoria
River country, splendidly grassed, stretches right into nor'-
western Australia. It is magnificent cattle country, probably
the very best in the world; rivalled, possibly, only by those
great plains of the Barkly Tableland that stretch away east
towards Queensland. The scenery of the nor'-west, in parts,
becomes wildly grand; wild gorges and sub-tropical lagoons
are made more interesting still by the black imps that walk
their shadowed trails.

The two rivers, the Victoria and the Wickham, are beautiful, flowing streams during six months of the year; in the
other six they are a succession of reaches and long water-
holes, such as the Pigeon Hole, and Longreach with its seven-
mile stretch of water and bird life. In addition the country
is watered by numerous lagoons and springs. This makes it
difficult at times to muster, as the cattle can get water anywhere and so are scattered over hundreds of miles of country
that affords them unnumbered "hide-outs". A water-hole on
the edge of the Victoria River Downs country, known to every
drover, is Murranji; a famous hole with tree-lined banks

where a hammered out kerosene-tin marks the resting-place of Jim McDonald. In that country, too, is the Eighty-Mile Fence, one stretch of fifty miles being perfectly straight, between Wave Hill cattle station and Victoria River Downs.

For many years this big country was practically valueless because of the great distance from market. The cattle steamers, when they began to call at Wyndham, not two hundred miles nor'-west, soon altered all that; while the meatworks, started in 1919, spelt prosperity. About three hundred thousand head of cattle have since been killed there; nearly a million sterling paid in wages; and more than a million for cattle. This country can carry fifteen head per square mile, twenty head in numerous parts. Undoubtedly, several large tracts, particularly in latitudes south from the Pigeon Hole, will be under sheep when the country is developed. Unfortunately crocodiles lurk in the lily-leafed water-holes.

The country is blessed with a good climate and twenty-two inch average rainfall. Supplies are brought from Darwin by boat along the coast approximately two hundred and fifty miles to the river-mouth, thence by luggers to the Depot within eighty miles of the station. From the Depot teams bring the supplies to the station every six months, just before or after the wet. The man who forgets to order his tobacco, or the woman her cotton, has to jolly well go without. Up there, you order the plums for the Christmas pudding in the middle of the year before. If you have a toothache you suffer it—or did before the A.I.M. came.

The Sisters had hardly got their quinine unpacked when a rider appeared holding to the saddle as if supporting the world. His face was so swollen that his eyes looked like little marbles. He had already ridden a hundred miles *en route* to Darwin: there and back meant a thousand miles to have a tooth extracted. He thought he was in dreamland when he found the station turned into a hospital. But when he saw the two Sisters he was sure there was a war on: when he

found they were capable of pulling teeth he collapsed altogether—as he had under the blacksmith. The shoeing pincers
had messed up the man's jaw, but after lancing it Sister pain-
lessly extracted the tooth. He slept for forty-eight hours.

Meanwhile the Birdsville Sisters were busily furnishing their
white-washed little home.

"It does look reminiscent of the 'night before'," said Sister
Ethel as she surveyed the sitting-room furniture tastefully
made out of beer cases.

"The chairs look jolly comfortable," smiled Sister Mary.
"They could tell a tale if they could only speak."

"Just as well they can't," replied Sister Ethel.

Their real furniture was coming away out on the tracks
of "Wait-a-While". It would arrive some time "before the
wet".

"It is rather wonderful how comfortable they have made
us," said Sister Ethel, "considering the labour involved in
carrying every nail to this isolated little home in the sandhills."

"How thoughtful they have been of the dental victims!"
remarked Sister Mary.

The hotel had contributed the rocking-chair.

"I'll have to hold their heads against the wall," surveyed
Sister Ethel professionally, "especially if any of those long
drovers come in. Hullo! What's this?"

"Only a hand," said Sister Mary. "He's shy too."

In shamefaced manner their very first case appeared: his
injured hand was in a lamentable state. Sister dressed it and
sent him away "All done up like a wedding-cake!" as he
dubiously expressed it.

Two days later Sister met him in the "street".

"Where are your bandages?" she asked severely.

"Me horse won't stand 'em!" he replied bashfully. "He's
too fresh!"

"Well, you come right along and get more," ordered Sister;

"and don't let your horse boss you about this time! We don't want you laid up for months with a poisoned hand."

Shrewdly she guessed his mates had been chiacking him about his "wedding-cake".

Time passed and patients began to dawdle in: "news was noised around". "Mulga wires" travel miraculously in the Inland. The Sisters found time to start a little social service which put girls within reach of the Home into the seventh heaven. A sewing-class was started in which each girl in turn was instructed in the duties of a "hostess". A service was held too—quite a success despite the hardness of the beer cases. The promise of a Christmas-tree for the youngsters made the district wonder what had happened to it.

On tenterhooks the Sisters awaited the arrival of the camel-team with their drugs and medical stores. A serious case, with the nearest doctor two hundred and fifty miles away at Boulia and neither telegraph nor telephone to reach him, would have been—well, serious. The local store was supplied by camel-team twice a year. That was the way the Sisters saw their furniture arriving: chairs, beds, oven, tables, and the stove balanced by two big tanks, on the backs of camels. No wonder the long necked beasts walked solemnly.

"They needn't have shown our little etceteras to the world!" remarked Sister Ethel reprovingly.

"The camels look rather disdainful," smiled Sister Mary, "but the camel-men have had a treat."

"Just let them come here with toothache," vowed Sister Ethel, "I'll treat them!"

Water used to give the Sisters qualms, every pint had to be bought, every drop was precious.

"Now you city people will understand why we outbackers drink beer!" observed the mailman cheerfully.

But the water alarmed the Sisters: impure water is not appreciated by a hospital. Lime or salts cleared it, but when cleared it was awful. Its compensations were small—as the Sisters found when they tried to bathe in a quart of it without spilling a drop. The hospital was now established, so was Victoria River Downs—two in one year!

Flynn was thoroughly prepared with knowledge when the first commercial companies started flying in Australia: he knew many of their hopes and the difficulties that would face them in organization and work. He could, when he liked, talk aviation and wireless with intimate knowledge. He had to learn these things and know them, otherwise he could never have approached experts to help him: they would have laughed him to utter scorn had he not understood the "innards" of his dreams.

No man hoped more than Flynn that all aviation ventures would prove a "Flying Success". Even before H. V. McKay assisted materially in promoting Western Australian Airways Ltd, Flynn went to him and discussed his dream. McKay was strongly of opinion that an actual start should not be made until aerial mail routes were strongly established. Then the dream could be based on those organizations.

So Flynn had gained another big friend who, as the years went by, helped very considerably in the materialization of the dream. The press of Australia again stepped in to his aid by sympathetically discussing the practicability of a flying doctor: thus broadcasting countless "seeds"; preparing the way.

Among doctors in all States Flynn had made numerous friends. A "Flying Doctor"? Why, certainly, such a scheme would interest doctors. They made him tell them all about it; then they discussed it among themselves; then they set to work to help him. But before Flynn tackled any doctors he trod cannily—he studied all the ramifications of medical etiquette.

He interested big pastoral companies, cattlemen, woolmen, banks, various businesses—certainly they would be interested in any scheme that might solve the problem of communication and quick transport in the Inland; any scheme at all that might help develop the country and business in any way.

He eagerly studied the operations and spread of the QANTAS pioneering flying company in Queensland, learning all he could from their experience. Seeking friends who could help the A.I.M. he became a close personal friend of Colonel Brinsmead, the man who was destined to do great things for aviation in Australia.

It is hard to realize now that the fine Nursing Homes, the patrol cars, the flying-doctor service, the wireless girdle, the publicity department, the powerful organization have been all built from the dreams, the quiet sincerity, the courteous work of just one man.

And he says it is the voluntary workers and the Board that have done it all.

CHAPTER XVIII

THE "BOUNDARY RIDER"

In 1924, a nursing service was started, unique in the history of the world—the "Border Sisters".

These nurses operated alone, each for a period of two years. Her district embraced seven thousand five hundred square miles. Scantily populated, this area could not then be safeguarded with a Nursing Home. It is a harsh district of gibber plain and sandhill, saltbush and coolabah, possessing a grim fascination of its own. On moonlight nights, one can see a surprising distance, though the shadows of hill and gully lie black as pitch. To the lonely rider the howl of a dingo or hoot of a night-bird draws the attention almost as an explosion would in a city street. By day the sun shining upon dry creek-beds sometimes deceives with haze and mirage; to the passing traveller it might almost hold the viciousness of the nesting magpie that swoops at him from the gum-tree near her nest. But when a man gets used to that land, he loves it. It holds him like a woman who has been hard to understand but who proves worth the heart-ache. When the scanty rains come the yellow-brown lands turn emerald-green and wild-flowers cover the sandhills with a rich embroidery. In the dry times, it is a long way between water-holes.

That is the country bisected by the South Australia-Queensland boundary, a bit of Australia where the sun tans a man nearly copper. Between Marree in South Australia and Boulia in Queensland are six hundred miles of track which occasionally, in parts, is obliterated by flying sand. An inexperienced man might easily, here and there, miss the track—it beckons away just around the bend and before a man knows where he is he is up a dry gully. And the low hills look all the same, and silence reigns—and there is no water.

There are no roads, no telegraph-wire. From Farina (S.A.) to Quilpie (Q.) it is nearly seven hundred miles by track and along all that track tiny Innamincka (S.A.) is the only township. Here for one hundred and thirty miles over gibber plain runs a private telephone-wire to a station at Mt Hopeless. A great stock route runs through this country from Queensland into South Australia. The dusty drovers meet with accidents at times as do the scattered stockmen. The stations are necessarily very large: a man working alone and thrown from his horse might lie for a long time before being tracked and found.

The job of the Border Sister was to help any sick or in-jured man in that vast loneliness. He might be lying hurt three hundred miles away—she must ride regardless of the hour. It might be the dry season with no water within a hundred miles; or the wet, with the probability of those huge old dry rivers the Georgina, the Cooper, the Diamantina, surging down in rolling brown floods to spread lakes for miles across the land—she started out just the same.

The Sister was generally stationed in turn at Innamincka and at Arrabury, Nappa Merri, or Cordillo Downs stations. And, as a rule, she was a guest of the Beltana Pastoral Company.

From these great stations she rode out when needed. It was a job that stirred the imagination and gained many friends for the A.I.M. The rides of the Border Sisters are a splendid Australian romance: it is a shame that the only record of those rides is to be found around the campfires of the Centre.

Far and wide the Sister came to be known as the "boundary rider". Stations are fenced with posts and wire, but this boundary rider fenced her station with the hearts of men.

After ten years' thought and five years' experimenting, John Flynn at last saw a chance of his wireless dream materializing. Perhaps only a practical expert can realize the apparent futility of Flynn's dream. This man wanted a tiny receiving and transmitting set which a bushman could sling on his back and carry across to the house, install in a few hours, and hear his wife chatting with friends a thousand miles away, or scolding the distant storekeeper for not sending the quarterly rations to time. This dream outfit must not cost at the utmost more than £50. He wanted it to cost £10. Utterly impracticable it seemed.

But Flynn scratched his head and carried on. By doing so, ideas seemed to come to him, the dancing little ideas, the means by which he solved the hardest of his problems. So, by 1925, he and his friends had evolved an outfit that could be slung on to the Dodge. Apparently it would work "with the help of the car engine". So they decided to try it out with a six months' test under service conditions, and loaded the car for the route, Beltana-Innamincka-Birdsville: thence back to Marree; then Oodnadatta and Alice Springs, on the maiden attempt to make the dumb Inland talk. Mr E. T. Fisk, Managing Director of Amalgamated Wireless (Australasia) Limited, helped them with apparatus; the government radio department lent a willing hand, and a whole army of wireless enthusiasts keyed up their sets to listen in.

That car looked like nothing on earth when loaded.

They called the outfit 8AC.

"You should call it the 'Ark'," advised a friend dubiously.

"Now, that's a good suggestion," agreed Flynn. "We are going to send out a dove, too!"

"Well—yes. But remember that little dove didn't get his message through straightway!"

"History repeats itself. Though it does look as if I'm asking too much of the old car. But it will go when I get in!" he added confidentially.

"Where on earth *are* you going to get in?"

"Well, I can climb on top. So long as I can reach the steering-wheel we ought to be all right."

"Um!" they said, "well you'd better climb in and see."

He did squeeze in somehow and started for the first Field tests at Beltana, three hundred miles north of Adelaide.

"With the definite objective," he observed, "of investigating the difficulties of wireless in the bush. And I'll jolly well find them out!"

He did—at a long dry creek with a mile of sand to cross. As the old car chugged comfortably to a full stop Flynn heaved himself out with the light of expectation in his eyes.

"Here's where the invention comes in," he mused. "Now, will it work?" He rummaged down among a heap of tarpaulins and cases and shovels and things. The sun was warmly sympathetic, shining far away across the sandhills. Finally, with painstaking care Flynn pulled out the "Wonder of the Age". He smiled just a little dubiously as he rigged that invention; it looked like a canvas road with cleats of wood nailed across it. Invitingly he spread it out in front of the car. With labour and sweat that disdainful machine was induced to "step" upon it, after which Flynn pulled one end of the "road" up over the front of the car, the other end up over the rear, and padlocked the ends together. He surveyed his masterpiece, wiping the sweat from his brow.

"A tank!" he murmured. "My kingdom for a tank. But I wonder just how I'll get into the blessed thing?"

It was a shin-scraping problem, to crawl back into the car under that enclosing hood. When he finally pulled his legs in and tucked them away somewhere he got his breath and ruminated: "They say, if I remember rightly, that the first tank tried out in France went up in smoke—and I've got no fire extinguisher!" He wiped some caked dust out of the corner of his eye and blinked around for the starting-gears.

The car started right enough, or rather it tried to, with a rumbling and a snorting that nearly capsized it and sent the sand flying. The miniature duststorm gathered itself together for another attempt then plunged desperately forward to a thunderous ripping of canvas and rattle of flying battens.

In the midst of a deep silence the invention lay beautifully wrecked all over the place.

"Rip, tear, and bust!" mused Flynn. "It might have gone; it nearly did!"

He gazed around. A disreputable crow surveying him from the topmost branch of an old creek gum remarked "Quark! Quark!"

"Croaked the raven!" mused Flynn. "Well you're not much of a dove but I'll make this Inland talk yet! After I cross this creek that is, and those sandhills beyond!"

It was a problem. He overcame it as he did other problems. He solved it.

All the same, Flynn's invention was only a few years before the times. The idea, applied in a caterpillar form to the wheels alone, is a successful method now used in sandy country to get a motor across any sand.

The tests proved a "successful failure". That six months of heart-break, thought, and hard work left their mark on the wireless history of Australia. A month after the event, he learned that while he had been experimenting at Oodnadatta his speech through wireless telephone from Cordillo Downs station eighty miles north of Innamincka had been picked up by Mr Hall—a visitor with a roughly made receiving set— at Murnpeowie, about three hundred miles away by air. That was a triumph indeed! It proved that the machine *would* talk anyway, sometimes, somehow, under some sorts of conditions. He also managed to get a few morse messages put over the air from Beltana, Innamincka, Cordillo Downs, and Birdsville. It was really a grand achievement. He was on the track. These experiments actually proved the practicability of keeping in occasional touch with places nearly a thousand miles away, and of phoning by air to a distance of three hundred miles—with the machine aided by the car and money. That cruelled the experiment with Flynn—the expense: he knew, as he sweated at the outfit, that the bushman could never run it.

He used to jack up the car on one back wheel on which a special pulley had been mounted, and so drove the belt for a generator mounted on the specially strong splashboard which had been substituted for the ordinary mudguard. Thus he secured ample high tension current for four U.V.202 tubes in the transmitter. He carried extra accumulators, two short-wave receivers, and a four-valve broadcast receiver. The last instrument gave him great encouragement and more problems. In fact, he found that bush wireless created problems quite its own.

Gratified with these little sparks of success he left Oodnadatta for the two hundred and ninety mile run to Alice Springs, counting on the Nursing Home being far enough advanced for him to use the electrical equipment being installed and the 50-watt transmitter lent by the A.W.A. Eagerly Flynn thought of the added power to be given to the tests by that electrical apparatus, backed up by the knowledge and enthusiasm of wireless friends.

But he was in the land of lots of time. When Alice Springs was reached the hospital was hardly started, the foundations were only just in. It looked like twelve months before the walls would be completed; most of the timber had to come by camel over a hundred miles. Flynn sighed; he must work at the wireless in his head only for the time being. He rolled up his sleeves and rushed into the work of building the hospital.

As he worked at the building the wireless was in his mind —and on the tip of his pen as through the long quiet nights he wrote to his fellow-experimenters in Adelaide. These unseen workers were toiling to materialize the dream that would make the Inland speak and eliminate distance and loneliness. They toiled in vain. Then Flynn decided on a compromise, namely, crude I.C.W. transmitters capable of morse signals only. The idea was that all outgoing messages could be sent by voice, obviating the difficulty in reception by inexperienced listeners. The bush folk would have to morse inward messages. These could be called back by voice for them to check, thus practically eliminating error in their sending.

Experiments were conducted in which the I.C.W. transmitter drew its high-tension current from a spark coil provided with the usual make-and-break. The original spark coil used was from an old Ford car. It is rather fitting that this old Inland pioneer should play an important part in still further progress. The wave was not truly continuous (hence the name, short for "interrupted continuous wave") and was of no use for telephone purposes. But the experimenters found the advantage gained by driving the whole transmitter from a 6-volt battery to be irresistible. Flynn then set out to find a suitable primary battery, and decided eventually to test Edison cells as used extensively in automatic railway signalling. These are of low voltage, only 65 volt per cell but their duration of 500 amp. hours, with absolute "rest" when not in use, made them most attractive. The dreamer worked with an eager smile at each fresh promise of success, a sigh at every failure, and a thoughtful pause before once again carrying on with an energy more dynamic by far than his "continuous-interrupted-current". The history of the evolving of that, eventually successful, Baby Wireless Set will some day be pieced together into an entrancing story.

In its experiments with wireless, the A.I.M. produced a wireless wizard, a young man who lives in wireless, a slim, quiet, thoughtful-looking young fellow with a smile at times that lights up his horn-rimmed spectacles. He is not a talkative man at all, but just mention "Wireless!"

It was Mr Kauper of Adelaide who first recognized Alfred

Traeger's genius, and soon had him completely immersed in experiments to solve the great-little problem. Traeger quickly found, as had the others, that it was not only a question of building a wireless receiving and transmitting set. It was a problem of inventing it first, followed by the problem of making it, then of solving the correct materials to make it with, and then the making of *them*.

CHAPTER XIX

THE BATTLING OF MANY MEN

FLYNN's dream was a dream no longer in 1926, when the A.I.M. opened three more hospitals—Alice Springs, Lake Grace, and Marble Bar. Alice Springs is in the centre of the Centre of the continent; Lake Grace is in the southern corner of Western Australia; Marble Bar is in the nor'-west of that huge State. From Marranboy, the most northerly Home, to Lake Grace is fifteen hundred miles, while a nearly similar distance separates Port Hedland on the western coast from Innamincka, destined to be the most easterly. The A.I.M. was now a strong organization benefiting the Inland, and its work was attracting the attention of the statesmen of the Commonwealth. Distinguished travellers from overseas who had seen the work being carried on were staggered at its ramifications. The State Governments now recognized the A.I.M. as a disinterested organization doing a practical work for Australia; while to the Inlanders the name of the A.I.M. stood for service and sincerity.

Flynn's dream had come true, his hospitals had materialized. But they were the dream of the Camel-man—a dream of the past. He had long since been toiling for his Chain of Dreams. And as he sweated at the building of his pet Nursing Home he saw the links welding into reality. In every State, men who had doubted now shook him by the hand, only to be surprised when he sought their interest in these other dreams. Some gave readily, some reasoned doubtfully, most murmured: "Impossible, old man; I'm afraid it's fifty years before the times!" Flynn smiled to all, softly gave his reasons, and passed on. As time passed, all these men would be convinced, all would help, each in his own way, to rivet a link in that Chain of Facts.

One evening he stood by his just-finished hospital at Alice Springs. That unbuyable happiness which comes to those whose hard-fought-for wish comes true filled his heart, and paid in great measure for the labour of half a lifetime.

The tiny town, with its little white houses surrounded by gardens and graceful trees, was quiet in the hush that comes after the day's toil. Sunset tinged with gold smiling flats among small hills whose rocks cropped up like great chocolates. Over-shadowing the flats, the hills, and the town, were the Macdonnell Ranges now wreathed in moving purple robes.

Flynn breathed deeply as the peace of the evening settled upon his face. Gazing out into the hushed silence he heard the fading drumming of a camel's feet, gradually silenced by the growing rattle of machinery, the clang of the black-smith's forge, the creaking of the tumbling scoops as they ploughed through the hard red earth. He saw a shining steel ribbon come creeping fast as the toiling gangs laid the rails which would make Alice Springs a town and settle this land with many homes. Unconsciously he faced towards the darkening north: it was second nature for him to throw his mind a thousand miles away. Here he visioned the northern construction camps in the white of the new moonlight, red fires all along the fresh-dug line. He strained his ears for the rollicking chorus of navvies' songs. Yes, they were coming down from the Katherine. Some day they would bridge that thousand-mile gap. And then—markets to north and south, markets across the seas to east and west would be at the service of the Inland.

Flynn came back to his Chain of Dreams, the links following the first Dream Transport! The motor was fast developing the old tracks and bringing new people. Flying machines!—The first flying service in Australia was the mail-service over an Inland route. Why, people could hardly call his flying doctor a dream now. The QANTAS people had flown three hundred and fifty thousand miles without a mishap. The flying doctor would. be a reality immediately sufficient "grains of sand" flowed in. Wireless!—His face clouded over. Wireless had come right enough, but—that dream Baby Set. The set the mother could use when she needed to call the flying doctor. He straightened himself and smiled: the set would come, every link in the chain would materialize.

"Well, stopped thinking at last?"

Flynn stared at the publican, then slowly smiled. "I'm afraid I'm late for dinner."

"You're never late," assured the publican. "You work to a time-table all your own. But the fowls have gone to roost long ago. Better come over and have a bite."

The gardens of Alice Springs grow luscious oranges, juicy grapes, and huge water-melons. As for onions! Pepper-trees, like weeping willows, shade dray and motor-truck. Two miles north of the township the Todd River emerges from the hills in rock-holes of calm beauty. Sixteen miles west is Simpsons Gap, a precipitous gorge whose frowning walls draw in so close that a horse and dray could hardly pass through. Man dreams of one day utilizing that gorge as a huge reservoir, simply by damming the Gap. One day a party of surveyors interested in the water catchment was inspecting the site, their guide being the oldest inhabitant amongst the natives. The chief surveyor asked him to show them the highest point the flood-waters ever reached.

"Up longa this way!" replied Jacky, and led the party up the almost inaccessible mountain.

"By Jove," said a linesman as they scrambled ever higher up, "I don't believe the waters ever reached this height."

"Yeh! One feller time him did!" assured Jacky.

"Did you see it?"

"No, boss, but I been told!"

"Whoever told that damned lie?"

"That what I bin think!"

"Well, who told you?"

"Misonary. He been tellum us feller flood one time cover hills altogether. Drown him man, drown him wallaby, drown him emu, drown him everything."

Immediately to the south of Alice Springs is Emily Plains. Beyond the ranges is the forty-mile belt of Burt Plain. These plains, Burt particularly, carry saltbush, other shrubs of many kinds, and kangaroo and Mitchell grass. In good seasons an edible spinifex covers the plains like a waving wheat-field. When a passing wind rustles the spinifex tops the traveller may imagine he is gazing over one of the granaries of the world. But the country is not always so good as it looks. It is good for all that, providing the pastoralist has a large holding, considers conditions of transport, and bases his calculations on minimum capacity. In the huge Centre there are numerous plains, some "awful", some medium, some good. The farther away a man's holding is from the Alice railhead the more does the question of transport affect his chance of a living.

It is to be hoped that sub-artesian and artesian water may solve the question of water-supply. Alice Springs draws its water from numerous pure wells at a depth of from fifteen to thirty feet.

Droughts come to these lands, spreading disaster. But then droughts, like Christmas, come to every part of Australia. Much of this country was taken up years ago, and the proof of its supporting capabilities is that the people still thrive and won't go away. The children are healthy, self-reliant Australians, as strong as horses. I have heard men and girls who live in the "Dead Heart" whistling the whole day through. The one real dread comes with the thought—"If I met with an accident so far from a doctor——?

Unless a man goes "far out" there is little pioneering to be done as our pioneers knew it. Those tough old chaps would laugh now if they could see the railway at the Alice, and the motor-trucks lurching "farther out" with stores. Some of those trucks pass over dust that was once the bones of pioneers, men who perished in the days when it meant a six-month trip to come for and return with stores. Many of the pathfinders were of British stock, men fresh from the Old Country. It must have been the blood of a race of battlers in them that woke to life in the New Land and saw them triumphantly through.

On that map of Australia which Flynn keeps locked in his brain is a patch marked "No-man's Land"—a huge unoccupied portion of Australia. Its inaccessibility, its distances, and its true desert have barred occupation. Some men say it is all desert, others flatly contradict them. The railway to the Alice may help solve that question. Approximately speaking, the eastern boundary of No-man's Land starts a hundred miles west of Alice Springs, then runs six hundred miles farther west, and a similar distance touches its northern and southern boundaries. Some of it undoubtedly is the true Australian desert—desolation. But running through it, with sandy country in between, are grassy areas. These in part have been traced by explorers, by wandering prospectors, by cattlemen and by several geologists of world-wide repute. An A.I.M. padre patrolled rapidly through one section. These men found large water-holes here and there and several fertile valleys. Flynn visioned that even this country, in time to come, will be developed where possible.

With great joy in his heart Flynn opened the Alice Springs Nursing Home. It was the first of the modern Homes, with a little operating-room, surgery, wards, electricity, everything complete. Press a button! Shades of the pioneers!

From Port Hedland a little train runs inland once a week to Marble Bar, the centre of the Pilbarra mining district, thirty thousand square miles in the De Gray River neighbourhood. Seventy miles south of Marble Bar is Nullagine.

From Port Hedland a decent motor road also runs out to the Bar. Some stations one passes through have great country, the De Gray, The Bungalow, Warralong, Mulyie, and others, boasting pleasant homesteads and numerous comforts of modern civilization. Many stations in the hinterland of Port Hedland are gradually abandoning cattle for sheep; which speaks well of country where it was once declared sheep could never live.

The Pilbarra is inclined to be a hard country inland and calls for hard men. It gets them too: hardy station chaps run their holdings against the weather and country and anything that likes to come along. They do it with laugh and song and reckon life's "just grand".

The big Inland that embraces all is the home of that queer, rooting, burrowing animal—that never-beaten animal which defies thirst, hunger, and privation of every sort. He is the prospector, the man who always goes before, always fades before civilization. This strong-faced, strong-limbed, unknown individual is really lucky, for he knows one of the greatest joys man can ever know—facing new country, with only himself, his horses, his dog, and the "Unseen" for company. When the last map is drawn across the face of the earth, the last claim pegged out, the prospector will break his heart and die.

The tracks to Marble Bar were blazed by the prospectors pouring down from the Kimberleys, from the Territory, from the Centre, from east and west and south. Vision how far these men travelled "on their own", and marvel that so many "got through".

The white-roofed township of Marble Bar nestles among low hills near the Noongan River. Like most mining-towns, it was either "up" or "down": while gold was being won locally it was "up": when the miners rushed to other localities it was "down". The Western Australian government asked the A.I.M. to take over the hospital there—one was already built, but it could never be kept staffed.

Marble Bar was so called because of the unique jasper formation whose cliff-like blocks wall the river-bed. These, gleaming in the early morning sun, with the entrancing colouring of the jasper in its strange wild setting, and the eerie beauty of these "painted marbles" in the moonlight, reflected from a chilly, deep-blue pool, are among the most picturesque sights in the nor'-west. There is a local legend that if a warm-hearted woman bathes alone in that pool at moonlight her heart will grow cold, but her body as beautiful as Psyche. If that story were only known to the feminine world!

There may be something in it, judging from the slim Sisters who have returned from the Bar during the last five years. Anyway, the native women out there (they are thin ones) can do something the men can't—they can "yandy" tin-ore. They separate the heavier grains of tin from the dirt by a rocking motion of the dish. For centuries these women have been thus separating, in their wooden pitchis, the dust in the white-ants' nests from the pupae, which they eat. When the "mad" white man arrived, eager for the little black stone, the women commercialized their art.

Marble Bar has the reputation of being the "hottest place out of hell". But, then, I have heard the same thing said about Bourke and Townsville and Quorn, Broken Hill, and lots of places. Personally, I've lost just as much sweat in Brisbane as at the Bar.

The "Bar's" reputation though was upheld at a recent burial for the coffin was plainly labelled "HELL". "No need to have labelled it," observed a mourner meaningly.

"Course not," replied his mate, "all th' world knows where Tim's goin'!"

The explanation was simple. There hadn't been enough timber for the coffin so the end was knocked off a Shell petrol case—so was the "S"

The Lake Grace Nursing Home was in a district which has

proved among the best wheat-growing lands in Australia. The district was "springing up like a mushroom", and in a very short time the residents were able to take over the hospital themselves. For a rule of the A.I.M. is that any district could do so when financially able, repaying the A.I.M. only for the money put into the building. As the money was repaid, it was utilized in the building of a Nursing Home elsewhere.

Flynn was delighted with his three trim hospitals in the one year, the old dream was just galloping along. With mind and heart smiling and eager Flynn hurried south to his wireless experiments. His lieutenants were prophesying great things. Carefully he had watched the successful growing of the great Australian airways— safer by far than travel on land. QANTAS, for instance, flying forty thousand miles per month had not so much as a cut finger. Why, flying had proved to be considerably safer than riding a camel!

Eagerly he farewelled Dr Simpson who was going to London, and while there would discuss the proposed Aerial Medical Service with all the overseas enthusiasts he could muster. He would find, too, some of those "silent men" who had taken part in military aerial ambulance services in arid countries somewhere in or around the British Empire. He would work hard to link an Empire chain with the Chain of Dreams.

CHAPTER XX

THE LOVE THAT NEVER DIES

FLYNN made a hurried trip to Sydney and was cornered by the Board. They held him in conference, putting through a big accumulation of work in a very short time until one day he slipped away again. Steadily the Board built on, putting aside those matters necessitating Flynn's personal attention until they could corner him again. There would be a big reckoning "some day"!

Flynn had hurried to Adelaide, picked up Traeger with the latest wireless creation, and returned to Alice Springs—full of hope.

Apart from Flynn's dream, great things were hoped for wireless in the far north at this time. The government by arrangement with the owners of Wave Hill Pastoral Co. Ltd, was erecting a high-powered wireless station at Wave Hill cattle station in the Northern Territory, for the use primarily of drovers moving the big mobs down the great stock routes. And another wireless station at Camooweal away east on the Queensland side. While at Brunette Downs on the Barkly Tableland the station people were erecting a huge private station in an endeavour to keep their interests in touch with the distant "outside".

These propositions were, of course, vastly different from Flynn's little Baby Set which was to be available to the poorest pocket and yet must do almost the same work.

The enthusiasts now believed they had a great chance of success. With the engine-room in the Nursing Home they would command power and would work in a comfortable workshop more conducive to success than the sand and spinifex outside. In schoolboy haste they set up the 5-h.p. Lister, the 32-volt house-lighting outfit, assembled the 50-watt transmitter on the other side of the room, and felt confident and capable of sending wireless all over the world. This station, built by Mr Kauper, it was hoped, would be the main A.I.M. wireless station. The set tuned up, the usual tests made, and Flynn was delighted to hear the voice of Harry Kauper in Adelaide a thousand miles away. The fifty-watter was tuned to eighty-nine metres on which Kauper was able to hear and reply distinctly to both voice and music. A spare spark set was similarly tuned, and, with a separate aerial, was provided for work with distant amateurs. Thus 8AB was born, and a case established round which might be built success. (This mother station was dismantled later.) Now, how about the little Baby Set?

Flynn and Traeger hardly dared breathe of it as they made final preparations to test whether their "Baby" could answer "Mother".

The weatherbeaten old car was loaded with one of the field transmitters on which were built such great hopes. Flynn and Traeger then set off for the Hermannsburg Mission eighty miles west, a locality strategically important in their wireless schemes for the Centre. From there they would press the buzzer and see whether "Baby" would call up "Mother" at Alice Springs. Between hope and anticipation they dodged the ruts along the foot of the beautiful Macdonnell Ranges. As the ranges faded into hills Traeger grew very quiet, brooding on this wireless transmitter upon which he had set his heart. And as the car jolted into the mulga and old familiar spinifex Flynn found himself dreaming of a lonely Camel-man. He stared far over towards the sandhill country. In the haze he saw the Camel-man taking shape as he rode into a mirage dreaming of a day of motor transport, of wireless, and aeroplanes. Vividly he remembered the dream. How far away its realization had seemed to the Camel-man!

Flynn looked at Traeger with a laugh in his eyes.

"We are going to succeed," he smiled eagerly. "We just are! Whether today or tomorrow or next year, we are going to succeed!"

Traeger smiled boyishly from behind his horn-rimmed spectacles.

"Of course we are. But, look out! We're right into that gully!"

"Not yet," chuckled Flynn as he swerved the car. "There's no sense in breaking our necks until the Inland speaks anyway!"

At Hermannsburg, Superintendent Albrecht and the teacher greeted the newcomers hospitably. The welcome was tinged with lively curiosity, growing to fever heat as the apparatus was installed. This station they christened 8AD.

They called up Alice Springs: results were bitterly disappointing. After many attempts they returned to the Alice and took another crude transmitter out to Arltunga, a gold-and mica-field, in ruggedly wild country seventy miles east. This set was installed in the police-station (a friend of the A.I.M.) and called 8AE. They worked this tiny station while the Hermannsburg people were endeavouring to call up from 8AD and the Alice Springs station was trying to call them both. They got quite a number of "buzzes". They hurried back to Hermannsburg and the three stations went at it hammer and tongs—with sparks of success. Alice Springs was intermittently in touch by signals which were always clear about sunrise, generally more or less satisfactory between 9 a.m. and 3 p.m., but hopeless in the evening.

The experimenters sent and received signals only now and again 'tis true, but the very fact of receiving an occasional answer proved that a cheap transmitting set *could* be made. They were getting "hot", but the ideal was far away. Their wonderful set was crude and bulky and inefficient. Keenly disappointed, they recognized all its faults and determined to eliminate each in turn. They would keep on and keep on. They soon found that the set of primary batteries and spark coil to produce high tension for the transmitters were quite unsuitable under the climatic conditions. Among other faults the batteries were far too heavy and evaporation from them was severe. An entirely new set would have to be devised.

"It's a successful failure!" voted Flynn, his blue eyes sparkling.

"It is," answered Traeger, "a failing success!"

"Better luck next time," said Flynn.

"We will succeed next time," answered Traeger. "If not, then we shall succeed the time after!"

"Let us get back to Adelaide," said Flynn, as they turned to the car, "and the workshop wherein we manufacture the Fruit of Dreams!"

And while they worked, the life of the Inland went on as ever, its hopes, its loves, its tragedies, all mixed up together in its great book of Life. And it tore a page from the heart of one man of the Inland, and left him bitter-sweet memories in its place.

When this man first walked into Mary's heart and stayed there, it is only fair to record that Mary waged a silent little fight to displace him—his invasion was a little terrifying. But he was a large immovable sort of person and he stayed.

No one would have believed it of Mary, she was such a quiet little thing. Her tennis friends, all her city pals agreed that she was very sweet and dainty; and, yes, very quaint, but timid and not very interesting.

The Man from the Inland was rather fine, he was a man's man too; and you could see that he had looked in the eyes of the Christ and found his manhood worth while.

He had expected to feel uncomfortably out of his element in the home of Mary's brother and sole protector. The brother, when on a trip through the Inland, had given the man a standing invitation to his home when his holiday became due. He had known the brother years ago at college; they had always been friends in a sort of way; one was very generous, the other rather overbearing; but they had chummed up diffidently, and he had rather hesitatingly accepted the invitation. Now, how glad he was! One glance at Mary and he was so thoroughly contented with his lot that he quite forgot to leave; he forgot all about there being an end to his holiday. His host grew restive. He thought it about time that he did his duty here. He was Mary's brother. Some people thought him "wooden"; but when he liked he could express himself freely enough.

"How much longer is that ass going to tail after you? He used to be a decent, level-headed kind of chap! Can't you see what you're doing? Stringing him on like that! You'll have to put a stop to it. The fellow's made a big enough fool of himself, surely, to satisfy you. He knows he can't ask you to marry him—no fellow would ask a girl to live in the God-forsaken hole he comes from!"

"Oh!" drawled Mary long and dryly, "it looks like that to you, does it? Well, you certainly have a right to be mad with me, though at least you'll admit it is the first time I've been guilty of 'stringing on', as you call it."

Her brother looked suspiciously at Mary. He hated sarcasm in women; so he felt relieved when she quietly continued:

"I'm sorry it looks like that to you; but as you insist I'll put an end to it."

A strained silence followed, and he felt a little uneasy when she left him. He had no idea what she would do. He could never understand her—no man could understand a woman anyway; it was sufficient that she should understand him.

The Man from the Inland looked well in his flannels. On the tennis court where they had so often played together, he was practising serves. How his eyes lit up as he saw her. Little he realized the turmoil raging in her direct little soul.

She herself didn't realize what she did until she found herself facing him with flashing eyes, all her being burning with a mighty courage.

"My brother says you'll go away from here without asking me to marry you. If you do, you're a sneak! I like a man who isn't afraid to make a fool of himself, but I don't like sneaks; and I think it's being a sneak to believe a girl's a coward and a funk just because she's taught to be, and because she's little, and—and because she has a nice complexion. And it's being a sneak to think a girl would let you make a fool of yourself if she—didn't care herself."

She turned and fled, and he gazed after her. When he ran it was too late, though he called with a glad cry:

"Oh, Mary, Mary, little girl, come here! Oh, Mary, you little goose."

But he started laughing and called after her as she vanished into the house.

"Your brother's an unmitigated idiot, a heaven-born idiot!"

On the veranda he found the good brother, feeling benign from a sense of duty done. He even felt a little sorry at the smiling face of the Man from the Inland as he came stamping along the veranda.

"Sit down, old chap," he said rather kindly. "I've been asking Mary her intentions, a fellow can't help seeing how things are going. Awfully sorry, you know."

"Thanks, old man," laughed the Inlander, "I'm really grateful. Do you know, I've often wondered what was in the mind of Providence when you were created. At last I know: You were made that you might give Mary to me. Your mission is accomplished, my brother!"

"What! D'you think I'll allow Mary——"

"Did you ever succeed in preventing Mary from doing anything she wanted to do?"

"Mary has never wanted to do anything I was opposed to," fumed the brother, "and she won't now. She will do as *I* wish!"

"Good! Forces of opposition all intact. I'd put a high estimate on them if I were you," added the Man from the Inland as he remembered Mary's eyes as he had seen them last.

Mary went to the far Inland. She learned there how little the external things of life really have to do with the things that count. If sometimes in those first sweet years, horrid little fears clawed at her heart and left her weak and sick, one look into the steadfast eyes of the man was always enough to dispel them. Just his eyes would make her smile: she loved him so.

The Man of the Inland now works alone. His heart would break if it were not filled with a great love and a great memory.

You understand? Little Mary was all courage and sweetness, but she was not very robust—and his Inland was a three weeks' drive from the railway line.

"I've had my heaven, boy," she sighed. Her arms tried to cling round his neck when she knew they would never get to the railway in time.

"Boy—I know—I'll just—be let sit on the steps—till you come—I love——"

CHAPTER XXI

WIRELESS!

THE wireless men in Adelaide once more concentrated on the problems of the Baby Wireless Set. Each attained results slowly and by great labour. "Seek and ye shall find!" they proved meant work, and more work. Each man's smallest success brought him a delight above anything that money can buy.

As Traeger toiled he was visualizing the future operator —bushman, mother, or child ignorant of wireless and mechanism. Hence the Baby Transmitter must be simple. It must both receive and send messages. That problem was more important even than weight and expense. The generator had proved a recurrent trouble. Kauper had experimented in a new thing—a crystal control. By means of a crystal, it is claimed a continuous transmitter could be evolved, eliminating the weight and other disadvantages of a generator; including the fluctuating current, produced by the uneven turning, which had made signals quite unreadable. This crystal control ultimately proved the key to the problem: they toiled upon it as men who begin to see the light. In twelve months a new set was designed, greatly improved and lighter.

Flynn and Traeger again set out for Alice Springs, made arrangements there for the trial, then went on to Hermannsburg and installed the set. Eagerly Flynn put on the earphones, then tapped the keys. The Lutherans and he and Traeger listened in breathless silence. No reply. Flynn tapped again, and they all listened—to silence.

Finally they gave up: if they had been schoolboys they would have jolly well cried. Next day they tried again—no result. So they left instructions with the Lutherans what to do, and gave them strict schedule times in which to try and communicate with Alice Springs. Two down-hearted men drove back along that disheartening eighty miles. They arrived at the hospital just two minutes ahead of the first schedule. Flynn walked to the machine, put on the earphones, and tuned in to the correct wave-length. Traeger stood quietly by the machine, his eyes on the clock, his ears listening for the faintest sound.

In the tension of that small room Flynn's thoughts raced away seeking relief. He visioned another small room at St John's, Newfoundland, and Marconi there, with his assistant, Kemp, in almost unbearable suspense as they awaited schedule time. Outside the old barracks the wind roared a howling gale which whined its fury right across the Atlantic to where, in Poldhu, Cornwall, the great dreamer's assistants waited ready in another little room. All the world was one vast room; all in suspense. Could this dreamer Marconi really send wireless messages across the earth? This 12th day of December 1901 would tell.

Marconi picked up his telephone attachment and listened while Kemp caught his breath. The unbearable minutes dragged slowly by—three faint clicks sounded in Marconi's ear. He listened again. Kemp stared at his face——

"Can you hear anything, Mr Kemp?" Marconi asked.

Kemp snatched the receiver. His face laughed.

"Three short dots—the morse code—the letter S——" he whispered with triumphant eyes——

"Near schedule time," said Traeger in a queerly strained voice. "Dreaming again?"

Flynn came to earth with a start.

"Buzz—buzz—buzz—buzz"—Flynn's shoulders humped over the machine. Traeger leaned forward and the men's eyes met, dancing with triumph. Strong and distinct came the

Hermannsburg signals—"buzz—buzz—buzz—buzz". Delightedly Traeger tried a voice message in answer, but power was not strong. Quickly he rapped out a morse signal. Breathlessly they listened — it came—"buzz—buzz—buzz—buzz—zzzzz", a jumble of dots and dashes. Laughingly Traeger buzzed out: "Space your letters. Send more carefully." The reply buzzed in indecipherable dots and dashes. In smiling triumph Traeger sent again and again, slowly and distinctly: "Space—your—letters—Send—more—carefully." But the reply wavered back in fainter morse until Traeger buzzed "Cheerio."

"We've got it!" exclaimed Flynn huskily. "At last the Inland speaks!"

"Next schedule," smiled Traeger.

It was a wild—almost hilarious—triumph. Success was assured! If they had been men who drank they would have painted the town purple and scarlet.

There was much more to perfect yet, but Flynn knew that the longed-for link in the chain had been forged.

The pastors at Hermannsburg had been so excited at the answer to their dots and dashes that they could not intelligently reply; so, instead of deciphering the "Space your letters—Send more carefully", they just wrote the message down in its dots and dashes and decided to decipher it "afterwards".

Which they did; and at following schedule time next morning they sent and received messages perfectly.

Flynn walked on air. Traeger's quiet smile masked a burning triumph. The initial failure had been due to the operator placing the incorrect coil in the receiver and listening in on a different wave-length.

But Flynn was reminded that though he might be lost to the world in wireless experiments, there were other important matters going on.

"What is the trouble?" he smiled at Sister.

"Goats."

"H'm, they're always butting in."

"Not this time; I wish they had butted a native."

"Why?" asked Flynn mildly.

"Because then we might still be getting our milk. You're so taken up with your old wireless that you miss the really important things. We're in the midst of a milk famine because there is no grass which of course you would not have noticed—until you take your tea tonight."

Flynn listened patiently.

"All our goats are put in the compound at nights with other people's goats," explained Sister distinctly. "There are wild dogs, you know."

"Sensible idea," murmured Flynn.

"Really!" inquired Sister.

"But surely the dingoes don't milk the goats?" asked Flynn.

"Sammy *does*."

Flynn raised his eyebrows.

"Sammy," explained Sister, "has been bringing us a full jug of milk every morning while other people have been complaining that their milk boys can't get any milk at all."

"They're unlucky," murmured Flynn.

"They were!" replied Sister grimly.

"But I don't see——"

"Of course you don't! Well, Sammy has been getting up very early each morning to milk."

"That's unusual of Sammy," said Flynn approvingly. "I trust others will follow his example."

"They have!" snapped Sister.

"Well?"

"They caught him milking their goats."

"Oh!"

"It will be, oh! when you get no milk in your tea tonight!"

Flynn and Traeger returned to Adelaide as cheery as

schoolboys. They had proved that even to the inexperienced, wireless transmitting was practicable in the Inland. Complete success was to be born from the thoughts of Traeger: he it was who designed the Pedal Transmitter.

They landed in Adelaide so dazed by the rapid day and night travelling that, as Flynn shook hands with his welcoming friends, he smiled vacantly and turning on his heel shook hands, still smiling, with the air. They held Traeger up and carried him inside before he went to sleep in their arms. An almost unbelievable effect of that continuous rough travel on the wireless apparatus was that a number of brass nuts, generally the very devil to unscrew, were found rolling about in the bottom of the box.

With keen regret Flynn heard of the death of his old friend, H. V. McKay. Shortly afterwards, his trustees offered the A.I.M. £2000 towards an experiment in furtherance of the flying-doctor scheme, providing adequate support was given in other quarters. Thus do seeds planted in the minds of men bear fruit.

The General Assembly of the Presbyterian Church of Australia authorized the A.I.M. Board to take all necessary steps towards the consummation of this long-cherished ideal.

A special Aerial Medical Service Committee was constituted, and a sub-committee set to work. The Wool Brokers' Association entered into the campaign: many other citizens quietly put in their weight.

The sub-committee, centred in Melbourne, was composed of men, each an expert in his special branch. Their job was to work out the many problems which beset the initiation of an aerial service. Among the experts were Colonel Brinsmead; Colonel T. White, President of the Victorian branch of the Australian Aero Club; Mr Sam McKay, of the H. V. McKay Charitable Trust; Mr L. W. Thompson, of the "Wide Spaces of the Gulf"; Dr Dunbar Hooper (possibly the

"Father" of the scheme from the medical side); Dr George Simpson, and the Rev. J. Andrew Barber, Honorary Convener for the Victorian Council. The sub-committee were to ascertain definitely whether Flynn's "Flying Dream" would be a practical success.

The dreamer was in high delight.

CHAPTER XXII

DISTANT PLACES

THE A.I.M. had grown to a far-spreading organization in 1927. In that year the Rev. J. Andrew Barber, Honorary Convener for the Victorian Council, was appointed Patrol Organizer. In carrying out his duties he must travel at least ten thousand miles per year—at times he was called on to travel twice that distance. Besides superintending the work of the patrols, he was required to investigate the fast-growing claims of the Inlanders for hospital sites, organize for the flying-doctor scheme, and penetrate into the wilder haunts of men and remind them that man does not live by bread alone.

Barber was a fine type for the job. Brainy and tactful, he was also a merry-eyed humorist, with a great voice that compelled his hearers' attention. And, what was almost equally important, he was a man of tremendous physique. All the men of the A.I.M. in their distinctive ways have been endowed with a strong personality—a potent factor in the building up of that unique organization.

Immediately the sub-committee had investigated all data they planned an experimental twelve months' Aerial Medical Experiment. A final organizing and investigating patrol across the continent and over four thousand five hundred miles of country was entrusted to Barber and Dr George Simpson. These started out immediately the doctor had fitted the old A.I.M. car. He made it as good as new—it needed to be. Even so, before the trip was over they registered a dozen punctures, broke an axle, three springs, one back wheel, burnt three exhaust valves, and suffered minor ailments. They started out thoroughly prepared for Inland motor travel, chains for slippery tracks, shovels for bog, mats for sand. With all aboard the old Dodge looked like a load of things.

From Adelaide their troubles commenced on the Flinders Range and continued for five hundred miles. It had rained inland: so they dug the car out of bogs, camped by the roadside on bitter nights, pulled others and were pulled out of bogs. The chains worked splendidly: when fixed around the wheels they gave grip on slippery ground. After a hundred and fifty miles of "digging" they called a halt at The Pines until the road dried a bit. The Pines is an out-station of Arcoona where the old bush hospitality reigns. The homestead is a big old stone house with long outhouses built of solid pine logs, the interstices being filled with mud and lime. The doctor and Barber strolled across when a big old bell rang "I'm th' cook!" That individual introduced himself as "th' busiest man in Central Australia!" He looked it, too, judging by the hungry sixteen who trooped in with the two latest "mud angels". It was a whopper old kitchen with a whopper old table and a similar stove on which steamed a whopper kettle. On a strong side table were big plates of meat and vegetables. "Bog in!" called the cook; and all hands "bogged in".

When pushing on to Arcoona the investigators missed the turn coming from Bon Bon station. The black night grew filmed with a fine, driving mist which made things that were really still "move". The car poked along like an antediluvian tortoise resigned to flop into a bog-hole at any moment. Suddenly the spotlight shot a dazzling radiance on some huts by a woolshed.

"Hooray!" exclaimed Barber.

"Who said we were bushed?" said the doctor.

"We'll try and sneak in somewhere for a camp," suggested Barber, "without waking anyone, otherwise we'll be frozen meat by morning. Hullo, what's this?"

This was a lanky youth who strolled across from the sheds: time, 2 a.m.

"My word," greeted the doctor, "you rise early on Arcoona!"

"Not so early," yawned the youth. "When your lights shone through th' mist I reckoned th' sun was getting up on th' wrong side so I crawled out to bo-peep. Better come erlong an' doss inside or you'll wake th' fowls."

Arcoona homestead was typical of a developed station: a good house, all rooms opening on to the veranda, kitchen separate: a large woolshed, store, men's quarters, garage, and sheds: comfy bath-room and good wireless set. The homestead is on a treeless tableland, over which Fords and a Brockway truck do good work, except in the boggy wet. The station covers thirteen hundred square miles and runs twenty-seven thousand sheep—fine, big, healthy animals. No vermin, except blowflies in occasional seasons. Saltbush is the feed; lack of water the main drawback. Existing supplies are drawn from wells and dams. A dam generally costs £1000, but will pay for itself in a good season. The station work is done by camels, horses, and cars. Mules are unsafe for one man to work alone with on the big runs. Little work is done in the wet. Camels are then useless, horses bog, and cars have continually to be dug out. Lamb-tailing was just starting—big lambs they were, too. Both the doctor and Barber were extraordinarily popular with the youngsters, who thought them princes of story-tellers. The youngsters are educated by correspondence school: each fortnight a set of lessons is received and supervised by mother. Results are good.

Such is a typical, well-developed station in those parts.

The investigators pushed on again when they thought the roads were dry, got fast in a few crab-holes, broke a back axle, and strained their nerves and tempers. A couple of days later they met Mr Moy in his Rugby, and thereafter right to Coober Pedy took it in turns, the Dodge to pull the Rugby out of the bog, reciprocated by the Rugby yanking the Dodge out of the crab-hole. The arrangement worked beautifully—until both cars bogged gracefully side by side. One morning the run rose red, so they mounted in haste and pushed on, delighted when mulga and gidgee appeared growing in nice, firm sand. When it rained they chuckled at their wisdom: the tablelands behind would be impassable for a week. They rolled merrily through East Well sheep station, then on to Coondambo and filled up from a bowser. The Shell people have been quick in placing depots throughout the Inland. When they at last reached Oodnadatta the doctor reckoned the innards of a car held nearly as many surprises as the mechanism of a human. Before reaching Oodnadatta they ploughed their way across country to the Coober Pedy opal-fields, delighted with the quaintness of this place, where a hundred men lived like troglodytes in holes in the ground.

Coober Pedy is a native name meaning "man live longa hole in the ground". Prospectors in 1915 found this rich South Australian opal-field. They and those following had to bring their water to it from Giddi Giddinna Spring, thirty miles distant. The old camel-prospector is a tough boy.

The country is strewn with gibber stones and suggests a gigantic cobble pavement, spreading beyond the horizon, relieved only here and there by dwarfed shrubs. The surface rock under the gibbers is desert sandstone, at one time the sands of a sea. Under this old probable sea-bed, have slumbered for a billion years those fascinating gems waiting to adorn the beauty of the women of the twentieth century.

The main street of Coober Pedy is a camel- and wheel-track meandering between holes and dug-outs. On a board by a big dug-out was nailed this legend:

POST OFFICE

COMMONWEALTH BANK OF

AUSTRALIA

SAVINGS BANK DEPARTMENT

Another board by another dug-out said

STORE

Both were commodious subterranean apartments in the soft opal rock.

The men all live in dug-outs and pop up out of and disappear into them like rabbits in a warren. They popped up at a shout from "Scotty", who introduced himself with the yell:

"I'm Scotty! I've been forty-five years in the Territory. It's th' best country God ever made. It's produced men! I'll race any blanky man backwards!" And he made a wild run backwards towards the car.

"Good day!" acknowledged Barber politely. But Scotty answered with a wilder yell and, bounding round, raced backwards again, talking at the top of his voice.

"He's reversing gear!" exclaimed the doctor, as Scotty leaped round and came at them again, to the chuckles of the gougers observing from their holes.

Scotty is a "character" of those parts: his speciality is "running backwards". A number among outback characters have their "speciality": some are rather quaint. "Taffy's" speciality, for instance, is "nipping horses' heels".

Life in the dug-outs is roomy, rentless, and cool. Very little furniture is needed. When a man requires a shelf on which to place his cooking-gear he simply digs it out of the soft opal rock. That is where he cuts the "pocket" where he places his pipe, when he yawns himself to sleep. Timber for fires is very scarce.

The hospitable crowd gave the travellers a "feed" in a

subterranean room, the roof of which sparkled like diamonds. In view of the possibility of the opal-field supporting a growing population in the future, the A.I.M. men were here to investigate the suggestion from the men for a hospital.

Dentists being so far away, as is usual in an inland camp, a number of the boys wanted molars "yanked out".

A row of petrol-cases was quickly arranged, on which sat half a dozen men with faces of varying expectancy. The doctor started at the more nervy end of the line and had relieved the last man's apprehension in less than half an hour: twenty-three teeth all told.

After a discussion on A.I.M. business, Barber held an evening service to which all hands rolled up.

Next morning the investigators struck north again, running through Anna Creek and Annandale, two of Sir Sidney Kidman's places, mostly under Herefords. The rains had filled a big water-hole at Annandale for the first time in years. It was already alive with water-fowl and grown frogs. Probably the frogs had been waiting deep down in the hard caked mud—a queer process of hibernation.

Sheep and cattle station etiquette out there differ a shade. On a sheep station the warning-bell rings at 7 a.m., repeated a few minutes later; then half an hour later the breakfast bell rings. On a cattle station morning tea in bed is sometimes the order at daylight. The bell is often a crowbar, bent into a triangle, a cattle-bell, or a short length of railway line. Small holdings of either sort indulge in no "frills", and they generally start work at sunrise.

The doctor was voted the "biggest-feller" medicine man in Centralia when he came to Alice Springs. A worried police sergeant met him:

"Seven prisoners," he explained. "Murder and little things like that. Three have been discharged, but the other four old bucks are in gaol—at least, three are: one died. They're all dying. Reckon they've been 'boned', and no power on earth can save them. I've done all I could. I've even dosed them with kerosene. But they've thrown in their bundles: they just lie down and want to die."

"We'll try the white man's magic," said the doctor. "The only chance apparently is to un-bone them."

The three prisoners were lying miserably waiting to die. Doctor knelt by one, thumped his chest, turned him over and thumped his back, in an endeavour to trace the extent of the lung trouble. The old warrior took not the slightest notice; just lay like a limp sack. The doctor took out his stethoscope, fixed it to his ears, and stared at the dying man. Craftily he introduced the fearsome instrument to the black chest. The patient's eyes bulged: the doctor's widened in a listening glare. The patient struggled to sit up; his mouth opened; he watched that uncanny instrument searching his chest for the "bone". The doctor located it—the patient could tell that from his "Ah!!!" Voicelessly he pointed to his swollen ankles. Solemnly the doctor ran the stethoscope over those dropsical members.

It was quite a new "magic". All three dying men sat up and took notice. When they were given brandy as medicine their smiles told they were on the highway to recovery. When he visited them next morning they greeted him with man-sized smiles and shirts flung straight over their heads so that he could get through the stethoscope part as quickly as possible.

A teamster here was cheerfully setting out on the seven-hundred-mile trip to the Katherine on the off chance of getting loading, looking on the tremendous trip as being all in the day's work.

Leaving Alice Springs the car plugged its way over the Macdonnell Ranges, then came down into the grass country and landed in fine trim at Ryan's Well. Mr Nicker owns two thousand miles of country there with the same number of cattle and horses.

"By Jove!" he greeted the investigators, "you chaps don't look it, but you're really angels in a motor-car. There's a sick man coming in outbush: his mate has been crawling along with him in a buggy this past week."

They hurried out and met the sick man, fixed him up, then travelled on to Barrow Creek along the overland telegraph. Three punctures at sixty-five miles brought them at about 10 p.m. to a big deserted homestead. After which they lost the track and camped, narrowly missing the experience of Mr Nelson, the member for the Northern Territory, who had also missed that turn-off and nearly perished. He had ridden a motor-bike and lived for two days on the oil out of his crank case. The trackers found him at his last gasp. But that episode gained him more votes than all his speeches.

Barrow Creek proved a rough country, heavily mineralized. Here the doctor attended a patient—the mother on a cattle station. She had lived eighteen years there and only needed a change, but refused to take it. She could not imagine being happy anywhere else.

Her daughters, both not long of age, were happy types of strong, lively, good-looking girls. They had never seen a train, but wanted to know all about one; while their interest in feminine things "down south" was almost embarrassing. These girls "ran" the station, including Dad. They roped steers, did the branding, built windmills, shot wild dogs, attended to the mustering, and could track any beast on the run. And their brains were as active as their bodies.

As the investigators travelled, the doctor attended to patients here and there, and here and there Barber held a service. Throughout their whole journey they were taking data as to the possibilities of forming the Aerial Medical Service.

The farther north they got the more obvious became the need for quicker transport for commercial as well as for medical purposes.

Twenty-five miles out they met two old-timers camped at a well on the edge of the "desert strip". One was Mr Purves, the other a waggoner employed by Charles Todd in 1872.

Several hundred beasts perished near this well, in one night, from eating poison weed. Out past Wycliffe Well they passed the Devil's Marbles, gigantic granite stones, balancing one on another—a landmark held in superstitious awe by the natives. At Kelly's Well they were entertained by thousands of little birds. Some of these wells were built by Chinese masons forty years ago, and the work was done to last. Through Tennant's Creek the car went on to Banka Banka, and, of course, ran out of petrol when within half a mile of the homestead. This was the edge of the Barkly Tableland.

One morning the two were very quiet and thoughtful as the car rattled along. A bush mother had told them she was quite happy now. Before the Nursing Home had been built at Alice Springs she had had to travel six hundred miles and back for the birth of each of her six children—her only companion the Afghan camel-driver. In future, she would only have to travel a hundred and fifty miles.

As the investigators cruised along towards Newcastle Waters they ran alongside a white water-hole extending for fifteen miles. From this water-hole the huge station enclosing it gets its name. A Police Post half a mile away is full of romantic stories. Passing Daly Waters they ran into a subtropical forest. By the side of the twisty track was a camp, the waggon and harness set out neatly in the shade of a tree. Squatting by the fire, luxuriously drinking tea, was a black boy. He regarded the car with a contemplative eye.

"Whose team is that?" asked Barber.

"Mister Macpherson's."

"Where is he?"

"Marranboy."

"What he go there for?"

"He got bung eye."

"H'm!" said the doctor, and drove on.

Marranboy was reached a hundred and forty miles from Daly Waters. The neat little Home here was perched upon a hill, across on another was the battery, while the police-station commanded a third. Mining-shafts, huts, and tents were dotted in between. The doctor was kept busy here.

One Sister had just come in from the bush, bringing a man with a broken leg. During her absence the other Sister had been "carrying on" with the hospital, mending a chalky bone with the aid of the railway-camp doctor seventy miles away, and a specialist on the end of the telegraph line three thousand miles away.

"There's one old chap here," said Sister, "a grumpy old dear with white whiskers right down to his belt. He ought to be in some nice comfy old home instead of working in the mines. They had to carry him here by force. He can't stand 'wimmen!' We had an awful row tucking him in, but he's quietened a bit now."

"Let's have a look at him," said the doctor.

The greybeard looked very comfortable albeit he stared up with a distrustful eye.

"How's the bed?" asked the doctor cheerfully.

"It's a nice bed to die in!" growled the ancient.

But the very next morning he had forgotten all about dying. Eventually the Sisters could hardly "shoo" him away from the hospital.

The doctor was taken aback by the next patient. This man was a lively looking little bushman answering to the name of "Taffy". Born and bred in the Gulf, he was proud of and noisy about it. He had recently ridden a half-broken colt after cattle and broken his leg as a result. He could still smile after a hundred miles of agony.

"Have you been here all your life?" asked the doctor.

"No, not yet!" flashed back the answer.

All the Gulf knows Taffy. His speciality is the "Dog Act". Riding up to a station where the yard is full of unbroken horses, he will glare round and yell to the crowd:

"I'll do what no mother's son here is game to do!"

"What's that, Taffy?"

"Never mind; drinks all round if I do it!"

"Right!"

Taffy hitches up his horse, then his pants, then crawls into the stockyard on hands and knees—dodging the flying hoofs of the flabbergasted animals while manoeuvring until he gets behind the hunched-up legs of some shivering beast. Taffy's head darts out as he bites the horse's heels and ducks instantly as the animal lashes out. Taffy flattens to the ground as it kicks out again.

He always wins his bet.

He has never "stopped one"—yet!

CHAPTER XXIII

GATHERING DATA TO FLY WITH

CONSTABLE CLAPP waved them a cheery farewell as, with bells jingling and mounted troopers laughing, he rode out-bush from Marranboy into uninhabited land on a long patrol. Later the doctor read with keen regret that this fine type of our Northern Police had been accidentally shot dead.

Starting north again the investigators reached the Katherine, fifty miles on, and ran right into a "Wild West" show. Seven hundred navvies were working on the line, and what they did at the Katherine would have startled Bret Harte. The Katherine is a big stream, but not as big as the thirst of the men who were working to bridge it. Most of the work was contract and piece-work; big money was being earned—spent, too. But the line was going ahead rapidly and more cheaply than any other line built in recent years. The big hotel was built of corrugated iron, a portable mansion run by Mrs O'Shea, husband, and daughters. There was no shilly-shallying at the hotel of Mrs O'Shea. Barber and the doctor arrived just in time for a wild and woolly night.

This line was pushing south across Centralia towards Oodnadatta, about nine hundred miles away. The first sod of the Oodnadatta to Alice Springs railway was turned in 1926, and that same year saw the Northern Australia Act come into force. That Act renamed the Northern Territory "Northern Australia", and also brought "Central Australia" into being.

The investigators left Katherine by train for Darwin. It

was a great little old train, the engine fifty years old. Presently it developed a hot-box, luckily near water. The driver pulled her up, got his pipe going well, and slung a few buckets of liquid over the wheels. Clouds of steam responded, to the shrill delight of a truck-load of abos, who were "travelling free". Then the little old engine puffed gamely on, to cheers that startled the parrots on the bloodwood trees. The guard proved to be stationmaster, paymaster, postmaster, guide, philosopher, and friend to all along the line. "Hellfire Jack" was on the plates, and he kept the engine puffing. Stops were made to fit the meal-times, but the guard brewed tea every now and then "just to keep our insides warmed, so to speak". A free and easy line, with passengers' comfort the first consideration. No traveller could make a complaint on that line. They pulled into Pine Creek and enjoyed lunch at May Brown's famous hotel, then hurried on, for they were going to make the run to Darwin in one day instead of two. On both sides of the line rose enormous ant-hills; some round and terraced like wedding-cake; some buttressed like cathedrals. There is a story in the north that white-ants have "tapped" the telegraph line. Barber pointed out some mounds that actually rose above the telegraph-poles. This showed the possibility of ants being able to "tap" the wires—by building their nest over them. Linesmen, however, would have to be asleep a long time to allow them to do it. Distinctive nests were narrow and tall, the long axis pointing true north and south—the work of the magnetic ant.

The two hundred mile run to Darwin was made in twelve hours—good going. The railway men there declare they have the best record of any line in the Commonwealth, despite stops by the wayside to boil the billy.

Some important organizing work was concluded in Darwin. The people there have publicly stated that, though they have planned and dreamed for years to develop the country, Flynn's dreams are the only dreams that come true. When the two returned to the Katherine, the doctor interested himself in the chronic complaints of the car, while Barber staved off the boys who insisted he must have a drink.

"Well, then, just one! Just to show there's no ill-feeling." To dodge the boys the investigators jumped into the Dodge and sped out for lunch to Manbulloo, Vestey's place, prettily situated on the Katherine. They were now bound for Victoria River Downs, two hundred miles sou'-west. At Willeroo station they met travellers all aboard a derelict car, its wobbling wheels bound with greenhide. The noises that car made as it groaned along sounded like muffled bells in a cattle stampede. The drivers were quite cheerful, and declared they were "living in hopes"—one hope being the car, and the other their chance of getting to the Katherine.

A heap of stones off the track marked the resting-place of "Great" Scott, "Great" because he had been a man of giant physique. He had been stoned to death by the blacks many years ago. Numbers of station people are attempting to mark the many scattered resting-places in that country. Recent ones are all known, others are being investigated. But sleepers are there who have left behind them no memories except their bones. The A.I.M. hope that in time the last resting-place of all the early travellers will be marked.

Willeroo is proud of its two-story homestead and of the excellent tropical and sub-tropical garden created by the Chinese cook. Ah Chong wouldn't swap places with the Emperor of China—if there is an Emperor. When forty miles on, through rough country, well grassed, they came within sight of Delamere homestead and heard wild yells ringing out from the hill behind the building.

"Sounds as if there's a war on," remarked the doctor.

"There is," answered Barber. "Look at 'em, all done up in feathers and nowhere to go."

As the car got closer, they gazed up at the hill-top. It was arrayed with two ranks of stamping, shouting black figures, their bodies "dressed" in ochres of fantastic patterns emphasized by white birds' down stuck on with blood. Spears were being waved to blood-curdling yells, lubras were shrieking and gesticulating and urging their men on.

"You'll have a job soon," said Barber pessimistically.

"Nothing like keeping my hand in," agreed doctor; "although this car gives me all I want. We'll ask this half-caste what the hullabaloo is about."

The stockman was gazing up the hill, the call of his mother's blood showing in his dilated eyes.

"B—— good fight," he could only say, and pointed staring.

Another half-caste came running down from the hill waving his arms in a tumultuous state of excitement.

"Stretcher-bearers," said Barber, laconically.

"Looks like it."

"You won't collect any fees: they'll expect a stick of to-bacco for your doctoring them up."

"Then they won't get it. I'll give them some if they let me film that war-dance. It looks fine."

The messenger had arrived.

"Man speared," he gasped, "through the kidney."

"What has he been up to?" asked Barber, sternly.

"Only run away with another man's wife."

The doctor reached for his instrument case.

"Might as well be in civilization," he sighed.

They walked up the hill and into a mob of wild, hysterical figures brandishing long spears with a total disregard for the anatomy of any man. Every warrior amongst them had forgotten his trousers—if he ever wore any—and what the women lacked they made up for in plastered mud. A hundred or so myalls had come in from the wild lands to corroboree with the station blacks and stir up what mischief they could.

The speared man sprawled in a pool of blood, waiting for his brains to be knocked out and stoically listening to the fierce arguments for and against him. Barber and the doctor pushed into the crowd just in time to stop them from starting an all-in mêlée.

Doctor had a look at the wound, then shoved three fingers

into it and fished around seeking the broken-off spearhead. The abo never quivered an eyelid; the crowd looked on breathlessly, their grease-daubed bodies smelling like an animal pen. The wound was soon fixed up. The operation was a wonderful sight to the abos: it would be "sung" at their campfires for many a long moon to come.

As a great reward, the doctor was invited to witness them "making a man" at next sun-up. Reluctantly he declined the honour. Vehemently they pressed him, declaring he could perform the operation himself. Declining this still greater honour, he took some Cine-Kodak pictures instead.

Down at the creek they washed their hands and pushed on to the station where a cloud of dust told of hot work in the stockyard.

"They've got all the horses in," said Barber: "must be shoeing them preparatory to mustering."

"Yes," answered the doctor, and he spurted up to the yards.

Thump of hooves, snorts, warning yells, clatter of scattering sliprails, and the mob with tossing manes and tails stampeded almost over the car.

After a spell and a yarn the investigators ran on into the Victoria River country of fine grassy downs, crossed the river, then ran on to the pretty Hostel on the Wickham. The Sisters had made friends of thousands of little finches with blood-red beaks, who arrived in noisy battalions at "crumb time". Here, too, was the bower-bird who cannily came to steal a spoon or any bright transportable object that might be lying about. Kingfishers, like flying opals, sped along a river that was the home of wild duck and geese. At night the Sisters had other lovely visitors, though the lamp was the attraction. Moths of exquisite colouring fluttered round the lamp, and sandy beetles buzzed, similarly fascinated. In these parts even the grasshoppers grew coloured legs and wings. In the evenings, a brazier was lit on the front lawn of the big homestead and all hands from the station and Nursing Home gathered round for a yarn.

The investigators returned to the Katherine on a Saturday to find the wild little place in roaring mood. All hands had knocked off work in honour of the weekly booze-up—those that indulged that way. The derelict car had arrived, its tyres stuffed with grass.

The Church of England padre from Darwin was in town and he and Barber collaborated in a service enjoyed by the crowd, after which the boisterous lot entertained them, and Barber responded with yarns. He was at his best among a rough crowd like this, able to appreciate a joke and make one better; able to talk to the men in an understanding way about their own business, yet maintaining a high standard; so that an intelligent, useful, and entertaining conversation ensued.

A black boy had ridden in from Elsey station on the Roper. Mrs Giles was worried over a man who had been gored by a bull. When the doctor arrived his professional interest was keenly aroused. The goring had happened some time ago. The man had got a needle and sharpened it on a stone to the shape of a needle used for sewing through flesh. He had then selected and sterilized horsehair threads for the sewing silk, and calmly and with the stitches of a craftsman sewed up his own wounds. Several days later the stitches looked like bursting apart, so he pulled them out and stitched himself all over again, placing the stitches farther back this time.

From the Katherine the investigators ran south into the Barkly Tableland proper, crossing plain after plain of waving Flinders and Mitchell grasses, each plain stretching away for twenty and thirty miles. Patches of light timber and sand occurred between them. These plains run right into Queensland. They would make a stockman's heart glad. Across them runs a government stock route watered by bores with gigantic "Comet" windmills at every twenty miles or so, with earth tanks and troughs complete.

After passing No. 5 Bore some seventy-six miles from

Newcastle Waters they met two dusty, dejected individuals on the tramp.

"Got a drink?" they asked huskily.

"Plenty," said Barber cheerfully as he handed them the water-bag.

They nearly drained it.

"You're angels," sighed one. "Th' last bore was dry. We've just done a forty-mile dry stretch, an' passed a grave on th' side of th' road."

"Where are you making for?"

"Katherine—looking for work on the construction."

"Where did you come from?"

"Cloncurry."

"Great Scott! Just about an eight-hundred-mile tramp."

"Yes."

"Well I hope you get the best contract on the Katherine line."

"Thanks. So long."

"So long."

The grave at which the swaggies had glanced askance was Jack Brady's, one of the most fearless horsemen in the north until he was found lying by the roadside. Some years ago, a young colt had thrown him, breaking both his legs. He dragged himself on his elbows three miles to a water-hole where his black boys tracked him. They laid him on a ground sheet and dragged him some miles through the bush to the nearest track. And yet, Jack Brady lived and laughed and mounted many another horse before, at three score and ten, he set out on his last ride.

When one hundred and seventy-three miles from New-castle Waters the motor-men saw the dust of two thousand head of cattle by Anthony's Lagoon. A lonely looking settle-ment—police-station, house, and store, each a mile away from the others—but of bush importance. Anthony's Lagoon is a junction. Roads lead north to Borroloola, east to Burke

town, south-east to Brunette Downs and Camooweal, and
west to Newcastle Waters.

The investigators pulled up at the store and the Count
came out to them, a dark-faced, smiling man, geniality itself.
Residents swear Biondi is a real Italian count. A mob of goats
came up and smelt the car, then probed it with their horns.
With the goats were a flock of half-caste children, equally
curious; although, unlike the goats, they did not try to eat
the tyres.

On to Brunette Downs was a clear sixty-mile run with the
lofty wireless masts visible from afar. Brunette Downs is
regarded as one of the finest properties in Australia. Camped
at this big station was a married couple with their Hudson.
Our investigators had heard of them from eager women
hundreds of miles back. The wife sold dresses and the man
shares in New Zealand forests. "Mulga wireless" had advertised the coming of those dresses far and wide. At this pioneer
wireless station they had much to discuss with the wireless
men. And here they restocked with petrol from the big Shell
dump.

Then came another sixty-mile run to Alexandra station—a
huge place of twelve thousand square miles running fifty
thousand head of cattle—then a drive across the thirty-mile
plain to the Rankine River store at dusk. That store was then,
perhaps, unique among Australian stores. George Watson
prints his own notes, and their face value is equal to those
bearing Mr Collins's signature. Watson's is a huge store
supplying anything from a "fishhook to an anchor". The
nearest other stores are a hundred miles east and a hundred
and sixty miles west, respectively. A race-meeting is held
annually near this store. Once isolated, now forty cars a
month pass, and 'planes are seen overhead.

At fifty miles they passed through Avon Downs, then
sped on another forty miles to Camooweal, and were then
well into Queensland.

The station homesteads on the Barkly Tableland are mostly

modern dwellings replete with comfort; proving what decent country allied with transport facilities will quickly do.

Camooweal is a splendid little town, lively and prosperous. Here they watched the air mail depart for Cloncurry—a sign that Flynn's aerial dream could be brought to fruition.

So far, the possibilities and organization all pointed to success. After an enthusiastic meeting at Camooweal, the investigators set out for Cloncurry, where it was hoped to form the Flying Base for the scheme, if organization could be completed. They arrived in Cloncurry after twenty-six hours' run. From here 'planes fly once a week to Normanton on the Gulf, west to Mt Isa and Camooweal, and south-east to Longreach. The 'plane does in two hours the trip that the investigators did in twenty-six hours.

A big public meeting was held, and it was soon proved that the townspeople were strongly behind the proposed Aerial Medical scheme. Barber and Simpson were delighted with this augury of future success. Right at the psychological moment a case happened which proved the practical value of a flying doctor. A message came in from Mt Isa, two hundred miles away, of a serious accident. With Pilot Evans Dr Simpson flew out, attended the man, and flew straight back with him to the Cloncurry hospital.

Negotiations were opened up with the QANTAS people; details of cost, distances, practicability, satisfactorily gone into; aerodrome arrangements proposed; probable landing-grounds investigated with Pilot Evans; and the whole scheme discussed with practical men on the spot.

Now followed the long drive to Longreach through Birdsville, Windorah, and Jundah. At Longreach the four thousand five hundred miles' investigating trip was ended.

The knowledge gleaned produced swift practical results. Flynn smiled—he knew his dream must materialize.

The Board, as ever, built cannily and well.

CHAPTER XXIV

THE FLYING DOCTOR

THE padre of the Carnarvon Patrol tuned up his trusty old car preparatory to a long patrol. He must meet every stockman, miner, shearer, and settler wherever possible, along a belt of country seven hundred miles long by three hundred miles wide. His southernmost point was Shark Bay eighty miles south. The bay, with Dirk Hartog Island, looks oddly like a man's hand. That tiny settlement of seventy men fished the seas for pearl-shell, confident in two boasts: One, that "the island" (on Cape Inscription, at its northern end) marks the spot where the first white man set foot—the Dutchman, Dirk Hartog in October 1616; the other that their one little street is the only street in the world that is paved with pearl-shell.

Inland the padre must travel three hundred miles, north to Port Hedland three hundred and fifty, and farther north if time allowed.

The country south, its dry rivers lined with stunted gums giving a dull green edging to the tawny sand, includes well-fenced sheep country. Little homesteads, like dolls' houses, are scattered far and wide. Farther inland, and to the northeast, the fences gradually disappear. Camel-teams crawl along, winding through the distance like gigantic ants following a slow motion trail. These slow old desert ships bring the golden fleece to the sea.

The padre was a short, thick-set man with a happy face. Many bushmen reckoned he was the "makings" of a good mate. His car was loaded worse than any camel; the wheels hardly visible under boxes, baggage, tarpaulin cover, foodstuffs, medicines, books, toys, tools, mail, things that women love, etc. It was a regular Daddy Christmas car for all hands —and looked it. But the padre was a mechanic, so the old box of tricks would get through somehow and chug into Carnarvon triumphantly ahead of the next "wet". Man is fast solving the Inland transport problem: he has yet to solve the problem of the "wet". As the padre buzzed off he thought a moment on the difference between this patrol and those of the old camel days. He would accomplish in three months what it would have taken him a year to do before. During the last four years he had averaged three thousand miles per year, and he knew he had accomplished a tremendous amount of work with it. How times were moving for the Inland! And there was forethought behind it all. As to his own particular job—well, no lone missionary could set out and do it now: it required the strength of a continent-wide organization behind him.

He looked back on Carnarvon because he loved it. How prettily it nestled on the banks of the Gascoyne! Right up to date is Carnarvon; with its electricity, its beautiful gardens and bungalow homes. The climate too is ideal. The padre caught sight of the little cemetery and smiled, remembering a local identity who had recently been putting it "up to date". This man is a fine type of the old "fight your way through" pioneer. He has won out, too, despite his lack of education.

Some of the local wags thought they saw a joke in the cemetery, so they approached him reproachfully: "I say, Bill, what have we done to you?"

"Why, nothing," replied Bill warily—"not that I darned well knows of yet!"

"Well, why are you shutting us out?"

"How?" asked the puzzled Bill.

They pointed to the gate. "You are only building one gate! Where do the other denominations come in?"

Bill scratched his head and gazed around the fenced-in cemetery—there was only one gate.

"It looks all right to me," said Bill. "Lots of good coves I know were planted in places with no gates at all!"

"But that was a heathen planting," they explained. "You ought to build this place like Karrakatta, the big cemetery down in Perth. They give all denominations a chance down there; one gate for each!"

"Yes," frowned a dubious lad, "it'll be hard enough to pass Peter. Give us a chance down here!"

"If Peter knew as much about youse as I do," answered Bill meaningly, "you'd never get through *his* gate!"

However, although Bill was doubtful he decided to "give th' boys a chanst".

So he wrote the secretary of Karrakatta cemetery asking if "all the dominions" of Karrakatta go in the one gate?

"They do," replied the secretary. "Why shouldn't they in Carnarvon?"

"They might here," muttered Bill darkly, "but I know some as won't 'up there'!"

The padre smiled again and set the old car buzzing. It was men like Bill who had helped make the little heaven down here that is Carnarvon. The padre's inland trip would be nearer four hundred miles than three; straight east, over low sandhills much of the way—strange-looking country on which to stock sheep. But it held rich native grasses and, above all, the parakelia, the "chunga" (milk) and "junga" (water) plant of the natives. It is a sort of ice-plant on which stock thrive without water for months. At shearing-time mustering sheep is a difficult problem where this plant abounds, for the "woollies" scatter in small mobs all over the run and do not come in for water. The parakelia is found for seven hundred miles right across into Centralia. Mitchell and Flinders grasses would rustle under the padre's tyres, and many other plants—few of which are not eaten by stock at some season of the year. Over large areas much of the timber is stunted, snake-wood and minariche predominate in places, and the wanya bean, which sheep love, also sampan leaf, the drought resister, and purple vetch like wild lucerne. If it rained in May the sands would appear like a cloth of gold under wild flowers of wonderful hues.

Portions of this country were once considered desert. Men then didn't know. A man must "learn" the country before he can successfully battle against nature. Upon some areas, half a million acres are needed to run twenty thousand sheep. But as time goes on, and we learn more still, the acreages will shrink and the sheep multiply.

Some five hundred miles out the real desert begins, running into No-man's Land. If the padre kept straight on east another eight hundred miles he would strike Alice Springs— if he was bushman enough to do it. He would have liked to chance that "Keep on!" which always drew him when nearing No-man's Land. The call of unknown lands stirs the heart of every man. When the padre reached his eastern limit he would head straight up north and battle on into the nor'-west.

Just one of the dreamer's patrol men. There were others. Some were working thousands of miles away; working by car, buggy, camel, horse, donkey, or foot, each doing his bit, each forging a "link".

Occasionally in their travels these wanderers met wanderers of other denominations hundreds of miles from the regular haunts of man. That night would mean a cheery campfire yarn. Possibly they would work together for a while. The A.I.M. has always accepted the hand of any denomination, and has always given a hand when opportunity occurred.

The padre hummed along a fairly good road into the sandhills country leading to the Junction, a hundred and twenty miles up the Gascoyne River. Here and there he deviated as his business required. Of course, he never missed a wayside

letter-box—a petrol case, generally, with a tin roof, nailed to
a tree. He always carried the letters on, or dropped some in
the box, as every traveller does. He "tooted" at a tiny bush-
store and the dog immediately ran for its master. That dog
answers the phone. Each time the bell rings it wags its tail
and is away down the paddock after its master like a shot.
Out towards Mardalthuna station he ploughed gaily over a
desert strip, only a very short strip, but it takes camels two
days to plough through it with half a load of wool. The soil
is a soft red sand, fine as ashes, but should rain come in May
it grows herbage and sweet-scented wild flowers of striking
beauty.

There are some fine stations in the Carnarvon district.
Lower Clifton Downs is the largest. Bidgemia has a beautiful homestead with lawn, flower-borders, concrete paths, telephone, typewriters, motors, water and sewerage system. A
number of other stations live under practically similar conditions—the reward of the pioneering stage. But we know
that the grandchildren mostly benefit. That is why the
dreamer always planned communication and quick transport
for those farther out. With those blessings the battlers would
pass the pioneering stage faster and have a chance to enjoy
the fruit of their labours.

Evidence of much motor traffic was plain around the
Junction; the day of the camel was done. Here too was the
last pub in a four-hundred-mile stretch. The Junction is a
small place of scattered iron houses on a flat where trees
show here and there; but its road-system is of strategic importance to the Inlanders. Here the sick men come—too late
at times, worse luck. The padre discussed business with the
people here: they desired the A.I.M. Nursing Home.

He drove on then into less settled lands, creeping farther
and farther out towards his farthest east!

One night he camped with old Abdul Khan. Sorrow had
come to Abdul with the greying of his beard, and poverty
too. He still owned his string of a hundred fine camels, but

his beautiful gold was gone! A woman had taken it: "May Allah bring her peanuts instead of children!" Abdul spat. Then in pious fashion he poured forth his woes to the padre who, however, knew all about them, as the courtship had lasted nearly twelve months.

It appears that Abdul had developed matrimonial ambitions ("Shame to the hairs of wisdom—was ever man such a fool!"), but not only that—he desired a white woman. A man of his position and wealth was worthy of a white woman. ("May she grow bristles on her chest! May her face turn into a water-melon and melt in the sun!") As Abdul progressed with the gist of his story, it appeared that a station manager had inserted an advertisement for him in a Perth paper: "Gentleman, assured position, eastern appearance, well set up, desires correspond young girl, pretty, well-developed, cook, view mat. Send photo."

Abdul had received two hundred and seventy-nine photos. What a month he had spent poring over those promises of delight, what entrancing hours with those white beauties on cardboard, the fires of his youth revived. How hard it had been to discard the last dozen. "What a fool country this was where a man could only have one wife!" ("I was the fool!" he groaned.)

At last he chose his Dream Lily. She had hair like the raven, skin like the lily, and big soft eyes that could melt a man's heart. Her limbs—well, Abdul sent her the £100 she wired for. That was for her fare and wedding garments. Then he sat and smoked his hubble-bubble and waited. He did not wait long, a wire came for another hundred. She had fallen off a tram and was caught—by doctors. Abdul wired the hundred, cursing trams and doctors in one breath. He cursed the doctors hardest. If people rode on trams instead of camels more fool them, but as to doctors—the thought of those "troubles of the earth" handling his good gold fairly pained his breath. ("May they eat their own needles! May their breath turn into stitches and choke them!")

He waited while his Dream Lily convalesced, the fires of his impatience burning fiercer.

When she did convalesce she did something else—went and stayed in a fool boarding-house that got burned down in the night and burned all her clothes and her fare and nearly herself. She had sent him the Perth paper with the picture of the burned house in it. She marked with a cross the spot where she had fled in her burning nightdress. Secretly, Abdul thought that a little judicious heat applied on the right spot might not be amiss; but he sent her the £100 she asked for, then bowed his head and wept.

It came—the letter asking for another hundred. She was under the doctors again! ("May she be under the sea! May she swallow the ocean and turn into a shower of rain!") She had been hurrying to catch the train when the taxis collided. She sent him the photo, cut out of the newspaper, with a cross to mark herself on the stretcher.

He sent her the money—after long travail.

She wrote again, poor girl, lying there all mangled and torn in bed, she could not scream for help because the bandages blocked her—("May they choke her!"). Her wicked brother had crept in and stolen all her money, vowing no sister of his should wed a coloured man no matter how big a gentleman he might be. He was coming back to cut her throat, so promised her loving brother. She wanted £100 quickly to get to the safety of Abdul's protecting arms.

In a raging fury Abdul wired that hundred. ("Oh! if he could only get that brother out here for just a few minutes he would slit his throat from ear to ear and feed him to the pigs!")

Abdul had peace for a while and enjoyed it by churning over in his mind just how he would get his money's worth when this elusive queen did fall into his protecting arms. Time passed and he grew anxious, gazing at her photo many times a night. What seductive promises she used to smile him out of that photo! Just when he was going to send her a wire he received *her* wire. She was stranded, had fallen among thieves yet again. A piteous explanatory letter followed. But she was coming this time! Nothing on earth could stop her. She was flying to the arms of her beloved—immediately she got another hundred!

Abdul Khan sat long, and spat longer. Many a time he looked at her photo; long he chewed the cud of reflection; then he sent the money. "It was like plucking the hairs of my beard root by root," he wailed to the padre. ("May wasps nest in her ears! May she bite her lying tongue until her eyes fall out! May her feet walk backwards and run her into every tram in the land!")

The padre smoked in silent sympathy, wondering why it had been so long before people of the little town had awakened to the "joke" and stopped it.

For just £600 did the city siren bleed old Abdul Khan. The padre thought of a white man he knew away north. He had paid just 2/6 (the price of the advertisement) for *his*, and he had got his money's worth. He would have envied old Abdul Khan his luck. His city siren had turned out to be a man!

When the padre turned on his long trek north he was travelling parallel with No-man's Land though considerably to the west. Seven hundred and eighty miles east, travelling parallel to him, on his trip up the Centre, was a camel-man on patrol. What really did lie in that mysterious No-man's Land in between? Often the padre wondered.

One night he was heartily welcomed at a station homestead, not because of the mail he carried, but because he was a man. It was a station of large acreage where only four white men were employed. One man was always "dying", so he was not employed much except when he was "alive". Then, his wizardry with tools made his liveliness useful.

"How's the 'Deadman'?" inquired the padre when enjoying the evening meal.

"Oh, he's all right," growled the manager. "He's 'dying'

again, just when I wanted him to erect that oil engine for the water-supply. Sometimes I wish he *would* die and be done with it."

"What is his particular complaint this time?" asked the padre as he waded into a meal wholesome enough for a king.

"Oh, just 'pains an' pains an' pains, pains everywhere: in me head, in me toes, in me abdymen, in me stummick, in me heart'. Pity he wouldn't get pains in his brains and be done with it."

"I'll have a look at him," said the padre, "after dinner. Just in case, you know."

"Case, it *is* a case. I say, padre, though, I wish you *would* do something!"

The padre looked up as the manager leaned across the table.

"Why! is he really ill?"

"Ill, my eye! Give him something with a *kick* in it that will sting him for a while: it might do him good!"

"I would hardly like to do that."

"Why not? It might make a man of him: he's useless as he is. When he gets 'relapses', that is, when he does work, he is the cleverest mechanic within hundreds of miles. He can make anything out of a piece of old iron—just the type of man a station like this needs. By Jove, I have never thought of it before!"

"Don't you get giving him anything," warned the padre. "You might over-do it."

"Kill or cure," mused the manager. "Perhaps I'd better not; I was thinking of giving him just a taste of sheep-dip."

"Heavens alive!" exclaimed the padre.

The manager laughed.

"I must get that oil engine working—somehow!" he declared grimly.

In the evening the padre walked over to the men's quarters. The strains of a hornpipe came in lively tones through the door.

"Just trying to drown th' Deadman's groans," laughed the player as he put the concertina aside.

The padre walked to the bunk on which a man lay. His freckles and red hair shouted the health his long face was trying to deny.

"Goo' day, padre," he moaned. "You're just in time; I'm a dead man this time!"

"Not quite," said the padre.

"But I'm goin', padre. I'm goin' to die. I'm goin' to die."

"Well, hurry up!" agreed the padre briskly, "and I'll bury you before I go."

The woebegone face looked amazement.

"What?"

"Die before I go," advised the padre. "It will save trouble and you look all out this time. I'm not going on until the day after tomorrow, so tomorrow afternoon would do nicely. There's a restful spot down there under the coolabahs. We could have it dug out by midday."

In the silent hut the Deadman's eyes were nearly shouting; his ginger hair showed signs of erection.

"Struth!" he whispered, "you're a nice parson *you* are!"

"Why?" asked the surprised padre.

"Lookin' to bury a man!"

"But that's my job!"

"You don't get a job here anyways!" roared the Deadman as he seized his trousers and stamped straight out of the door.

"He'll put them on down by the coolabahs!" laughed his mate. "He'll sit there half the night swearing at you."

Next morning at daybreak the Deadman was whistling triumphantly at the oil engine.

The manager was in excellent spirits over breakfast.

"I'm going to get Charlie and Jim to mark out a grave under those coolabahs," he chuckled. "Just dig it down a foot or two so that he won't relapse. Say, these are great chops. You'll go a long way before you get chops as juicy and tender as these. Hey! Jacky," he yelled, "when did you kill this sheep?"

"Me no kill him," yelled Jacky, from the kitchen.

"What you do then?"

"Me find him dead, boss."

The padre went on his way with a laugh in his heart and one for the manager and the Deadman.

At the instigation of the Board Flynn hurried to Queensland to conclude preliminary arrangements in the Field. Flynn has been a toiler all his life; he has lived side by side with physical hardship, mental worry, and sometimes heartbreak; but he is really a man to be envied, because his sweetest dreams are coming true. His heart was singing as he hurried off for Queensland.

The Board had decided to commit themselves to only one flying station for one experiment for one year. The result would prove whether the work could be developed further. The objective was to provide an Aerial Medical Service to outback districts, at present isolated, thus linking them with existing ambulance and hospital services. Cloncurry was to be the base of operations, as mapped in Flynn's latest map.

QANTAS had a flying service there and an arrangement was to be entered into for an aeroplane, capable of being used as an ambulance, with a pilot in charge, and with accommodation for doctor, nurse, and one patient; to be available for use within the flying radius; such radius to cover three hundred miles.

Dr Constance had expressed the hope of installing a laboratory at every three hundred miles. This touched Flynn very closely. His own brother had been treated for influenza while he was dying of typhoid!

A skeleton telegraph and telephone service already exists throughout the district as far west as Avon Downs, south to Boulia and Urandangie, north to Normanton and Burketown; while Brunette Downs had wireless. Thus a fair portion of the district, when in need, could call a doctor. Still, most of the stations were totally isolated. The hope for these was that the Baby transmitting sets would soon reach perfection.

In the Cloncurry district, too, there is the excellent Queensland Ambulance Brigade, which would enthusiastically co-operate with the A.M.S.

A "Mother" wireless station would be erected in anticipation of the successful invention of the Baby Wireless Transmitter, of which Traeger's latest experiments gave every hope of final success. Should the invention materialize, then every portion of the district, and far beyond, could communicate with the Mother station.

That circle on the map meant that a "mantle of safety" would be cast over an area exceeding a quarter of a million square miles. This Aerial Medical Service represented a truly national movement. The Queensland Government immediately approved; the Commonwealth Government gave a practical benediction by a subsidy of half the running expenses of the 'plane; the Defence Department was already interested; enthusiastic public meetings of support were held throughout the Cloncurry district. In addition to the £2000 from the H. V. McKay Trust, the Wool Brokers' Association voted £1000 towards "the dream"; interested companies made grants and numerous friendly individuals offered substantial donations. Seven thousand pounds was raised without making any appeal to the public: the money was a free-will gift from the people concerned.

As Flynn hurried north he was anxious, not over the flying doctor, for to him that part of the dream was completed, but over that Baby Transmitter. Would it, in time, be perfected, or would it leave them "in the air"? Unless this problem of communication was solved, further extension of the A.M.S. would be almost a mockery. The doctor must be told he was wanted before he would know where to fly.

Smilingly Flynn greeted the great reception accorded him at Longreach (the headquarters of QANTAS)and Cloncurry. He showed no sign that his mind was tick, tack, tick, tacking away back in those little workrooms down south.

In May 1928 Dr K. St Vincent Welch and pilot Arthur Affleck set out without any fuss on the first flight that inaugurated the Aerial Medical Service, one of the most important flights in the history of aviation in Australia. And a world flight historically, for it inaugurated the world's first flying-ambulance service. The doctor's first case (calling immediately he reached Cloncurry) was to save the life of a man who had cut his throat!

As the *Victory* (D.H.50) soared up like a swift white dove the dreamer watched her Red Cross speeding away on its errand of mercy. And as he listened to the vanishing hum of the engines he again heard the soft padding of a camel's feet.

In that year's test the doctor flew twenty thousand miles, saved ten lives, saw two hundred and fifty patients, held fifty consultations with other local doctors, made fifty flights, and visited twenty-six different centres. There were no mishaps; and on only one occasion was it found impossible to answer a call, owing to weather conditions. Then the case was succoured by car. A two-hundred-mile flight before breakfast, operation, and back to the base for lunch, was in his regular routine. He flew by night on urgent calls.

A representative conference of Cloncurry district people, broadcasting their appreciation of the A.M.S., added: ". . . notes with satisfaction that the work was carried out in complete harmony with all existing medical services."

Such was the practical record of the first flying doctor having the largest practice in the world. A fascinating twelve months, well worthy a book in itself. But what is *not* recorded is the security felt in the hearts of the people as they watched the Red Cross flying over their lonely lands.

An urgent call from Davenport, two hundred and fifty miles south of Cloncurry, sent the flying doctor soaring into the air, roaring away over hill and valley and river bed, then over sand ridges that showed up like a brown sea all storm-swept where hot winds blew the dust. Over the country the doctor gazed down looking for tree or grass, and seeing none, thought how safe he was up in a 'plane, while down there two men had recently been lost for four days without water.

Pilot Affleck was doing a hundred and thirty miles by compass while grimly realizing that "down below" would be no place for a forced landing. Above the big old Diamantina they flew and swooped down like a powerful hawk to make a perfect landing before Davenport Downs homestead. A kindly-faced old lubra was nursing the sick woman while consoling two frightened little children.

As the 'plane rose with the patient and roared straight up towards the sun, the doctor, with a queer little feeling, noticed the perfect shadow of a cross moving along the ground. He leaned over the fuselage watching the course of that shadow and saw it glide directly over a little enclosure near the homestead. He looked closer and saw it was a tiny cemetery with two white headstones!

The patient was landed safely at Boulia hospital in time to save her life. That flight represented five hundred and ninety rush miles and prevented the digging of yet another grave in that cemetery of the Cross.

CHAPTER XXV

THE BREAKER-IN OF SOULS

A WAYFARER drove along a lonely track, breaking no speed records despite his reputation. Before him stretched a pack-horse-pad that, like a broad blotched snake, wound in and out as it dodged rocky bars and fallen slabs from the sandstone wall above. Evenly on each side of the pad deep-cut wheel-ruts twisted and turned round spur and ledge, disappearing down shingly watercourses to be found again climbing into the timber on the opposite bank. The man in the sturdy old Dodge drove with the caution of a practised hand. If he snapped an axle—well, the car would stay there until after next "wet" as likely as not.

Lucky man, even though all his skill and energies were concentrated on safely negotiating the track, for he was driving through country of primitive grandeur, seen by few. He was just passing the end of the Great Wall, a towering labour of Nature where jagged rocks seemed flung one upon the other by some fierce and mighty hand. To his right the wind moaned through a valley whose lovely forest shielded a foam-flecked torrent. Across the valley arose strange mountains, striking in form and individuality. In one outstanding clump there rose seven bare pyramids, three abreast with the last standing back in isolation, the freakish folly one might easily imagine of long-dead Titans. In striking contrast to the bareness of "The Pyramids" were the surrounding peaks, clothed in timber to their summits. Jumbled strata of shales and basalts and quartzites. Among those siliceous pages were pressed countless fossils and imprints of tracks of animals that had lived when the world was very young, of plants and birds, fish and shellfish, and long channel things that were really the tracks of worms crawling long before the first man set foot upon the earth. Other beings than man have footprints in the "Sands of Time". Some hills even were composed of coral rock, proving that they had once been coral colonies busily working in ocean depths.

But the patrol padre was not thinking of the past. On this trip his special job was to leave tracks in the minds of men, men as "wild and woolly" as this country that had bred them. He had come from the coast and was now hundreds of miles from "anywhere". He had been twice out here before preparing the way: this time he must act: time was precious and life short. His present object was to put the reality of spiritual existence directly before the men of these regions. They were a tough lot: prospectors who roamed these lonely mountains seeking gold, and cattlemen from the grassy plains that began thirty miles away out through the gorge. But they were big-hearted men, on the lawless side perhaps, living "wild" and dying wild when the time came. Their God was "mate"! The padre thought them the makings of fine men, and it was his burning desire that these fine men in the making should know and understand the great Mate.

Occasionally numbers of them collected at a little pub strategically situated at a mountain base, past which ran the track to the gorge and the faint trails leading to the inside fastnesses. The pub was a pub and store combined, as is common with the inland hostelries. From this little log cabin the prospectors drew their supplies.

The padre had "left religion alone" on his previous visits, had sought their confidence until his breezy personality won him the respect and promised friendship of "th' crowd". They all had a very warm regard for the A.I.M.—one of whose little hospitals was now doing good work some two hundred miles to the west. They realized the good in an institution which came to mend their broken bodies when accident or sickness demanded, but they could not understand "religion". They could not explain why: they were just against it.

In their tiny mountain community they had boasted that "no damn parson will ever preach here". This padre, however, had determined to make them one of his congregations. It was his special job. They could accept or not, but he must "explain"; and he judged the time ripe.

Towards evening he neared the pub. Thankfully he cocked his ear to the scattered tinkle of horse-bells telling that the boys were "in".

They were—and something else was "in" too. He heard the shouts, the rollicking song, as his car crawled along still half a mile away. Now and again from a valley a pad would join the track. He wondered what tales those pads could tell! Pads disappearing among the whispering pines and leading to craggy heights and mountain retreats far away. What wild rides must have been taken along those pads, rides echoing to wider songs, bottles clinking in the saddle-bags, and Death racing behind! He had heard tales of men at night driving in the spurs and thundering over a precipice, clinging to falling horses.

As he drove up the last bank he took in the scene in a flash. About thirty-odd men in front of the pub, others in the bar most likely, and lying about elsewhere. "Hooray!" he thought grimly. "They're mustered anyway." The pub and store was one long, low building of rough hewn logs of cypress pine. Smoke coiled lazily from a huge stone and mud chimney: the wooden shutters that served for windows were propped open. On a low, shingle-roofed veranda, khaki-trousered men in leggings lounged against the posts and on rough wooden forms. Other tough-looking chaps in shirt or sleeveless flannel and dungarees smoked "with th' mob". Numbers wore cartridge belts, for men generally go armed in the north if travelling through "bad-nigger" country.

The songs ceased as the car drove up. Without moving they eyed the padre. It had been a warm day and some of the boys were stripped to the waist. The padre stepped from the car with a sigh of relief and stretched his huge frame, eyeing them as they eyed him. Then he smiled from twinkling eyes.

"Good day, boys," he said cheerily as he strode towards the veranda. "How's things?"

"Not bad," several growled. "How're you?"

"Fine and fit."

He stamped into the bar where the publican greeted him genially by reaching a big paw across the counter. It was of planed pine, stained by many drinks, deep cut where knives had been playfully thrown into it, initialled deeply with names, with station brands, and names of mining claims. On shelves behind the bar were bottles of all sizes, shapes, and colours, and all spirits. An old-time picture of the king held pride of place above the bar, supported by a military cross and a photo of a strikingly pretty bush girl.

The publican was a friend of the padre, and leaned his big elbows on the counter while cheerfully asking news of "th' track". After the usual local conversation the padre whispered mysteriously.

"Say, George, can I have the use of the store tonight? I'd like to speak to the men."

"Sure! I'll get a couple of them at it now and they can clear away things. You couldn't swing a cat in the place as it is."

Confident of the publican's co-operation, but keeping him in ignorance of the real objective, the padre took his swag off the car and joined in with the mob as they stampeded into the dining-room. It was a fairly riotous dinner, rough and ready maybe, and eaten with similar appetites. The table, long pine planks, around which were forms; the cutlery, tinware and enamel with pannikins like buckets; the "fodder", roast beef and corned, with "spuds" and onions, baked bread, tinned butter, and jam. As a preliminary, any man who had anything to say against the cook was invited to step outside or "have it where he stood". Uproar greeted this challenge with an intimation that the cook would be attended to "as soon as a man has his insides lined". The waiters were black boys who when not laughing were kept in a hurry. All hands sat down with much shuffling into places, stamping of feet, clinking of spurs, and light-hearted badinage. All reached for their tools and set to straightaway; one man facetiously bawled for his serviette ring, and another for his finger-bowl. Both were accommodated. When the serviette man grew too uproarious he was man-handled against the wall and handcuffed there with a pair of old-time police 'cuffs.

"Have your 'serviette rings' then, an' be done with it," panted the publican as he glared at the manacled dude. "An' you!" he roared to a black boy, "bring th' Count his finger-bowl."

The grinning boy hurried away, to return with a cow bucket.

"An' just make another complaint," roared the publican, "an' I'll dip your flamin' head in it."

The padre battled in for his share of food and ate a hearty meal. He exchanged banter with the boys to such advantage that soon he had all the table listening to and laughing at his jokes. He could give and take with the wittiest of them; while his big voice, his powerful physique, and personality dominated the whole crowd. The conversation rose to a considerably higher level, and the eating went on the merrier.

After the meal he went out to his car and got busy on a repair job. He made that an excuse when the boys asked him to referee a fight. About nine o'clock the publican edged along and whispered—

"Come on, I've most of them mustered in the store. Red Mick wants to give you a speech; better let him spout a bit. We'll have to hurry or there'll be breakaways."

The padre whipped on his coat as they hurried to the bar.

"All out, boys," called the publican cheerily. "Th' parson wants a word with all hands over in the store. We'll adjourn for refreshments later."

Quite willingly they ambled out, anticipating further good yarns.

"We won't bother about these three," said the publican as they scruffed them out into the passage. "They're dead to th' world and wouldn't hear a word you say. I can close the poker-school all right," he explained as he led the way to the kitchen, "but I'm not too sure about th' two-up school. Two-up is the national pastime and not to be interrupted lightly."

However, with rush tactics they closed both schools, though not without aggrieved protest from the two-up enthusiasts. The padre followed the last of his future congregation into the store. Now would come the test. The publican shut the door. The padre made up his mind to take them by surprise immediately it was his turn to "spout".

The long smelly room was dimly illuminated by a hurricane lamp strapped to a rafter. On tiers of shelves were stores for many men for twelve months: bags of flour and sugar, cases of butter and jam, cases of tea and bags of salt, tins of soda and tartar, and whatnots. From poles along the walls hung hobble-chains, surcingles, saddles, pack-bags, branding-irons, rings of horseshoes, picks and shovels, prospecting dishes, horse-bells, stockwhips, etc. On the slab floor lay bags of "spuds" and onions. Some of the "fruit" was loose which provided a roaring "Encore! 'Core!" when an unsteady newcomer trod on an onion and fell with a crash.

When order had been restored Red Mick rose solemnly from his bag of onions. The dull light shone on his hard brown face and turned his heavy beard aggressively red. His mop of fiery hair would have defied a currycomb. He had hands like hams and a savage gleam in his eye. He looked hot, but his speech was hotter. Its peroration ran:

"He's th' greatest thing in saints ever come this way: th' A.I.M. knew its job in sendin' him to youse blighters. Now th' —— old —— will speak to you."

The padre rose and bowed to the applause:

"Gentlemen," he replied, "I must thank Red Mick for the courteous manner in which he has introduced me to you, and I especially thank him for the kindly references to myself—which I fully reciprocate. Above all, I am pleased at this appreciative reference to the A.I.M. But I regret the chairman has made no reference to the One in whose service I am. Now, boys, we can make amends if we all bow our heads while I lead in prayer."

An astounded hush held till the prayer was finished.

The padre spoke on mateship. His theme was readily followed, for every man present had experienced the worth of a comrade; some among them owed their lives to the devotion of a "cobber"; in several instances that cobber had since "gone west", leaving a deathless memory behind him. The padre's impressive tones filled the dimly-lit room with memories. "One-eyed Bogan" saw again that terrible Madman's Track, heard again the voice of Shirtless Charlie: "Keep on going, One-eye, keep on. 'Tis a long lane has no turning—water may be at the next bend! We'll pull through."

Bogan lived again through the hopelessness of those miles of spinifex waste, under a pitiless sun, his one eye dimmed as Charlie's voice croaked cheerily at his elbow, pushing him on and on—Charlie who collapsed when they had battled within sight of Anna Plains station.

Others were there, too, who had had mates, the grand mates that stick to a man to the very last. Diggers were there, too, who saw again their cobbers of the A.I.F.—It was a Deathless Army that the padre gathered there.

He spoke of Charles Kingsley and other fine men who have admitted they were what they were simply because "I had a friend". Then, quite naturally, sincerely, because he knew it himself, he went on to tell them of the Greatest Friend of all—He who made friends and kept them too. And because they knew what mateship was, the parallel told. They dimly realized the transformation that came to those who followed the great Mate: they felt how weaklings under His inspiration could become strong, become men who could do something for the world. The preacher appealed to his hearers to stand up to the claims of mateship, to help all hands as well as their mates, just as does the Great Mate to whom all men are mates.

"We are our brother's keepers," he continued earnestly, "and we are 'kept' in proportion as we seek to keep others. The Rule is simple: 'Do unto others as you would have them do to you.' It is a wonderful Rule—one that works. If we help others then we are helped; if we don't, then we get what is coming to us on the rebound. What are you fellows doing? What is your influence over your pal? Is he any the better man for knowing you? Any happier? Can he look into your face with a smile and feel glad to shake your hand?"

Finally the padre got them singing. But he knew his men. Had he offered them a hymn-book they would have refused to open it: to deliberately sing a hymn from a book savoured too much of looking like "Holy Joe". He got them as he had won their breathless attention.

"You fellows could have a 'break' if you could only sing a hymn," he suggested. "I was thinking of—but," he broke off, "of course you don't know it."

"We don't know what?" came inquiring voices.

" 'What a Friend we have in Jesus'," answered the padre —"a rollicking good song and a true one!" As he stared at them some memory awakened in the mind of one man. He had known Sunday School in the years of long ago.

"Cripes! I know parts of it," he burst out. "Same here!" came another voice.

"Well, have a go at it," called the padre, "and I'll stick to you, though my voice is better for driving bullocks. Now give us a start and all hands join in."

They got it going. Other hymns followed in happy succession: everybody sang. The influence of that service changed the life of that wild place in the hills.

At the conclusion, the padre told them stories of the A.I.M. After that he held them in the hollow of his hand. They wanted to take up a collection. He refused.

"You birds would say afterwards I came for what I could get."

He rolled himself in his blanket that night thoroughly pleased. He had won through on a most difficult job. They would be ready for the muster on his next visit. They were.

The padre drove straight on and out through the Gorge into a plain that was a sea of grass. He camped at a bachelor cattle station and received congratulations over the "roping in of th' crowd". Next morning as he drove on they called after him—

"Hi, padre, if you see the Hairy Caterpillar send him along to help us with the muster."

"Right-oh! So long."

"So long!" came the shouted farewell.

Twenty miles along the track he suddenly remembered the Hairy Caterpillar. He had forgotten to ask the man's name. All he knew of him was that he "ran a shack" eighty miles down the track. It was midday when something wee and weedy pushed out of the long grass beside the track. The padre pulled up, staring. Two small eyes in the quaintest human he had ever seen stared back. From his head, his face, his skinny neck, his little arms, hair sprouted profusely like the bristles on a well-worn broom. Tufts of hairy growth sprouted even down his nose. A glimpse of his chest spoke of ancestors.

"Good day," said the padre.

"Goo' day."

"I've a message from the boss. They want you up there to give a hand with the muster."

"How th' —— hell do you know me?"

The padre hesitated, then being a George Washington replied—

"They mentioned your nickname!"

"Ho, did they! The —— —— cows!"

On his return to the outskirts of civilization the padre advised his colleague who was following on his tracks:

"They're wild and woolly, but the rough edge is taken off them. They'll pester you to take up a collection, too. Well, take it!"

In due course this padre arrived. The boys trooped out to greet him. One lovingly tried to embrace the car; another the padre. When he had firmly but tactfully turned down the offer of numerous drinks, they said—

"Well, then, will you give us a —— service like the big padre does?"

"Yes, I'll give you a better!"

"Oh, will you! An' will you take up a collection?"

"Certainly! You can regard yourselves as an organized congregation now and you pay for the privilege. Just give me a hand to jack up this car if you will, the wheel is squeaking like——"

"Hell!" broke in Red Mick.

"No," replied the padre—"not as hot as——" and he glanced at the fiery beard—"that! It squeaks like iron which requires oil."

"Drinks are on me!" declared Red Mick. "Give him a hand with th' car, boys."

At the evening service they gave him a good hearing. Then the publican was deputed to take "th' hat". When he returned to the store with a saucer in his hand Red Mick immediately kicked it to the ceiling.

"Git something!" he roared.

The publican retired to return with a soup-plate.

"There's th' Count's finger-bowl outside!" he advised, with a nasty rumble in his voice.

Red Mick snatched the plate.

"Git busy!" he ordered the "Lame Cassowary". That individual accepted the plate lackadaisically and limped across to the nearest man. The Lame Cassowary was elongated and thin, with bony shoulders perched under his ears like a sick fowl's wings. His hooked beak, dreamy eyes, and long mournful face belied the chuckling heart within. In mute sorrow he shoved the plate under the nose of the nearest victim. That person straightened his back, stretched out bow legs, and shoved a hairy hand deep into a trousers pocket. With a grunt like a tooth extraction he pulled out a florin and dropped it in the plate. Red Mick's roar hit the roof.

"What!!! You ain't been to church for thirty years an' you sling in two bob! Now, what are you goin' to do about it?"

"There's a ten-bob note in me other pants!" growled the victim.

"Git those pants!"

With protesting grunts the man complied. Uproar greeted the flourishing of the ten-shilling note. He dropped in the note with one hand while reaching to collect his 2/- with the other.

"Keeps!" snarled Red Mick, while cheers greeted the Lame Cassowary as he snatched away the plate. Imperturbably he limped from man to man, the lamplight shining on his tired brow, trickling down his long hooked nose. Red Mick followed step by step lest "sundry birds" be tempted.

It was the first collection ever taken up in those parts and it was a record. The plate was all "wafery" with pound and ten-shilling notes.

"If there'd only been a few more of us," announced Red Mick with a baleful glare at the publican, "we'd ha' wanted th' Count's finger-bowl."

The Lame Cassowary bowed as he handed the plate to the padre.

Cheers hit the roof.

CHAPTER XXVI

THE BABY TRANSMITTER IN ACTION

TRIUMPH came to Flynn and Traeger—the latter had discovered the wireless link that welded his Chain of Dreams! In desperate anxiety they hurried to test out the completed instrument. They took it to the Centre, and when it "worked", their overstrained faces glowed, and with wild shouts they threw their hats in the air and joined hands in an hilarious "merry-go-round" with the little machine in the centre. The old Dodge, packed with its boxes, its swags and dusty tarpaulins, its tools and mats and water-bags—their tried and trusty old friend—was forgotten. Eagerly they rapped the little instrument again, and the morse shot out to the distant amateurs who were listening in to the test. The Baby Wireless Transmitting and Receiving Set was a fact! Very materialistic the little instrument looked, squatting on the sand; hard to realize that it was actually built by the thoughts of men.

The machine could be easily carried, easily installed: it could be easily mastered by the bush mother. It was worked by pedal. The generator was simplicity itself and a marvel of efficiency. It could be phoned up from any mother station, but transmitted its own messages by morse. Those technically interested might like to know the following details:

The generator which supplies the power for the transmitter is operated by foot, like a bicycle, and can generate a power of about 20 watts at a pressure of 300-400 volts. The gears are enclosed in an oil-tight casing filled with oil: thus minimizing wear.

The transmitter is "crystal controlled", the crystal maintaining the wave-length at a definite value, and keeping the note steady; thus making the signals easy to read even if the generator is driven unevenly.

The receiver is a two-valve regenerative circuit usually known as the P.1.—Tetrode valves being used. The "A" battery is a 1.5-volt dry cell, and the "B" battery consists of two 4.5-volt "C" batteries connected in series; thus giving nine volts. One set of batteries gives from four to six months' service. By plugging a larger coil into the receiver, broadcast programmes can be received. Ear-phones are used. A small loud-speaker can be used. The cost of the instrument is under £60.

The experimenters hurried back to Adelaide. Here Scott joined them. Arrangements were made to make some of the machines immediately. Then Traeger and Scott hurried to Cloncurry to install the Mother Station.

Flynn's dream was realized. Australia in her most isolated areas girdled by Nursing Homes; a Flying Doctor established at a Base Station; and now the perfected wireless machine to link the doctor with his patients!

Six more flying doctors, each at their base station, and all isolated Australia would be under the Flying Red Cross!

The reaction had come for Flynn, the old fighting light left his eyes. With their blessing and the necessary cash the Board sent him overseas on a twelve-month holiday.

The Rev. J. Andrew Barber carried on as Acting Superintendent. Scott and Traeger loaded up the old Dodge and set off north for a year's work, installing the first transmitting sets.

In 1929, the acting superintendent and Dr George Simpson, in a modern motor-car, drove up under a big old tree whose gnarled limbs bear deep-cut testimony to Australia's pioneering history. B was clearly cut in that old coolabah-tree. And

DI

under

ee

on the reverse trunk. Originally this message, left by Burke, read, "Dig under 40 feet W".

On the tree, facing east, is still clearly seen—

B

LXV

This was the camp under 65, and Burke's initial. On the left branch was cut "December 16th, 1860". This is the Depot Tree, still with a few palisades left in silent testimony to "Fort Wills". Within three miles of the Nursing Home they were *en route* to open, the two men drove up under the old coolabah in whose shade Burke was buried. Its trunk is carved—

R.O'HB

21/6/61

AD

and on the third branch was cut "MK". The early explorers generally marked any particularly outstanding tree with one letter of their initials. Thus, B stands for Burke; AH (A.H. conjoined) indicates Howitt; MK, McKinlay.

The Innamincka district is rich with such traces of the ill-fated Burke and Wills expedition. What remarks those men must have passed if, from another life, they were watching these men in the motor-car reading their names on that tree!

Close by the Nursing Home are acres of sharp, rough stones, unlike the smooth gibber which induced Sturt to label the country The Stony Desert when he was seeking the centre of the continent to find whether sea or mountain range lay there. A cairn of stones, built by Sturt near Mt Poole, is visible from a great distance today, while the old beef-wood tree, still alive and healthy, carries the epitaph of John Poole—"JP, 1845".

Historical Innamincka, in lonely South Australian country, is close to the Queensland border fence. The border has no customs officials now, but it has its problems for all that, as the Queensland Methodist padre found when he rode over the border and found a couple in Innamincka very anxious to get married. The padre couldn't do it—there. His licence only allowed him to officiate in Queensland. So he drove the couple fifteen miles back to the border fence, through it, and into Queensland, where he triumphantly married them under Burke's Depot Tree. At a later date a Presbyterian padre came along and reaped the first fruits by baptizing the baby.

The township lies across Cooper's Creek, about three miles from the old cattle station, at a point where the Strzelecki branches off from the main channel of Cooper's Creek.

The Nursing Home was named in gratitude after Elizabeth, the daughter of Sir Josiah Symon, K.C., who for years had been quietly helping in the good work. This Home saw the last of the Border Sisters. It took in their country, and the "Boundary Rider" rode no more.

Scott and Traeger, loading up the old car at Cloncurry, had a pleasant surprise in a gift from the Queensland Country Women's Association of the cost of four of the little Baby Transmitters. Full of cheer they motored the hundred and eighty miles to Augustus Downs station and installed the maiden set. The Rev. G. M. Scott was another typical A.I.M. man, cheery always, with a stock of good jokes and ready to take one against himself. The type of man who can understand the other man's point of view, give him a hand, then interest him in a good sermon. An ingenious fellow, too, who can rig up a wireless on a bush car, transmit a Sunday School story to youngsters two hundred miles away, then whip off his coat and help fight a bushfire, side by side with the station-hands.

A woman stood by to test this maiden set. The Mother Station call was VJ1. That was received O.K.

"What shall I send?" asked Mrs Rothery as she sat before the machine.

"Send anything!" replied Traeger eagerly.

"Oh, I don't know what to say!"

"Send, 'Hello, Harry!' " suggested Scott as he watched the keys.

Mrs Rothery started "H-e-l-l-o".

"It's too jumbled," broke in Traeger. "See, the 'H-e-l-l' is a jumble of dots, but you have spaced the 'o' correctly. Try again."

She did.

"That was better, but it's not good enough yet," declared Traeger. "Send it again. That's better; a lot, but not quite right. Send again."

Yet again that mighty atom buzzed out into space "H-e-l-l-o!"

"O.K.," declared Traeger triumphantly. "The 'o' was spaced a little too far from the 'l', but it is O.K., lady!"

"You're sending a 'Hello!' that's shouting all through Australia," laughed Scott. "Now send him the 'Harry'."

"H-a-r-r-y!" buzzed out into space.

"O.K.," they both cried together, "O K."

Eagerly they listened for the acknowledgment.

It did not come through "O.K." It came, but a trifle diffidently.

The lady had sent: "O hell! Harry!"

Well satisfied with the result, the wireless men started again from Cloncurry on the four hundred and fifty miles south to Birdsville.

This sparsely inhabited area was cattle country. The wireless would serve the stations and the drovers, and travellers along the lonely Boulia-Bedourie-Innamincka-Marree tracks.

Scott and Traeger were heartily welcomed at Birdsville where all hands and the cook gathered at the installation: the natives strolled along, too, and the goats rolled up, just on the off chance. There is nothing like a Birdsville goat for picking up things. (In spite of all precautions, they managed at a later date to pull down the wireless mast.)

If you also are interested in rigging up a bush wireless, just look on while Traeger scouts around outside for a suitable spot for the pole, and makes sure that the guy-ropes will be out of the way of wandering horses and cattle. The aerial-pole was of light piping in five twelve-feet length, each length screwing on to the other. Diameter of the pole at the bottom 1½ inches, at the top one inch. It was laid on the ground and screwed together; then four guy-wires were fixed, each to a joint; two of the guys were then fixed to pegs set at a certain distance at opposite sides of the pole, while the pair of opposite guys were left loosely coiled. The long slender pole thus lying on the ground raised a discussion that threatened to become heated. Some were positive that the pole would "buckle", others as sure that the A.I.M. men "knew their job".

It did look a problem; and all watched curiously while the little pulley block and halliard were fitted and the jib erected. The jib was an upright pole eight feet high. With block and tackle fixed to the top of this jib, as it was pulled down so the much longer pole was easily raised, the already fixed guys preventing buckling. As the pole rose the loose guy-wires slowly unwound and, when the pole was up, were fastened to their respective pegs. When the pole was erect the jib of course was lying on the ground.

"So help me bob!" gazed a greyhead who had been loudest in prophecy of disaster, "I'm jiggered! Drinks are on me!"

The next job was connecting the aerial wire to the set and adjusting the condensers; then tuning the transmitters to the correct wave-length.

Traeger pressed the buzzer and Birdsville was "on the

air". Yet another link was forged in the dreamer's Chain of Dreams.

Just as Traeger finished a successful try-out, a drover came winding his way among the sandhills from the Diamantina, riding a flea-bitten grey, and looking more worried than the horse. He dismounted at the pub, nodded absent-mindedly to the crowd, and slouched into the bar. The grey, lowering its head, arched its muscles for a sneeze. "Look out!" cried a lanky bushman, as he turned side-on to the blast of dust from the grey's red-rimmed nostrils. It shook itself until the saddle rattled to the clinking stirrup-irons. Then it subsided with a long sigh, closed its eyes and aimed a beautifully-timed kick at a stray dog. With dreamy eyes it listened to its master's thirst.

He was thirsty, that drover, and a worried man as well. Several weeks back he had posted a cheque to his sick wife at Hughenden. He would not know whether his wife was better or dead until he arrived at Boulia, two hundred and twenty miles north. He was uneasy, too, about that cheque.

"A man might as well be in th' Sahara desert," he drawled as he finished a bottle of beer. "He'd find just as much to drink and a telegraph station every thousand miles."

"We're modern now," replied Mr Afford, quietly. "It's you who are out of date. We have wireless in this township."

The drover's eyes opened like his mouth.

"It's all right," explained mine host, "I haven't got 'em. Our wireless will put you in touch with Hughenden within minutes. Come on and we'll send a message to your wife."

With deep suspicion the drover followed him across to the wireless room at the hospital. He stared at the instruments as one seeing things. Traeger tapped the keys and buzzed out the message.

He received a reply that the wife had recovered and thanked her husband for the cheque.

"Hell-an'-Tommy!" said the drover. He passed a hand

over his forehead, then returned to the bar. This sudden modernity was just a bit *too* sudden.

Ordinarily, he would not have got a message through until the mailman made the trip; now he had received it in two hours. So he had a few more, nodded over the bar, thumped it with his fist, and declared that the bush "was done". He threatened he would go "farther out!"

Scott was on the veranda laughing at the bushman's surprise, thinking how John Flynn would enjoy the joke, when a nuggety chap in flannels and broad-brimmed hat walked across from the little hospital. He carried a pipe in his mouth and was rolling tobacco in his sun-tanned hands. He nodded and smiled as he came up to Scott.

"Say, mister," he said in a soft drawl, "them blokes in the south know the kind of religion that's good for this country. Their hospitals is better than preachin' every time."

The padre, in his working clothes, looked at the man's blight-rimmed eyes and remembered how much of Christ's teaching was embodied in healing. He came to the conclusion that perhaps the bushman was not so far from the Kingdom after all.

Birdsville races, to which all hands roll up from near and far, are famed in the Inland. Stations within three hundred miles send their representatives. Mailmen, drovers, teamsters, well-sinkers, all send in their "prads" and would bet their reputations on the result. Birdsville race-meetings are as enthusiastic as the Cup. The horses just love it. Some speedy horses run there at times. They are as hardy as kangaroos, and every one is a trier. There is no "pulling", no dope, no electric batteries, no deadening injection, no weighted saddles. When the judge says "Go!" then every moke "Goes!" And every jockey is out to win. If he can't, then he goes his hardest to keep the dust out of his eyes.

There is a "lawn" at Birdsville, too, and ladies grace it— some fine-looking girls amongst them, their eyes shining with the happiness of meeting other people.

The refreshment booth is a happy affair: a bough shed
in whose homely shade friends and old-timers, youngsters and
roamers, meet once in twelve months on the heartiest
gossiping ground in all the great Inland.

The judge's box is fitted up from four upright saplings;
and the judge has to keep wide awake to see the finish of
those races. Sometimes the prads flash past the post with
"only a whisker" between them.

It is generally a two-day programme, with a couple of balls,
fancy- and evening-dress, to finish off with. A great turnout
that for fleeting moments brings the breath of companionship to many lonely Inlanders. How the women appreciate
it, what it means to them, only they know. Men don't quite
realize.

The A.I.M. party were present during a race-meeting that
coincided with the installation of an auxiliary set; a particularly joyous meeting, for the drought had broken and the
river had "run". Mrs Scott, fresh from the city, was surprised
at the ladies' dresses—the latest of race frocks, all the way from
Adelaide.

At the ball the ladies wore evening-dress, and wore them
well. The secret was forethought, that forethought which
the Inland people acquire by hard experience. The dresses
had been ordered months before. Some were bought, some
came on hire from "Buttonhole". The hotel being the centre
of the social life of most bush hamlets, the dresses were
mostly directed to Mrs Gaffney. When the ladies rolled up
for their dresses the hotel was the hub of activity; about the
only sanctuary for the men was the bar. Women who only
have a chance of personally choosing their frocks once in
twelve months will, however, realize that on such an occasion
the women did not care twopence where the men were.

Cars were poked here and there; buggies and buckboards
were stabled out in the open; horses were browsing everywhere; ambitious dogs, with hair erect and teeth gleaming,
were trotting all over the town seeking some likely looking

tyke on which to pounce. Several days before the meeting old Abdullah, the Afghan, loomed up over the sandhills with his solemn camels laden with forethought in the shape of crates of whatnots to sell at the races.

The big race was for the Lady's Bracelet and the horse that carried that off would not say "Good day" to Phar Lap.

One of the most energetic jockeys was Joe Hagen the mailman, the most picturesque rider there and the liveliest. Joe is seventy years young and still going strong. He raced against his own son and beat him. Joe was in double delight, both because of the races, and because the river had come "down". The drought had broken; which meant that the only real animals in the world could be ridden again. Old Joe is the mailman travelling the Betoota to Birdsville track, a track noted for its lonely dangers. Joe has always got his mails through. When the drought barred horses Joe had relapsed to camels and his opinion of those beasts was as "rorty" as a local dust-storm. When the long-necked runts didn't bolt in daylight they sneaked away in the night, expecting him to track them across the waterless sands. The camels were more atrocious than the pinkest devils; behaved worse, too, especially in a sand-storm when it was so easy to get bushed among those barren hills all looking exactly the same, the faint track twisting and turning to vanish altogether where sand blew on it. Conditions in a storm were hell; pale-red sand swirling like driven rain-sheets to blot out the hills or film them in unrecognizable shapes. And all the time the mailman's neck stretched like the camels' as he tried to watch them and the track and keep the dust out of his eyes. No wonder old Joe brushed the sand out of his moustache when the river came down, and with a wild exuberant yell booted his astonished camels in turn, then galloped into Birdsville for the races.

There were fifteen women and fifty men present—and one bookmaker from Windorah. Natives of course weren't counted, nor Abdullah. Young Jack Gaffney was recklessly proud of his Ford car. Jack was modern, his car was as good as any horse he reckoned; it would take anything, any sandhill in the country. One not far from the pub was pointed out as a "beaut". Jack immediately accepted the challenge, leapt into his steed, and charged the sandhill at a roar, the Ford snorting up and up to completely somersault back at the top. The crowd rushed across to pull the rider out of the sand. He spat it out, blew it out of his nostrils, shook it out of his ears, and opened his eyes to remark—

"I'm not hurt, just a little upset."

The dance was a wonderful success; it could hardly have been otherwise when everyone was so wonderfully happy. The piano and accordion were brought over from the pub and banged music in the little hall: old-time dances were the favourites, although there was a jazz or two.

Scott had a Cine-Kodak outfit with him and screened some jolly scenes. On his return patrol the following year he showed Birdsville itself at the races, and the enthusiastic audience augured well for the coming success of genuine Australian-made pictures.

However, we always get our biggest disappointments when things are going best. The A.I.M. now experienced a bitter disappointment. The well-known Northern Australian "millionaire" Felix Holmes died, and was reported to have left the A.I.M. a residuary legacy of £300,000! For hospital work in Northern Australia. What visions there were of quickly equipping another circle in the Chain of Dreams! Alas, the dead man's estate had been lamentably over-valued by popular opinion. There was no residue at all!

CHAPTER XXVII

THE "VOICE OF THE BUSH"

THE wireless men returned to Cloncurry via Boulia and crossed a plain on which stood one solitary tree whose riven bark bore witness to collision.

"The tree won," nodded Traeger.

"Yes," said Scott, "I wonder what happened to the corpse?"

They met him in Boulia. He was that dear old chap known as "Old Everyone's Friend".

"What happened?" inquired Scott.

"Well," explained Old Everyone's Friend, "I was worried because I was driving so fast; the speedometer said twenty-five miles per hour. I looked at the ground, then at the speedometer, then looked up and saw a tree. I said a little prayer, put both feet on the brake and held on. Then I hit the tree."

Farther along was evidence of a more serious mishap. A station man and his black boy were riding to catch the mail 'plane. He was one of those unfortunate chaps to whom things happen. Riding a quiet bush horse, a sudden wind flapped his coat, and the horse threw him and he lay unconscious. The abo dismounted, took the letters from his master, and calmly rode on to meet the mail. He knew that it was the policeman's job to look after accidents.

At Cloncurry the wireless men loaded up again and headed north to Lorraine station. One of the finest bushmen in the north lives there. He has a splendid station home, and a family of girls who magnificently advertise the Gulf country.

Trailing up along the banks of the Leichhardt with its lovely Leichhardt trees they came to Burketown, right on the Gulf, and took lugger across to Mornington Island, a hundred miles out at sea. Missionary Hall had been clubbed by the natives there some years before, and Owen wounded. After a siege of several days Owen and the two women managed to reach the cutter at night and sailed for Burketown. A wireless transmitting set on this little island would mean that if such a siege occurred again help in a 'plane would arrive within four hours—as it did shortly after the wireless was installed, when the serious epidemic broke out.

On a previous visit, Scott had taken a moving-picture of these natives in a corroboree war-dance. He advertised the film now. The mission natives turned up, but the myalls kept suspiciously aloof. They wanted to see what this "big feller corroboree" was all about first. Lured on by the excited yells, they gradually drifted in just in time to see their own warriors take the screen. As they recognized themselves excitement "ate them up": they screamed and yelled to the throwing of imaginary spears and banging about with wommeras. It was a great joke for the whites; but they turned off the picture in time lest that seething mob of bulging-eyed humanity became uncontrollable.

The wireless men recrossed the Gulf, keeping constantly in touch with the Mother Station, as they did when travelling by car. Eighty miles west of Burketown a set was installed at Turn Off Lagoon (now Corinda). Corinda is an amalgamation of cattle stations, eight thousand square miles of country, running twenty-seven thousand cattle on decently grassed flat country, sparsely timbered. The homestead is built on piles, for floods there are of the "old man" variety. One bright day Mr Kemp left the station on business. He got just fifty miles away when the rain came in torrents, turning the Nicholson into a mighty river. It was six weeks before news reached the mother and daughter that "the Boss" was safe.

The wireless went up quickly on this station, livened by a laugh from Tom Chong. Tom is Australian, born on the run. Out riding with the boss one day they came on a steer caught by its horns in the fork of a tree. The animal was quite mad; the boss managed to free its horns and it charged him instantly. As they were galloping away Tom yelled—

"Bi cli, Boss, Tom Chong when he get all hot inside feel 'em wind, but Tom Chong all li when he all li inside no wind."

These widely scattered sets linked up an enormous area with Cloncurry and were immediately used not only for the flying doctor but for business purposes. Suddenly people reaped in practice what they had only believed before—the benefits in numerous ways of being in quick communication with a modern centre. Instead of waiting weeks and months for a mail, people within riding distance of a Baby Transmitter could now send a message all over the continent in the time it took them to get to the station. The Mother Station, morning and evening, was answering the calls of her "Babies".

The transmitting machine, with its generator and crystal control, was housed in a wooden box. This box, the wireless men found, warped very much in dry country. Also, at Augustus Downs, the white-ants played a merry tune on it not appreciated by the Mother Station. So the following year the sets were rebuilt of metal cases, and the wireless men hurried off to Hermannsburg.

Thus the Centre was given a definite voice through Cloncurry to the world.

This Hermannsburg machine soon proved to Australians the valuable work done by the forethought of the A.I.M. It wirelessed the plight of Pilot Coote at Ayers Rock, and soon afterwards awoke the world to the disappearance of Captain Pittendrigh and mining-engineer Hamre in Central Australia. But for the Hermannsburg transmitting set the ill-fated Lasseter gold expedition would have claimed more victims.

From the Centre, the wireless men struck nor'-east straight across country to Cloncurry, five hundred miles across a very little known part of Australia. Other men have written a book on less. From Alice Springs to the Arltunga goldfield and the Jervois Range was over ruggedly precipitous country that will be a favourite tourist trip in time. Its wild beauty is emphasized by a wonderful purple haze that steals over the mountains every evening. Crossing the Arthur River and the prettily grassed Plenty Valley they came down on to the flat country and the "bull dust" (finer than sand yet not quite dust), a greasy sort of dust in which, in wet or dry, beast and car can bog very easily if they break through the crust. A drive of a hundred miles through long grass that filled up the bottom of the car, and was on occasion set alight by the exhaust pipe, followed the bull-dust experience. Then across the old Georgina, and away on into Cloncurry.

The next set was installed in the old weather-board homestead at Gregory Downs; then on to Borroloola, four hundred miles north-west of Cloncurry.

When crossing the Flinders up near the Gulf they saw a man kneeling at the salt water bathing his gums. A doctor at Normanton had just relieved him of some teeth. Squatting on the bank was a lubra, smoking her master's pipe.

"What matter longa him?" inquired Scott.

"Oh, him mad," she replied scornfully. "Him bin drinkem brandy, now him drinkem salt water. Him pullem out teeth, now can't eat beef!"

"The lady has a poor opinion of white men," volunteered Traeger.

"Her eye is hostile," answered Scott. "We'd better 'buzz' off."

Borroloola is a tiny place with a history that would make any wild-west town crazy with envy. It is inland a few miles from the Gulf, on the McArthur, a broad stream. The wireless men no sooner arrived than they found that a parson was an object of abhorrence. Scott saw an old-age pensioner with whiskers fairly bristling as he rolled up his swag. His dog didn't dare say a word.

"Where are you off to, Jim?" asked the policeman as the ancient grabbed his billy.

"T' hell!" he snapped. "Wot with wimmen an' parsons an' wireless this country's done! I'm goin' bush."

He went, straight out into the west, his old dog humbly following.

As they were erecting the pole, a young gin was brought into the police station, suffering from yaws. The bashful smile told that she looked forward to the "white-man medicine". The sergeant retired to the kitchen to sterilize the needle. Now Polly's mother happened to be in the kitchen. With her eyes like onions she crept out to Polly.

"Sergeant him stickem needle into you," she whispered hoarsely, "big feller needle." (She spread her arms a yard wide)—"Fillem you up with water—You bust!"

Polly didn't—she took to the bush instead.

The blacktracker took after Polly. It was not the first time Polly returned under police escort.

At Newcastle Waters, Scott and Traeger had a real gala night, for, as somethimes happens in the lonely places, "all the world" had congregated there. Station people, half a dozen teamsters and drovers, three linesmen, two A.I.M. Sisters and Mrs Scott, passengers from the southern and northern mail-coaches, MacGregor, a wandering inland Methodist missionary, and Father Gsell from the Roman Catholic Mission at Bathurst Island, four hundred and fifty miles away.

It was a grand gathering and a perfect Inland night. Father Gsell is a well-known missionary priest; a fine type of man who has never made an enemy. A big man, with a high forehead, kindly face with an understanding smile, and a flowing beard that some day will be that of a patriarch, he looks what he is.

Bedourie lies in western Queensland, in the dry saltbush and sandhill country, about a hundred miles from the Centralian border. The Georgina flows (once a year) near by. When the water *does* arrive it comes in a rolling brown torrent that rapidly rises, spreads over its banks, and swamps the billabongs, that in turn overflow and flood the country with yellow-brown lakes. Bedourie then knows that the "wet" has come—from a thousand miles away up towards the Gulf of Carpentaria, and from the Barkly Tableland and Camooweal, right to the parched lands of the Centre. Teams cannot travel much until the "dry" season comes to harden up the boggy country. Then, for several months, the land for hundreds of miles will be smiling under grass and wild flowers, trees will put on new coats, animals and birds will buck and prance and whistle in the exuberance of a well-fed life. These extremes of wet and dry make a problem of their own for certain areas of the Inland. The "wet" actually occurs in the distant sub-tropic north and causes a problem for the Inland, in that its overflowing waters rush down the dry river-courses and cause floods and bogs.

Once when the Georgina came rolling down, George Gaffney had set out to ride to Cluny station, but the quaint old river suddenly turned the country into a lake. Gaffney did the trip over the sands in a boat—a seventeen-mile pull.

Thus Bedourie actually borrows its wet from northern lands a thousand miles away. Bedourie is really a land of the sun, a dry land of warm days and starry nights. Here the famous Bedourie showers roar over the land in walls of hissing sand that blacken the sky and moan as they come; while the women rush to shut the doors and slam down windows and poke bagging into every crack and cranny in a futile effort to block the dust fiend. It will creep through into the flour and sugar, cover the pictures and the floor, even creep into the beds. Luckily the big storms don't come very often.

These storms may give Bedourie undying fame. There, old bushmen declare, the crows fly backwards to keep the sand out of their eyes! At Bedourie a million gallons a day of warm fresh water gush up out of a subterranean reservoir and run down to the Georgina to replenish the water-holes for fifty miles.

It provided food for thought in that exceedingly dry country to see a little girl holding a cabbage almost as heavy and big as herself. Both girl and cabbage have thriven on the bore water. Perhaps nature has stored many reservoirs down below to help us solve the dry problem when we grasp the initiative.

The publican at Bedourie is of the Good Samaritan type. For over a thousand miles George Gaffney is known as a white man—which is the highest compliment the bush can give, and being endorsed by a bush parson marks its sincerity. It was this well-built, grey-moustached man who welcomed the wireless men.

Mrs Gaffney straight away made the party comfortable, while Gaffney cleaned out a room which he made over for the installation of the wireless set. Son Allan runs the set now, and has a daily yarn with his cousins a hundred and twenty miles south in Birdsville. He was an intensely interested student during the days that Scott and Traeger were busy with the installation.

"That looks an unusually solid sandhill," said Scott one day, "that hill across there with the goat-yard built upon it."

"That is a yard built upon a yard," explained Gaffney. "There is a cattle-yard underneath. Succeeding dust-storms piled sand against the fences until in time they were covered completely over and a new sandhill formed. I suppose it is the old fences underneath that bind the sand so tightly. That might have been the way those ancient cities were buried in Egypt and the Sinai desert. Sand is an overwhelming thing, once it gets a move on."

"Yes," answered Scott, "I've often heard John Flynn say that."

"I wonder why?" mused Gaffney. "He just smiled when first I pointed out that hill to him; seemed to know all about it, and yet I'll swear he had never been here before. Heard of it from some drover or other I suppose. Did he ever tell you of his first trip into this country?"

"No."

"Well, old Reece saw him coming. It was a blood-red sunset just after hell's own dust-storm. Out of the haze, a camel-man loomed up, man and beast with eyes bloodshot, their nostrils choked with sand, and gasping. Flynn was clinging to the saddle, all humped up like a sick crow. Crows followed him too. They flapped low overhead and settled on a withered coolabah just ahead of the camel as Reece watched. Flynn was all in when the camel lurched down, but he smiled at Reece.

" 'You don't mean to say you're this parson we've heard about?' asked Reece.

" 'Why not?' croaked Flynn.

" 'You're a sticker.'

" 'We are like that.'

" 'H'm,' said Reece. 'A parson is a rare bird out here, but you'll do. Come and I'll put the billy on.' "

Scott smiled.

"He *is* a sticker, one of the greatest in Australia. He has stuck to his dream until it has materialized: he is still sticking."

"Wonderful!" mused Gaffney, as he stared into the distance and then glanced at a heap of wireless tools on the veranda. "Only a few years ago a Camel-man crawled here in a dust-storm and now hospitals and wireless circle the Inland and a flying doctor speeds overhead! A man won't have time to die soon. I laughed at Flynn that evening he first told me of his 'Dream', and now I live to see the day when I benefit by it."

Late one afternoon a dusty horseman rode up to the hotel and smiled down upon a lad who raced out to the horse. Too excited to laugh or smile or talk he just gazed up from the stirrup-irons. Bobby Crombie's Dad had come home! Dad had been away all the long season droving; he had delivered the cattle and was now returning with the horses and plant. Only this afternoon he had camped his outfit at the crossing two miles away. Gaffney's wife had been looking after the boy— And Dad had come at last!

That evening while all hands and the cook commandeered the snug room and talked of bush life, of long droving trips, of cattle-duffing, of "dead men's secrets", of bonanzas lost and found, of stories of the A.I.M., Bobby sat on his father's knee and his eyes rarely left the sun-tanned face: his ears never missed a word.

Late that night the father rode back to camp, a lonely two miles through the dark. All hands turned in, and the hushed silence of the Inland wrapped the township in slumber. Among the ghostly gums down by the river a mopoke croaked eerily. Two miles away under a coolabah-tree a tired drover nearly awakened, but not quite: he dreamed that his faithful old cattle-dog was creeping in under the blankets. It was a cold night, with stars like diamonds.

At the first call of the galahs the drover awoke to find himself clasped in the arms of his little son.

Bert the cook was keenly interested in the wireless, it would give him a chance, he explained, to hear "some of them double-bed stories". Bert was the antithesis of old Peg-leg the famous western navvies' cook. Peg-leg stirred the porridge cauldron with his wooden stump, he rolled the dough with it, basted the beef with it, whittled off splinters with which to pick his teeth, and on occasion used it as a club when "roughies" among the gang proved "obstruculous". He despised men who grew ordinary legs for he could do so many things with his wooden leg that he wished he had another. The huskiest navvy in the gang hesitated to provoke old

Peg-leg, for a butt in the bingy from that wooden terror was capable of sending the toughest navvy to the A.I.M. hospital for many a painful day

But Bert of Bedourie was spotlessly clean, both in himself and the kitchen. He was a methodical fiend however: everything must be kept in its place, including the cat. Bert knew exactly where to lay his hand on every shiny spoon, on every pot.

"I likes the things," he observed, "so I can lay my hands on 'em in the dark, an' I never allows th' pot to call th' kettle black." Bert was such a fiend for cleanliness that he even beat the Bedourie dust. So far as is known no sand had invaded the kitchen of the Bedourie Royal Hotel.

Scott had made other trips through this country, had always been made welcome and had seen a lot of the life that ebbs and flows past a bush hotel. And here, as in other bush hotels too, he had never known a man "stripped". Hard drinkers found, even against their will, money in their pocket when they took the track again. Many a wandering bagman was helped from the hotel store often with no hope of payment. And that at a place where stores only arrived "dependent on the wet". The A.I.M. padres all tell of similar experiences with bush publicans.

One evening Mrs Gaffney remarked, "There hasn't been a service held in this hotel for fourteen years. The last was held by Hulton Sams."

"What!" exclaimed Scott, "the Fighting Parson?"

"Yes, the Inland loved that man."

"I'm afraid it is not many parsons who are remembered after fourteen years," said Scott. "I hope I shall be."

"He said that others would be sure to come and carry on."

"May I hold a service in the same room tonight, if the boys don't mind?"

"They have all spoken of it."

That evening all hands knocked off cards, the little card room behind the bar was cleared, and all hands and the cook turned up, including the old black dog who settled himself comfortably against the old-fashioned fireplace. A cheery little fire murmured approvingly as a cracked gramophone gave the anthem. It was a mixed congregation, not much larger than the original band of apostles. Lutheran, Congregationalist, Church of England, Roman Catholic—some did not know what they were "labelled"—but all Bedourie was there. Scott spoke in the way that the Inland loves, as man to man. Perhaps it is because the Inlanders live so close to nature that they so unerringly detect sincerity.

After the service came the inevitable yarn. Out came pipes and comfortable chairs, in came the cat with tail held high and a plaintive mew. Allan Gaffney cornered Traeger with eager talk of "buzzers". A long-limbed drover got nicely settled to start a longer story when Mrs Gaffney got in first.

"I don't suppose you A.I.M. men fully realize what this wireless means to us women of the farthest outback," she said dreamily.

"Why?" inquired Traeger.

"Well, last year I was taken suddenly ill, desperately so. The only hope was Boulia, a hundred-and-twenty-mile drive in a hurry. After an awful ninety miles we found that a storm had broken miles ahead making it impossible to pass the boggy country. The driver turned back and struggled on to the A.I.M. at Birdsville the same distance south. It was two awful days and nights but he just got me there in time. If this wireless had been installed on that occasion we could have called up Cloncurry and the flying doctor would have been here within a couple of hours."

Treager nodded.

"The wireless and the A.I.M. Homes will save many lives farther out," said Mrs Gaffney. "They will take away that awful dread that has been killing the women of the frontiers."

CHAPTER XXVIII

CARRY ON

FLYNN returned from a wonderful holiday, eager to rush his gigantic work to undreamed of conclusions.

Of course, he had taken a "busman's holiday" and learned much about his business. His particular joy was in investigating the methods of treating dry lands in Egypt, Palestine, and Arizona; seeing if he could pick up anything and apply the knowledge to his own beloved "arid lands".

He was surprised to find himself a centre of interest in many places he visited. He and his work were known. It appears that the military authorities of the world had been closely watching his flying-ambulance scheme and what they didn't know about it they wished to know now. His ambulance machines were successfully flying over great distances, over practically unmapped country in some flights. His men were putting up records and saying nothing about it. Great Britain had been quietly doing a wonderful work in this regard in the military line. The eyes of the world were on France who had accomplished military flying-ambulance work of which she was justly proud. Other nations were eagerly nibbling at the idea. But this Australian had pulled the job off in continuous successful practice. He was invited to the First International Health Aviation Conference (l'Aviation Sanitaire) held in Paris, May 1929. He found that the world knew far more about Australia's Flying Medical Service than Australia did herself.

In London Flynn availed himself of the sympathy of Mr

Amery, ex-Secretary of State for the Dominions, J. E. Wrench (founder of the Overseas League), and a host of other notabilities who might help some way or other with his great Chain of Dreams. And he availed himself of the chances offered of learning points about the modern construction of aeroplanes designed for medical work. Altogether he completed a busy, fruitful holiday. With head filled with fresh ideas and new knowledge for his work, he found the boat could not bring him back fast enough to Australia.

The Base on which he had to work was now a powerful organization with twelve outpost Nursing Homes erected, one nearing completion at Esperance on the sou'-Westralian coast, another proposed to be erected at Fitzroy Crossing, and others in course of investigation. On the financial side, welcome bequests were coming in—bequests urgently needed.

The A.M.S. was firmly established. The first flying doctor had increased the ordinary "radius" of the A.M.S. to four hundred miles, saved valuable lives, alleviated untold suffering, and brought a feeling of security to that particular portion of the Inland which the people had never experienced before. The area actually flown over by the Red Cross machine during the experimental stage was larger than New South Wales. The sum of the diagonals thereof was decidedly greater than the diagonals of New South Wales. The former were south-west to north-east over seven hundred miles, south-east to north-west twelve hundred miles.

Dr J. A. Spalding, with Pilot Affleck, was carrying on an enterprise which had captured the imagination not only of the Inland but of Australia. He had increased the airline to Darwin, just on a thousand miles straight flight; to Kooltah, north-east in Cape York Peninsula four hundred miles; to Birdsville, just under four hundred miles south; to Newcastle Waters, five hundred miles north-west; and pioneered numerous flights into previously unflown-over country.

The apparently insuperable difficulty of landing grounds had been overcome in the good old bush way. Stations pre-

pared their own landing grounds by knocking down a tree
or two and bowling over a few ant beds. Others when they
radio for help describe the "cleared paddock" or bare patch
that must serve for the aerodrome. Then, the doctor far away
asks a few terse questions:

"Have you four hundred yards clear run against winds?"
"Yes."

"Are there any trees close?"
"A few."

"Well, could you drive a car straight over that ground at
thirty miles an hour?—You think you could? H'm. Well
then, expect us in an hour!" And the machine roars up and
away.

When an accident happens in out of the way rough
country, where a landing is impossible, the difficulty is got
over in a number of ways. Perhaps you will read how in a
future flying-doctor book.

Doctors A. J. May and W. H. Cornford have carried on
the work that has made the *Victory* famous.

·   ·   ·   ·   ·   ·

A LEAF FROM THE FLYING DOCTOR'S DIARY

Flew "bush" to a locality where there was no landing
ground. Advised patient's friends to take him by car to a
meeting-place thirty miles distant. Patient very ill, but began
to improve when we got him to Cloncurry Hospital.

Called by telephone two hundred and twenty-three miles
to baby with malaria fever. Quick flight.

Called by telephone one hundred and twenty miles; found
husband, wife, and two children under poor conditions in
isolated situation. Parents simultaneously overcome by a
melancholic form of insanity and had been found wandering
at large in the bush. Advised removal to medical centre.

Called two hundred and twenty-three miles. Bumpy flight.
Saw woman suffering from malaria. Other cases: baby, two

sick women, aboriginal with septic hand, Japanese with syno-
vitis, contusions of foot and leg.

Called one hundred and seventy-five miles. Swift flight—
clear day. Baby fifteen months, acute enterocolitis(?) menin-
gitis. Transported to hospital. Patient's condition apparently
not adversely affected by flight.

Advised man by letter re tumour on face.

Advised Mornington Island by wireless re patient suffering from skin rash.

Heard of man suffering from fracture of humerus. Un-
able to go out owing to absence of pilot in Normanton.
Advised taking patient to Burketown Hospital. Two days
later flew to Burketown but patient had not arrived.

Advised Mornington Island by wireless—child suffering
from epilepsy.

Flew to Normanton on mail machine at request of local
doctor who was absent. Good opportunity to demonstrate
possibility of flying doctor's co-operation. QANTAS gener-
ously gave complimentary ticket for trip.

. . . . . .

Flynn found that the Radio Base was in constant touch with
its far-flung family by wireless telephone; the reply of the
Baby Transmitters now being audible from five hundred
and fifty miles away; a Chief Radio Officer occasionally
visiting each outpost to overhaul the gear; a radio patrol car
on active service and twenty radio outposts being established,
including Innamincka, Iffley, Lawn Hills, Rockhampton
Downs, Anthony's Lagoon, Beetoota, thus making the quarter of a million (now three hundred thousand) square miles
of country under the flying doctor animate with a "voice".
The Aerial Medical Service, the Patrol Padre, and the Wireless, working together; thus creating a triple A.I.M. scheme
over western Queensland and the Gulf area.

Flynn's first "Great Circle" was chained and complete.

As to the outer Inland he found great areas of it com-

pletely transformed under motor transport; the people, secure
in their hospital arrangements, eagerly anticipating the Baby
Wireless and flying doctor for themselves. As to the future,
well—experts were declaring that in fifteen years the south
will be compelled to look to the north for all the beef it can
produce.

Flynn eagerly flung himself into the job of completing the
work—the establishment of the five other Circles which
would chain the entire Inland with hospitals and
communication.

He met the Depression. That held back the A.I.M. It
proved something which dreams might bridge but not wireless, nor flying doctors, nor work, nor anything else but
Time. It was more deadening by far than the war, though
the A.I.M. organization, now being a power in the land,
has found it easier to hold on. So the Board, encouraged by
the General Assembly, kept consolidating, improving wherever possible, planning, installing more transmitters—including a set each with the Methodist folk on Goulburn and
Milingimbi islands; re-organizing patrols, making them two-
man now, one of whom must be a first-class radio and motor
mechanic; brought out the fine little A.I.M. *Frontier News*;
made larger and more modern the still existing Nursing
Homes. With the clearing of the Depression the A.I.M. will
complete the Six Circles.

After that?

They will carry on while they are needed which will be
many years yet.

The Nursing Homes are always available to be taken over
by local bodies or the government when the time comes.
The organization is not working for itself but for Australia
—and for all of us. The finger of Fate never writes Finis!

But Flynn is hopeless, on this earth he will never "wake
up". His friends have just found that he is not dreaming
of the Circles: he regards that dream as completed. He is
dreaming of other circles, far larger, far more comprehensive

circles that are to link all cultivable Australia with winged transport by land, sea, and air.

The latter dream only Flynn knows in its entirety; perhaps *he* does not realize it all. A few intimate friends know something of this "Greater Dream".

Who *could* follow John Flynn's dreams!

But the man cannot be laughed at now. Look what has come true!

His friends just study the little programme the Board has given them to carry on with:

THE AERIAL MEDICAL SERVICES OF AUSTRALIA

Incorporating:
- Frontier Medical Patrols (road):
- Frontier Radio Clubs:
- Life-saving Section.

OBJECTIVES:

1. To promote throughout the sparsely-settled areas of Australia:

(a) The establishment of *Aerial Medical Service Bases*;

(b) The multiplication of *Landing Grounds*, properly marked and duly charted;

(c) The formation and training of *Frontier Radio Clubs*, where "wire" facilities are lacking.

(d) The organization of the necessary *Service Patrols*, to ensure continuous efficiency throughout the entire system;

(e) The provision, at strategic centres, of *Special Equipment*, to be maintained always ready for the use of search parties when persons are lost.

2. Where locally desired, to assist kindred services within the areas influenced, with a view to the evolution of *District Medical Service Associations*—which might, ultimately, take over control of local sections of the Aerial Medical Services.

3. To provide opportunities for Post-Graduate Study for doctors who have served in outposts associated with the Aerial Medical Service.

4. To assist in creating adequate *Bureaux of Information* about the isolated areas of Australia.

5. To establish, and to administer *Development Funds* necessary for the attainment of the above objectives.

So the "Legionaries" gave up trying to unravel his dreams and set about inducing others to enrol in the Inland Legion and thus build his dreams with money. It is proved now that Flynn's dreams which have produced great things produce undreamed of things in themselves. For instance, recently he has seen the third flying doctor, Dr Allan Vickers, set off on a flight of mercy to Mornington Island—called up in haste by the Baby Transmitter there.

It sounds ordinary. But, is it? Mornington Island is an isolated speck lying three hundred airline miles out in the waters of the Gulf of Carpentaria. No steamers call there of course. The only touches of civilization are four white people: the rest are a host of partly tamed savages and sub-tropical jungle. There is no such thing as a landing ground, or any help whatever in case of a crash or forced landing on sea or land. Rough country, almost uninhabited, had to be flown over, before the sea was reached.

QANTAS people held a quick consultation; heads pored over maps; plans were quickly arranged. In minutes almost Pilot Affleck was in his seat and the flying doctor was soaring away on a new flight, a flight made as safe as lightning planning and human ingenuity could foresee; but, for all that, a flight never before attempted and one fraught with tragic possibilities—all with the object of saving life.

And they did the job with never a word. The world has not the faintest idea that this record flight has been attempted, achieved, and carried out again.

But then, Human Endeavour is a great thing. The lucky

men amongst us do things and the happiness of achievement is far above the blare of trumpets.

Just as the book goes to press the wires buzz with the record flight of the Flying Doctor beaten at the last lap by the Wings of Death. Mr Williamson, hotelkeeper at Croydon, was seriously injured by a refrigerator explosion. Dr Vickers and Pilot Donaldson immediately flew to Normanton from Cloncurry, took the patient aboard and flew back to Winton where the speedy *Atlanta* took him aboard and raced overhead for Brisbane. But he died when only 110 minutes' journey from the city, the first patient lost by the Australian Inland Mission since the inauguration of its Aerial Medical Service. But the patient was frightfully injured, a chest trouble developed almost immediately and a heat wave was also against him.

The distance flown was 1300 miles.

Traeger is now working on "something wonderful", a wireless set as simple and efficient as a telephone. You just pick up a gadget, speak into it, and you are heard anywhere. It is to be a Baby Miracle Machine.

It will be far smaller than the existing machine: a child can lift, carry, and operate it. It will do away with all necessity for training in operation: there will be no difficulty in installing it: it is to be ridiculously cheap. It will type out a written message like a typewriter and send out morse automatically; its receiver is as reliable as the most efficient telephone service. It will be an epic of modern wireless invention: you "just press a button and it speaks".

An improved gear is fitted which will make two-way telephoning possible.

Before this book goes to press the inventor will have registered the keyboard with the Postmaster-General.

Last year (1931) the Baby Transmitters sent seventy thousand words of private and business message to and from the Commonwealth Government's land lines. That in itself justifies their existence. Their messages of hope and healing are a greater justification.

With intense satisfaction Flynn saw the development of roads under motor transport; the ingenious devices for overcoming sand, bog, and distances; the greatly increased business in the area controlled by wireless, thus putting the settlers in touch with the outside markets; above all the sense of security cast over the Inland by the nearness of medical help and the quiet spiritual influence of the padres, the nursing sisters, and the work of the A.I.M. as a whole. In this connexion the A.I.M. never forgets the toilers of other denominations among whom they have often worked side by side and hand to hand.

An unforgettable chapter in the history of this grand movement is the years of toil given by the voluntary workers. They have gained nothing by it but the quiet reward of having helped others.

Such is the dream of a Camel-man, weather-beaten of face, a smile in his fine blue eyes as he gazes up to the flying doctor roaring overhead.

A wave of the hand from away up there, the shadow of the Cross upon the ground—and it is gone.

With the vanishing drone comes the drumming of a camel's feet.

THE SLEEPER IN THE CENTRE

THE years have marched by since this book was written. Flynn of the Inland now sleeps—or *does* he sleep?—in the very heart of his beloved continent.

He accomplished his titanic task, ringed the entire untamed northern half of the continent with his "Mantle of Safety": the Bush Hospitals, the Flying Doctor Services, the longed for transport and communication, that have saved and continue to save so many valuable lives, that have banished the deadening isolation of lonely men and women. It is impossible for us in the sheltered cities, the country towns, in fact almost anywhere in these swift days of speed, of rapidly growing population and developing security, to realize the mighty work accomplished by this man.

Not only did his vision succour in time of direst need the distressed ones in the wilderness: his far-flung work also came to his country's aid in her time of greatest need. For the knowledge gained throughout the years in the enormous task of selecting, erecting, and operating that chain of tiny air bases over that vast area of sparsely inhabited country helped Australia during the last Great War. And we know how very desperately we needed every helping hand we could get.

It is only as Time glides by that future generations will realize what Flynn of the Inland, and that tiny handful of helpers who stuck to him through thick and thin, accomplished for Australia. And the sweet thing about it (maybe the secret of the success of his apparently impossible scheme) was that he, and they, did all this for humanity, regardless of creed or colour. Their thoughts, their work, and later their money, were all devoted to humanity in distress—which is why the accomplished work is so much beloved.

Flynn of the Inland built his memorial out of a dream—and the unquenchable will to make that dream come true. His life was given to it. And how happy the man who sees his dream come true!

He sleeps now in the harsh Red Heart of Australia, so beloved of its people. But to me, who in all humility wrote this book about this man, he is awake; for I am one of those who believe that death is but the Doorway to Greater Life, that the Sleeper sleeps but briefly. To me, the spirit of Flynn of the Inland broods away up there over the Centre. What a happy Spirit!

Truly, the deeds of great men live after them. And Flynn was great.

His people remember his works in their hearts with love and gratitude; and for generations who will know not Flynn they have erected the John Flynn Memorial Church, to be opened on 5th May 1956 in his own beloved Centre.

Symbolic of his work and of the country which he loved, his memorial is built from the very stones of the age-old ranges that have stood since the Creator breathed life upon the earth. What *His* mighty plan may be we do not know. But the plan of the humble human John Flynn is accomplished. And now his followers borrow a few bricks from the Almighty Plan to remind future generations of a quiet seeker after truth who toiled past this way.

That memorial church has been created from the thoughts of his people to symbolize Flynn the Dreamer, to symbolize the Reverend John Flynn with his feet set firmly upon the firm red earth, to symbolize this man so beloved by many, so respected and admired by the pioneers of a vast area—Flynn of the Inland.

ION L. IDRIESS.

Sydney,
March 1956.